Great Sporting Rivals

Dear Dad,   (April 7th 2006)
This is a thankyou for helping
with my ucas and uni applications
while I've bin away, plus I thought
you'd like it.
                love
                     Marcus
                      xxxxx

Great Sporting Rivals

Joseph Romanos

Lothian
BOOKS

Thomas C. Lothian Pty Ltd
132 Albert Road, South Melbourne, 3205
www.lothian.com.au

National Library of Australia
Cataloguing-in-Publication data:

Romanos, Joseph, 1957- .

    Great sporting rivals.

    ISBN 0 7344 0720 3.

    1. Sports - History. I. Title.

796.09

Cover design by Dexter Fry
Text design and production by BookNZ
Printed in Singapore by Tien Wah Press

Front cover photographs
Top: Muhammad Ali punches Joe Frazier in the seventh round of their heavyweight fight in Manila, 1975. TRANZ/CORBIS
Bottom: Sebastian Coe wins the Olympic 1500m gold in Moscow, 1980, with Steve Ovett following in third place. TRANZ/CORBIS

Contents

Acknowledgements 6

Introduction 7

1   Fire and Ice: John McEnroe v Bjorn Borg 9

2   The Four-minute Wonders: Roger Bannister v John Landy 21

3   Showtime Comes to the NBA: Larry Bird v Magic Johnson 33

4   Chalk and Cheese: Margaret Court v Billie Jean King 46

5   'We Need Muscles Like Yours to Beat Germany':
Joe Louis v Max Schmeling 58

6   Dicing with Death: Alain Prost v Ayrton Senna 70

7   The Old Firm: Celtic v Rangers 84

8   The Rivals Who Wouldn't: Sebastian Coe v Steve Ovett 98

9   Ice Queens: Tonya Harding v Nancy Kerrigan 111

10   'Nobody Roots for Goliath': Wilt Chamberlain v Bill Russell 122

11   Rise and Fall: Jack Nicklaus v Arnold Palmer 135

12   Still Smokin' After All These Years: Muhammad Ali v Joe Frazier 146

13   Great Gareth, Super Sid: Gareth Edwards v Sid Going 158

14   When Opposites Attract: Chris Evert v Martina Navratilova 171

15   Enhanced Performance: Carl Lewis v Ben Johnson 185

Bibliography 198

Acknowledgements

During my 30 years as a sports journalist I have been fortunate to interview many of the people featured in this book, either at major events like the Olympic Games, Wimbledon and the world track and field championships, or in more private one-on-one situations. These interviews have provided the basis of the research for this book, but I have also delved extensively into the Internet and books on specific subjects.

Most sports stars have their own websites, which assist with essential basic information. Other sites are more specific. For instance, the Football Fan Census on www.footballfancensus.com provided fascinating details about rivalry in football.

Many of those profiled have written autobiographies or have had biographies written about them. I have credited these in the text when quoting from them, and this book includes a full bibliography.

Several sports journalists and sports followers helped me with information on specific chapters. To Bruce Holloway, Gordon Glen Watson, Gordon Irving, Keith Quinn, John Dybvig, Peter Marriott, Phil Murray and Gael Woods, particular thanks.

The photos and other illustrations have been culled from many sources, but most have been supplied through the excellent work of the Photosport and Fotopress teams. I have endeavoured to find the owners of the copyright wherever I could, even with photos several decades old. If there are any omissions, I apologise.

Joseph Romanos
May 2004

Introduction

Competition is the essence of sport, and the most fascinating type of competition is head-to-head rivalry. When two sprinters finally settle on their blocks after months of speculation about their meeting, when two old adversaries walk onto Centre Court at Wimbledon, when two great boxers put the hype and the insults behind them and climb through the ropes, when great basketball teams, each boasting a superstar, do battle in the NBA Finals … these are the moments that make big-time sport so compelling.

But what is it that makes a great rivalry? Here are what I consider to be the five big factors. Unforgettable rivalries will have most if not all of them.

- Top-level sport.
- Longevity.
- A contrast in playing styles.
- A contrast in personalities/temperament.
- Fluctuating fortunes, with each competitor dominating at different times.

They are the key ingredients. But there's also an X-factor. Most of the rivalries featured in this book have that extra element that lifts them above the many other memorable rivalries found in sport.

With Max Schmeling and Joe Louis, their heavyweight boxing contests took place in the shadow of the Second World War. When they fought, it wasn't just two famous heavyweights at war, but Germany against the United States. For figure skaters Nancy Kerrigan and Tonya Harding, the story is of more than just two American stars striving to win Olympic gold. The premeditated assault on Kerrigan makes it a uniquely riveting tale. Carl Lewis and Ben Johnson each wanted to be the world's fastest sprinter, but their rivalry also involved the spectre of drug-taking – and what a tortured and twisting road that has turned out to be.

And so it goes – John Landy and Roger Bannister were seeking not just to be the world's fastest middle-distance runner, but both also wanted to be first to break the elusive four-minute barrier for the mile. Supremacy on the Formula One tracks of the world meant so much to Alain Prost and Ayrton Senna that it endangered their lives. Rangers and Celtic clash several times every season. Each match involves far more than just a game of football because of the underlying issues of race, class and, especially, religion.

In scanning the history of sport, there are hundreds of examples of great rivalries. Some sports, such as tennis and boxing, lend themselves ideally to individual rivalry. But I have tried to spread the net wider in this book, dealing with rivalries from many different sports. They can range from the all-out warfare of Muhammad Ali versus Joe Frazier to the more gentlemanly clashes of golfers Jack Nicklaus and Arnold Palmer.

I am well aware that many other famous rivalries are missing here. Among the most obvious are Gene Tunney v Jack Dempsey, Pete Sampras v Andre Agassi and Bobby Fischer v Boris Spassky. These and many more were considered, but I'm happy with my final 15, which represent a range of sports, of eras and of personalities.

For me, a particular fascination about an individual rivalry is the contrast in personalities. I've always found that the way people play their sport mirrors their character. So Jimmy Connors was combative, brash and confident off the tennis court – and with racket in hand was aggressive and intimidating. Wilt Chamberlain was a Hollywood-type personality off the basketball court and on it was ever the centre of attention, full of flair and colour.

It's the difference in personalities that elevates a rivalry. Would it be possible to find people with more different upbringing, background and deportment than Tonya Harding and Nancy Kerrigan? But isn't that what makes their story so special? Or take Billie Jean King and Margaret Court: King – a stereotypical outgoing Californian who seemed to thrive on confrontation, and spoke publicly about having had an abortion and a lesbian relationship; Court – a quiet Australian, who married and raised four children. One clearly enjoyed being the spokeswoman for all manner of causes; the other just wanted to play tennis, then shrink from the limelight and be with her family. It was their vastly contrasting personalities, as much as their brilliant tennis, which made their confrontations so riveting.

Such is the nature of rivalry. Long may it continue.

1 Fire and Ice

John McEnroe v Bjorn Borg

O n 6 July 1980, Bjorn Borg and John McEnroe played the greatest match in tennis history. Borg, the ever-so-cool Swede, beat McEnroe, the passionate, hot-tempered New Yorker, 1-6, 7-5, 6-3, 6-7, 8-6 in the Wimbledon singles final. The 20-minute fourth set tiebreaker was an epic in itself. McEnroe, who saved seven match points in that set, won it 18-16.

It's quite some statement to claim a particular match is the greatest ever. But who would argue? There have been other tennis matches, though not many, as exciting and with as many swings of fortune. There have been a few matches, though very few, in which the standard of the tennis was as high. But has there been a match of such quality played on such an important stage? Let's face it: the Wimbledon final is the biggest of all tennis stages. The 3h 53min match was, as esteemed English journalist John Barrett wrote, 'a final fit for the gods'.

Billed as Fire versus Ice, the match was a promoter's dream. Like the first Muhammad Ali–Joe Frazier bout, in 1971, this Wimbledon final had tennis fans licking their lips in advance. And again like Ali–Frazier, it delivered, and more.

There was much to be excited about. Borg, aged 24, was attempting to extend his fantastic run of consecutive Wimbledon titles to five. McEnroe, 21, was bursting to prove he was the new big shot in men's tennis.

Borg was a mystery figure. He was the most self-contained of players, so difficult to read, so nerveless. McEnroe, a combustible personality, displayed every emotion. He had a fire raging within, and on court could swing from extreme elation to utter despondency within seconds. With his Nordic good looks, Borg was a heart-throb. He had a superb athlete's body, wore his blond hair long and invariably had a massive following. McEnroe cut nowhere near as elegant a figure. He was chubbier, tended to shy away from physical training when he could, and didn't seem to care what anyone thought of him.

Their styles were diametrically opposite. Borg played with two hands on the backhand, was superbly fit and fast and had the sort of stoic temperament that allowed him to rally all day, which explains why he won six French Open crowns. McEnroe was the classic serve-and-volley player. He had a one-handed backhand, liked to camp on the net and relied on wonderful hand–eye coordination. He had a potent, swinging serve, and delivered it from a more side on stance than anyone had ever seen. Borg was a right-hander from Scandinavia. McEnroe was a left-hander from the United States. In every sense the contrast was absolute.

They tested each other to the maximum on court. Borg felt McEnroe's serve was the most awkward he faced. As Borg explained in his biography, *My Life and Game*:

> All left-handers give me trouble by serving wide to my two-handed backhand ... McEnroe builds his game on his serve ... He is incredibly fast, great power volley, plus touch with a flipping wrist. He can drop volley on both sides. He is the master of the unexpected. I can never anticipate his shots. To beat him I have to keep him pinned to the baseline by maintaining perfect length on my groundstrokes. If I don't, he'll come in on anything.

McEnroe assessed their games like this: 'He is always at the ball early. I'm not. He concentrates on the whole match. You must be in good shape to play him, so you must prepare for the entire match and have the patience to mix it up with him.' The difference in their games was what made the prospect of their first Wimbledon clash so mouth-watering.

Borg had first been ranked No 1 in the world in August 1977, knocking Jimmy Connors off his perch, and had retained the top ranking through most of 1979–80. At the time of the 1980 Wimbledon tournament, Borg was No 1, but there had been a three-week period in March that year when McEnroe had leapt to top spot. Their Wimbledon showdown would decide the No 1 ranking, and McEnroe was eager to unseat Borg.

They had met seven times, but never in a Grand Slam tournament, and certainly never in a match where the stakes were as high. McEnroe had become the first player younger than Borg to beat the Swede when he'd toppled him in straight sets in his backyard in Stockholm in 1978. Thereafter they had met six more times and Borg had won four of the encounters. By the time their careers on the ATP tour were over, they had met 14 times. Appropriately for such a landmark rivalry, they scored seven wins each.

Their paths to the 1980 Wimbledon final were very different. The top-seeded Borg had over the years had some narrow early-round escapes at Wimbledon – names like Mark Edmondson, Vijay Amritraj and Victor Amaya come to mind – but not this time. He beat Ismail El Shafei, Shlomo Glickstein, Rod Frawley, Balazs Taroczy, Gene Mayer and Brian Gottfried – every one of them capable of an upset – for the loss of just two sets, and was never really in danger.

McEnroe, the second seed, eliminated Butch Walts, Terry Rocavert, Tom Okker, Kevin Curren, Peter Fleming and Jimmy Connors, but his was a much more tortured path. Rocavert, the durable Australian, pushed him to 6-3 in the fifth and the big-serving Curren foretold future glories at Wimbledon by going down only 7-5, 7-6, 7-6. In the semis, McEnroe and Connors staged their usual bad-tempered, tempestuous slugfest. They were about even on the insults and abuse, but McEnroe's tennis was a shade better.

There was speculation that McEnroe might taint the final with some of the cursing and bad sportsmanship he had displayed at Wimbledon previously. (By 1980 he had already been tagged Super-Brat. Soon his 'pits of the world' and 'you cannot be serious' comments would become part of tennis folklore.) But McEnroe, who was greeted with a noticeable amount of booing when he and Borg took the court, said later that there was never a chance of bad behaviour. With Borg at the other end of the court, he knew he had to be focused entirely on his tennis. There wasn't time to be distracted with side-issues such as errant linesmen or umpiring, or outspoken spectators. Besides, McEnroe, for all his brashness and youth, was well aware of the traditions of tennis, and he knew this was an occasion to honour.

And so it was that these two players, both of whom would be serious contenders for the title of greatest ever player, turned on a match of brilliance and drama. On this day Borg, recovering from the loss of the first set 6-1, was just a shade too good. He could have won the fourth set when he had two match points at 5-4, 40-15, but McEnroe stayed alive with two outrageously bold winners. How Borg managed to compose himself at the start of the fifth set defies belief. He lost two points on his first service game but then never put a foot wrong. He lost only one more point on serve and gradually chipped away at McEnroe until he broke through to win the set 8-6.

The match was outstanding, but what lifted it to the realms of the supernatural was that fourth set tiebreaker. Seven times McEnroe held set point during the tiebreaker and five times Borg stood at championship point. With the stakes so high, it was a nerve-jangling, desperate time. There were flashing passing shots, magnificent volleys, courageous returns of service. On and on they battled, taking the crowd with them on the sort of emotional rollercoaster seldom seen even in top tennis.

McEnroe and Borg knew they were involved in something special, and the crowd didn't want the match to end. The spectators, always pro-Borg at Wimbledon, began to acknowledge and then to support McEnroe. They admired his pluck and grit and wanted more tennis. How shattered must Borg have been to lose that tiebreaker. It was incredible that he was able to put it behind him so swiftly and play the sort of fifth set he did.

At the end of the match, Borg sank to his knees in his time-honoured victory salute. The crowd stood and round after round of cheering rocked centre court. They were acknowledging not just the superhuman Swede, but also the brave and brilliant American.

Borg let his mask slip slightly at the press conference following that great final. 'I couldn't believe it when I lost all those match points. It was a strange feeling and I felt terrible and disappointed – especially when I lost the fourth set. I was also below my best at the start of the fifth and said to myself, "I'll have to forget and try to go forward, hold my serve and break his."

'I gained more satisfaction winning a great match like that than winning an easy one. It was a great contest. We both played well. It was certainly the best match I've ever had at Wimbledon. I was very steady in the fifth set, especially in my last three service games. I kept telling myself not to get tight or nervous. This was the toughest of my Wimbledon finals.' And then, prophetically, in response to a question about his American challenger: 'I suppose McEnroe could be a worthy successor to me. He has given me some of my best matches.'

There have been many great tennis rivalries down the years. Tennis is a sport that lends itself to rivalry because players can meet often and results can be so topsy-turvy. There have been passionate but short-lived rivalries such as those of Suzanne Lenglen and Helen Wills, Don Budge and Gottfried von Cramm, and enduring rivalries like those of Ken Rosewall and Rod Laver, Margaret Court and Billie Jean King, Martina Navratilova and Chris Evert, Andre Agassi and Pete Sampras. But none surpassed McEnroe and Borg. And though they were to meet six more times on the ATP tour and many more times in seniors events during their tennis twilight years, it came to a head that day at Wimbledon.

It was Borg's finest hour. McEnroe would go on to greater tennis glory and eventually would win seven Grand Slam titles. He was to beat Borg in five sets in the final of the 1980 US Open and in four sets in the 1981 Wimbledon and

US finals. But it was during that 1980 Wimbledon final that McEnroe showed his finest qualities. No temper, no tantrums. Just hour after hour of unrelentingly fine tennis, and the sort of tenacity and back-to-the-wall courage that only true champions possess.

The curious thing about Borg and McEnroe is that they were not always true to their stereotypical behaviour. Borg first came to international tennis prominence in 1972. The 15-year-old from Sodertalje, a smallish town about half an hour south-west of Stockholm, was selected to play in the Swedish Davis Cup team against New Zealand at Bastad. He shocked by winning both his singles, including a come-from-behind five-set victory over Onny Parun, a respected professional who reached Wimbledon quarter-finals in 1971–72 and would reach the final of the 1973 Australian Open. Borg went on to win the 1972 Junior Wimbledon, beating Buster Mottram 7-5 in the third set in the final.

Already he was noted for his cool temperament. But three years earlier things were different. 'When I was 12, I was a cheat on the court,' he once said. 'I was always throwing my racket, hitting the ball over the fence. I was a real nutcase.' Eventually his parents became so embarrassed by his antics they refused to watch his matches. Shortly afterward, he was suspended for six months by Swedish tennis officials. It was a salutary lesson, for Borg went on to epitomise self-discipline and control on the court.

Thereafter displays of emotion from the Swede were rare. For the most part, he satisfied himself with looking twice at a linesman and, at times of huge importance, perhaps indicating with a fleeting gesture where a ball had landed. He seemed to have channelled those early emotional outbreaks into stubbornness.

Borg was the most obdurate of all players. He would rally endlessly on the clay courts of Roland Garros, simply determined to stay there longer than his opponent. His stubbornness came out in other ways too. In 1991, when he was making a brief comeback, he refused to adopt the new generation of carbon fibre rackets, preferring to use his old wooden rackets – never mind they were obsolete and did not enable him to generate the power he needed to survive on the modern tour.

Borg showed his unyielding nature when he played local idol Adriano Panatta in the Italian Open final at Rome in 1978. It was a threatening situation for the visitor. Before the match, the umpire appealed to the crowd to be fair to both players, but the spectators desperately wanted Panatta to win and would do almost anything to ensure he did. The linesmen and the umpire bowed to the pressure of the vocal and parochial crowd and soon the odds were slanted outrageously against Borg. Still the Swede persevered, and he took the match to a fifth set.

Even more outlandish behaviour followed and three times Borg was hit by coins thrown by the spectators. He appealed to the umpire, but the loutish behaviour did not stop. The Swede calmly picked up the coins, went back on court and beat Panatta 6-3 in the fifth, thereby extracting the sweetest revenge possible. He vowed then he would not return to the Italian Open, and he never did.

There was one occasion when the temper Borg must have displayed as a youngster was seen in an important match. In the final of the Masters in New York in January 1981, Borg beat McEnroe 6-4, 6-7, 7-6. During the second set tiebreak, which was very tight, the umpire overruled the linesman on a call. Borg must have felt unusually strongly about it because he walked to the umpire and quietly protested. The umpire wouldn't change his mind and Borg refused to continue. Even after quite a delay, Borg wouldn't carry on. The umpire finally warned him for time-wasting, then penalised him a point. Still Borg wouldn't play, and he was penalised a second point. That made it set point. Sensation of sensations … Borg was within a whisker of being defaulted. Only then did he resume.

He lost that set and just won the third. Afterwards, in a classic understatement, he said, 'I was very, very angry.' The episode threw McEnroe, who was shocked and unsure how to react to Borg's display of anger.

There were many times when the boot was on the other foot, however. The pair met in the semi-finals of an indoor tournament in New Orleans in 1979 and at 5-5 in the third, McEnroe got himself into a rage about a decision he felt was wrong. He seemed to have lost control of his temper to the point where it began affecting his tennis. Then he looked up the court at Borg who, palms down, quietly waved his hands up and down, in effect telling his opponent to calm down. 'It's okay, just relax,' was the message. Surprised and chastened, McEnroe regained his composure and went on to win 5-7, 6-1, 7-6.

There were few people McEnroe openly looked up to, but Borg was one of them. McEnroe has always been unstinting in his praise. He says the Swede was the best athlete he has seen on the tennis court. More, he feels Borg understood him. 'He thought I was a little crazy, but it didn't seem to bother him,' McEnroe wrote in his autobiography, *You Cannot Be Serious*. 'The way I saw it, he went out of his way to show me respect.'

Amazingly, the first time they met in the flesh – though meeting is probably not the right word – was during a US Open in the early 1970s, when Borg was a boyish-looking teenager and McEnroe a ballboy in one of his matches. McEnroe recalled the moment:

I thought he was incredible-looking – the long hair, the headband, that little bit of scruff on his face that he'd get from not shaving for a couple of weeks. And the Fila outfit – the tight shirts and short shorts … I loved that stuff! I would trade anything, back then, to get a Fila striped shirt; a jacket was a really big deal …

I thought Borg was magical – like some kind of Viking god who'd landed on the tennis court. I can't explain, exactly. It certainly wasn't his personality, that's for sure. You've seen the interviews. He didn't have much to say, on or off the court – back then, he didn't *have* to say much. The way he looked – long, tan legs, wide shoulders – and the way he played, the vibe he gave off, all that was more than enough.

Borg had just turned 17 when he reached the quarter-finals at Wimbledon in 1973, losing to Yorkshireman Roger Taylor 7-5 in the fifth. He became the object of Borgmania, and developed a following – thousands of teenage girls who treated him like a rock star. He had to play all his matches on the show courts and had to be hustled on and off them. Watching Borg play a tennis match was like watching the Beatles or the Rolling Stones do a live show.

Borg made the leap from talented junior to great player remarkably quickly. By the time he was 17 he had won the Italian and French Opens, and two years later won the first of his five straight Wimbledons, beating Ilie Nastase in straight sets. He did not lose a set throughout that 1976 championship.

He went on to compile a fabulous record. In 1975 he had led Sweden to that country's first-ever Davis Cup victory. During this campaign, Borg was unbeaten in singles, scoring wins over such good players as Wojtek Fibak, Karl Meiler, Alex Metreveli, Jose Higueras, Manuel Orantes, Jaime Fillol and Jan Kodes. It was quite an accomplishment for a lad who was 18 for much of the year.

Later he won 11 Grand Slam titles, six French and five Wimbledon. He never really attacked the Australian Open, which was a lesser event in the 1970s, but had a run of disappointments at the US Open. He was runner-up four times and a semi-finalist on another occasion. He claimed he could not play as well under lights, that he was at a disadvantage trying to pick up the laser-fast serves of such players as Roscoe Tanner and McEnroe. It's true he did lose a big match under lights to Tanner, and he had problems with injuries at times during the US Open as well. But perhaps more pertinently, the hard surface didn't suit him. The ball bounced more and forced Borg further back in the court, meaning he had to run further and that his passing shots had to be hit even more precisely than normal. The US Open title he should have won was in 1976, when the tournament was played on clay, but Jimmy Connors beat him 6-4 in the fourth set. Considering Borg's domination of clay in Europe, this was a Grand Slam title he let slip away.

Despite the holes in his tennis CV, and despite departing big-time tennis at the age of 25 (except for a couple of brief, aborted comebacks), Borg was one of the all-time greats. The American publication *Tennis* chose him as one of the 10 greatest players of the 20th century. He was voted Sweden's sportsperson of the century and *Sports Illustrated* picked him as the No 2 tennis player of the century, behind Pete Sampras. France's sports newspaper *L'Equipe* nominated Borg No 2 tennis player of the century, behind Rod Laver, and No 13 of all sportspeople of the century.

With his double-handed backhand and his heavy top-spin groundstrokes (sometimes he looked more like a table-tennis player, so heavily did he whip his top-spin), Borg's style was revolutionary, and a whole generation of youngsters modelled themselves on his game and his on-court demeanour.

Why did he retire so young? Well, he was young only in years. As with Martina Hingis, who in 2002 retired at the grand old age of 22, Borg had already had a full career in tennis. He had been a major contender in Grand Slam events for nine years, had locked horns with fine players like Connors, Vitas Gerulaitis, Guillermo Vilas and McEnroe, and had enjoyed massive success. He had made money and won titles, 62 in singles, four in doubles. Now he'd had enough.

He confided to McEnroe and Gerulaitis during an exhibition tour in Australia in late 1981 that he was quitting tennis. The Americans laughed – Borg was only 25. They simply didn't understand. Now, when he thinks back, McEnroe feels maybe he had something to do with Borg's premature retirement. When you've been king of the roost, No 2 is not an attractive proposition. Borg didn't want to grind away and not be top dog.

Borg's retirement was undoubtedly a blow for McEnroe. 'It was unbelievable,' he said. 'The matches between us had become really exciting. It took the wind out of my sails and I had a very tough time motivating myself and getting back on track.'

McEnroe was also a brilliant teenage player, though his serve-and-volley game was a lot more difficult to master than the Borg groundstroke variety. McEnroe had to concern himself more with slices as well as top-spin, approach shots as well as baseline strokes, and then there was the small matter of learning the finer points of volleying. He was always going to be an exceptional player, though. Attending Stanford University for an abbreviated time, he led Stanford to the NCAA title and became only the fourth player to win the US intercollegiate singles crown as a freshman.

By mid-1977, aged 18, he had won the French Open mixed doubles with his friend Mary Carillo, later to become a leading television tennis analyst, and had earned himself top seeding for Junior Wimbledon. He never did win Junior Wimbledon, however, because he also entered the senior event that year and, after working his way through qualifying, kept performing miracles to eventually reach the semi-finals. To get there, he beat Ismail El Shafei, Colin Dowdeswell, Karl Meiler, Sandy Mayer and Phil Dent. Not bad for the 233rd-ranked player in the world.

McEnroe's semi-final was billed as Jimmy Connors versus John P. Who? The odds before the two semis were Borg 2-1, Connors 3-1, Gerulaitis 7-1, McEnroe 250-1. Connors was mighty happy to get through with a 6-4 in the fourth victory. That tournament propelled McEnroe into the big time, and for the next 15 years he was major tennis news.

McEnroe won three Wimbledon crowns and four US Opens. He never won the Australian Open, his worst defeat a four set semi-final loss to clay-courter Mats Wilander in 1983 when the tournament was still held at Kooyong's grass courts. And he never did conquer the Roland Garros clay courts, though he went desperately close to winning a French Open. In the 1984 final, he led Ivan Lendl 6-3, 6-2, but at 3-1 in the third set blew the match when he let his temper get the better of him and allowed himself to be distracted from the task at hand.

McEnroe excelled in many areas of tennis. He was a brilliant Davis Cup player, maybe the best in history. He played in 38 ties from 1978 to the early 1990s, winning 41 of 49 singles matches and, incredibly, 18 of 20 doubles matches. He made his Davis Cup singles debut in a Davis Cup final, beating Britain's John Lloyd 6-1, 6-2, 6-2 at Palm Springs in 1978, the first player to make his singles debut in a Davis Cup final and win the match. McEnroe made six appearances in Davis Cup finals and on five of those occasions the United States won. He played two of the longest matches in Davis Cup history, beating Mats Wilander in 6h 22min in 1982 and losing to Boris Becker in 6h 21min in 1987.

McEnroe was such a good doubles player that for years the world's No 1 combination was said to be John McEnroe and Anyone. He won 77 professional singles titles and 77 doubles titles, including nine Grand Slam doubles – with Peter Fleming (seven), Mark Woodforde (one) and Michael Stich (one).

McEnroe took a sabbatical in 1986 and when he returned was never quite the same force, though he remained an outstanding player, good enough to win the Wimbledon doubles in 1992 with Stich.

It always seemed McEnroe enjoyed the tennis scene more than Borg. The Swede was extremely self-contained, cocooned by a small entourage headed by his girlfriend/fiancée/first wife, Romanian Mariana Simionescu, and his coach Lennart Bergelin. McEnroe was good mates with some of the other American players, including Peter Fleming and Vitas Gerulaitis. There was always an edge to McEnroe and he tended to comport himself like a rock star, but there was no denying he loved tennis.

For some years after he quit major tennis, Borg was hardly seen and any time he was in the news, it was for disastrous happenings in his private life – his companies going bankrupt, marriages and other relationships failing, even a reported suicide attempt.

McEnroe didn't have the most peaceful of lives after his big-time tennis days either, but the New Yorker seemed more suited to a frenetic pace. He continued playing on the ATP tour, and kept getting into trouble for outbursts of bad behaviour, to the point where he was defaulted while playing Michael Pernfors in the round of 16 in the 1990 Australian Open. His marriage to Tatum O'Neal crumbled spectacularly amid all sorts of accusations, including drug-taking.

McEnroe turned to television commentary where he was a natural. His intelligence, insight, willingness to be outspoken and sense of humour made him compelling listening. He also had a shot at captaining the US Davis Cup team, but didn't enjoy the experience. McEnroe loved the Davis Cup and when he was a top player committed himself unconditionally to the competition. He was miffed when the next generation, players like Sampras and Agassi, didn't care to offer such wholehearted support.

For some years, Borg and McEnroe's paths didn't cross very often, except perhaps for the odd function to honour past greats. Then came their involvement on the seniors tour and the two old warhorses lined up against each other again all around the world, from Asia to England, the United States to Australia.

They were true to themselves. Borg had remained in terrific shape and gave a whole new generation of spectators a glimpse at the characteristics that had made him such a special player. They saw his athleticism, his matchless passing strokes and his unnervingly calm demeanour. And McEnroe still had the slick serve-and-volley game, the brilliant winners … and the outbursts of temper. Sometimes it seemed just part of the show and McEnroe had to suppress a smile, but there was plenty of shouting and complaining, plus some fantastic tennis.

They've settled down now, as much as two sports super-celebrities can. Borg, for many years a tax exile in Monte Carlo, has returned to Sweden. His third wife, Patricia, is a stockbroker. He is busy cultivating a clothing and apparel line bearing his name and coaching promising youngsters. McEnroe will always rush about at 100 miles an hour. He has his tennis commitments, plus his music – he has his own band – plus his art gallery interests and his and his second wife Patty's extended family.

They say that modern tennis players are too concerned with money, and too protected by agents, partners, coaches and advisers to enjoy the sort of camaraderie that was normal in professional tennis during the 1970s – therefore it was nice that one of the people McEnroe made sure he invited to his second wedding was Borg.

When McEnroe and Borg see each other now, there's a soft, mellow feeling, two middle-aged men who put each other to the sword all those years ago and brought out the best in each other.

	Bjorn Rune Borg	**John Patrick McEnroe**
Born	6 June 1956, Sodertalje, Sweden	16 February 1959, Wiesbaden, Germany
Career titles		
Singles	62 (finalist 26)	77 (finalist 31)
Doubles	4 (finalist 4)	77 (finalist 23)
Grand Slam titles		
Singles	French Open: 1974, 1975, 1978, 1979, 1980, 1981. Wimbledon: 1976, 1977, 1978, 1979, 1980.	US Open: 1979, 1980, 1981, 1984. Wimbledon: 1981, 1983, 1984.
Doubles		Wimbledon: 1979, 1981, 1983, 1984, 1992. US Open: 1979, 1981, 1983, 1989.
Mixed doubles		French Open 1977.
Davis Cup wins	1975.	1978, 1979, 1981, 1982, 1992.

HEAD TO HEAD

	Place	Surface	Stage of tournament	Winner	Score
1978	Stockholm	Carpet	Semi-final	McEnroe	6-3, 6-4
1979	Richmond	Carpet	Semi-final	Borg	4-6, 7-6, 6-3
1979	New Orleans	Carpet	Semi-final	McEnroe	5-7, 6-1, 7-6
1979	Rotterdam	Carpet	Final	Borg	6-4, 6-2
1979	WCT Final	Carpet	Final	McEnroe	7-5, 4-6, 6-2, 7-6
1979	Canadian Open	Hard	Final	Borg	6-3, 6-3
1979	Masters, N. York	Carpet	Semi-final	Borg	6-7, 6-3, 7-6
1980	Wimbledon	Grass	Final	Borg	1-6, 7-5, 6-3, 6-7, 8-6
1980	US Open	Hard	Final	McEnroe	7-6, 6-1, 6-7, 5-7, 6-4
1980	Stockholm	Carpet	Final	Borg	6-3, 6-4
1980	Masters, N. York	Carpet	Round robin	Borg	6-4, 6-7, 7-6
1981	Milan	Carpet	Final	McEnroe	7-6, 6-4
1981	Wimbledon	Grass	Final	McEnroe	4-6, 7-6, 7-6, 6-4
1981	US Open	Hard	Final	McEnroe	4-6, 6-2, 6-4, 6-3
Result: 7-7					

2 The Four-minute Wonders

Roger Bannister v John Landy

When athletics followers billed the mile clash between Englishman Roger Bannister and Australian John Landy at the 1954 Vancouver Empire Games as the Race of the Century, they weren't exaggerating.

Generally, sports promoters will do anything to hype an event. They tend to use the word 'century' liberally. When James J. Jefferies met Jack Johnson for the heavyweight title at Reno in 1910, for example, it was billed as the Fight of the Century, even though the century had 90 years to run! But Bannister–Landy met all the criteria. It was a seminal moment in athletics history. It featured the two greatest milers of the period, but what gave their clash a sharper focus was the magic of the supposedly unconquerable four-minute mile.

As long ago as the time of Walter George in the late 19th century, runners had dreamed of cracking four minutes for the mile. Paavo Nurmi, the Flying Finn, spoke of the prospect in the 1920s, and Jack Lovelock, the enigmatic New Zealander, moved closer to the barrier in the 1930s. Then great Swedish runners Gunder Haegg and Arne Andersson got stuck in during the early 1940s. Between them they trimmed the world record from 4min 06.4s to 4min 01.4s, which Haegg ran in July 1945. Sceptics who had claimed the human body could not stand the strain of a four-minute mile began to concede that it was possible.

But after the brilliant Haegg–Andersson era, the record never moved. The 1948 Olympic 1500m crown went to a Swede, Henry Eriksson, ahead of his countryman Lennart Strand. Neither ever got near Haegg's time for the mile. In 1952 popular Jose Barthel of Luxemburg collected the Olympic 1500m gold, but still the mile record was not approached, not by Barthel or the other medallists that year, Bob McMillan of the United States and Werner Lueg of

Germany. Who could have guessed, in mid-1952, what exciting times were just around the corner?

The key figures were Bannister and Landy, though others, such as Belgian Gaston Reiff and American Wes Santee, played bit parts in the drama.

Bannister, born near London in 1929, began attending Oxford University in 1946. When he arrived at the university aged 17, he had never worn spikes nor run on a track, but soon revealed a talent for middle-distance running. The first mile victory of his life came in the 1946 Freshmen's Sports at Oxford. His time was 4min 53.0s. When he was 18, he declined to seek a place in the England team for the 1948 London Olympics, preferring to wait until the next Games, when he felt he would be at his peak. Nevertheless, those 1948 Olympics inspired him, as did a run by Englishman Sydney Wooderson at White City in 1945. He dedicated himself to running, advised at times by famous Austrian-born coach Franz Stampfl. Two of Bannister's running companions were his Achilles Club colleagues Chris Chataway and Chris Brasher, both of whom were to play major roles in his career and become world-class athletes themselves.

Bannister trained relatively hard for those days, though he did nothing like the 100 miles a week workload advocated by New Zealand distance-coaching guru Arthur Lydiard. The Englishman preferred to run 'fresh', rather like Lovelock, another Oxford University student of a generation earlier, which meant that he was not able to sustain a long season of gruelling races. (The lives of Bannister and Lovelock were oddly intertwined. Not only were they both champion milers, but they attended the same college at Oxford and later worked at the same hospital in London. They first met in 1947.) The rangy 6ft 1in, 10st 11lb Bannister had a sizzling finishing kick and would try to shepherd his resources so that he had some energy left for his final burst. He finished his big runs absolutely spent, in contrast to what we see today, when even after running world records middle-distance athletes look relatively stress-free.

From 1948 to 1951, Bannister improved steadily, and as the 1952 Helsinki Olympics approached he was regarded by the English as a strong 1500m gold medal contender. Thoughts of a sub-four-minute mile were far into the background in an Olympic year.

Meanwhile in Australia, John Landy, born in 1930, was starting to come to public attention. Landy was a late developer as an athlete. At 19 he had run no faster than 4min 38s for the mile. At 20 he whittled that down to a still moderate 4min 19s. A year later he'd managed 4min 11s.

Encouraged, Landy set to work training intensively. He packed in far more miles than did Bannister, who was busy studying towards a medical degree.

Landy was a university student, too – he eventually gained a Bachelor of Agricultural Science degree at Melbourne University – but he made sure he ran two to three hours a day, and did lots of repetition 600-yard and 440-yard workouts.

Though Landy never had Bannister's raw speed, he built his strength with Emil Zatopek-like training and became a formidable front-runner. He would set such a torrid early pace that he sapped the kickers of their sting before the final lap. Landy was coached at this point in his career by the ebullient and eccentric Percy Cerutty, who a few years later would gain more fame as the coach of Olympic champion and multi-world record-holder Herb Elliott.

Landy went to the 1952 Olympics, but he was still a fledgling at international level and was eliminated in a first-round 1500m heat that included Bannister. It was their first meeting. Landy also failed to progress past the preliminary stage in the 5000m.

Bannister, however, went to Helsinki as a big name. He'd had a fine 1951 season, but had raced only lightly in 1952, a policy that hurt him when a round of semi-finals was belatedly added to the 1500m programme, as he had fewer reserves of strength than many of his rivals. 'With three races at the Olympics, their tougher training gave them an advantage,' Bannister said later.

The Englishman ran unimpressively in his semi-final and in the final never looked comfortable. While Barthel sped to victory in 3min 45.1s, Bannister barely held on for a disappointing fourth in 3min 46s. He was criticised in England for his unconventional training and coaching methods and left Helsinki shattered.

It was Landy who made the first big advance. On the back of his heavy training, and a wiser runner after his Olympic experience, he stunned the athletics world by running 4min 02.1s for the mile in Melbourne on 13 December, the third-fastest time ever and nine seconds better than his previous best. 'It was the most important race of my career and I think it triggered the race to the four minutes,' said Landy recently. So surprised were the officials that they delayed announcing the time until they had had their watches checked independently. They also had the track re-measured. The *New York Times* was equally sceptical. 'Please pass the salt. This is not to be believed of an unknown runner,' wrote their athletics correspondent.

Watching from England, Bannister was shocked. 'I could hardly believe the improvement from the runner I had known at Helsinki,' he wrote in his biography, *First Four Minutes*. 'Landy made no secret of the fact that the four-minute mile was his goal. The race for the first four-minute mile had really begun.'

Three weeks later, again running in Melbourne, Landy set a strong early pace and passed the 1500m mark in 3min 44.4s. He needed to run the final 108 metres in 15.5s to break four minutes, but the early pace proved too demanding and he tied up. Even so, he managed 4min 02.8s. Bannister: 'Wherever I went after Landy's two races, the inevitable question was broached. Was it possible for a man to run a mile in four minutes? The four-minute mile had become rather like an Everest – a challenge to the human spirit. It was a barrier that seemed to defy all attempts to break it.'

Landy's times, both achieved without any competition of note, emphasised what a fabulous front-runner he was and set the athletics world abuzz. For the first time since the Haegg-Andersson era, the possibility of the four-minute mile loomed large, and Bannister became determined to atone for his Olympic disappointment by becoming the first to run it. He was relieved when the southern hemisphere summer ended without Landy getting to the goal first. Through the northern summer of 1953, Bannister made several attempts. These were runs with little advance publicity and often took place on tracks of questionable quality in unfavourable weather.

Helping Bannister were Brasher and Australian Don Macmillan, who by then lived in England. Bannister had a serious crack at the famous Motspur Park track on 27 June 1953, and after passing the three-quarter mile mark in 3min 01.8s held on to finish in 4min 02s, the fastest mile since Haegg. However, the time was never ratified. Brasher began very slowly and allowed Bannister to lap him. As Bannister, a lap ahead, approached him, Brasher sped up and paced his friend. Because pacing was not permitted in the 1950s, British officials would not allow his time to stand as a record. Bannister had several other impressive miles through 1953, including winning the AAA mile in 4min 05.2s. He was unbeaten for the season, but cracking the four-minute mark had eluded him.

By now a genuine Bannister–Landy rivalry had emerged. It was an odd business because by the end of 1953 they had never faced each other on the track, except in that Olympic heat when Landy was a novice. Yet their rivalry was undeniable. They followed each other's times closely and sports magazines devoted page after page to speculating about who would crack four minutes first. Bannister said he spent the winter of 1953–54 following Landy's progress in Australia: 'I waited anxiously for news of Landy, who was getting into his stride again. This would be his second season devoted to record-breaking runs, and I felt it was only a question of time before he ran a four-minute mile.'

Bannister considered Landy had an advantage because he was running in a warmer climate. He conceded Landy's training regime, which involved weight-lifting and running every day, was more severe than that of any other middle-distance runner.

Landy himself could hardly wait for the 1953–54 Australian summer. Though handicapped because his attempts at the four-minute mark were in effect solo efforts, he peeled off race after race of brilliant running. At Melbourne on 12 December 1953, he ran 4min 02s, equal to Bannister's best. Despite this fine result, Landy was rather disheartened. 'If Haegg and Andersson, with several years of hectic rivalry, couldn't go below 4min 01.4s, what hope have I got here, with no competition at all? I can see now what a colossal task it is,' he said. 'Perhaps I can reduce my time by half a second.' Over the next two months, Landy made three more serious attempts on the record, running 4min 02.4s, and 4min 02.6s twice. He also ran several times under 4min 06s.

Landy's fantastically consistent running was applauded all over the world, and he became a real crowd-puller in Australia, but the man himself was frustrated. He said he had hit a brick wall, and wouldn't attempt the record again. He had nevertheless caught the four-minute fever, and was already planning to go to Scandinavia for the northern summer.

In England, Bannister readied himself for 1954, which would be his last year of running. He hoped there would still be a four-minute barrier to break, so close was Landy. Watched intently by Stampfl, Bannister trained with Brasher and Chataway. He'd heard about Landy's intended trip to Europe. There wasn't much time to lose.

An attempt on the time, dubbed Operation Four Minutes by the Bannister group, was scheduled for Thursday 6 May – extremely early in the season – on the dodgy Iffley Road track at Oxford, when the British AAA team would meet Oxford University. It was a low-key midweek meeting and a dicey venue for an attempt to achieve athletics immortality but, as Bannister said, time was critical.

The weather was unpromising (when Bannister arrived at the track, spectators were wearing raincoats and sheltering under umbrellas), and a decision on the attempt was delayed. Bannister and Stampfl caught the train to Oxford after Bannister had completed his morning shift at St Mary's Hospital in London, where he was a student of the medical school. In the late afternoon it began to rain lightly and the wind was gusting. Bannister decided against the record attempt. It required some swift talking by Stampfl, Brasher and Chataway to change his mind.

Then fate took a hand. As the six starters warmed up, the rain stopped and the wind died. Brasher set the early pace and Bannister fell in behind. Brasher was a smart runner – he would win an Olympic steeplechase gold medal in 1956

– and judged the pace perfectly, despite Bannister imploring him to go faster. After Brasher had done his work, the red-haired Chataway took over and towed Bannister until the back straight for the last time.

Then Bannister, who'd passed the three-quarter mile mark in 3min 0.5s, went into overdrive for his finishing burst. He passed the 1500m in 3min 43s, which equalled the world record. With the 1200 spectators urging him on, he forced his way down the straight and fell into waiting arms as he breasted the tape.

A few minutes later, Norris McWhirter (who with his twin brother Ross was for years to edit the popular *Guinness Book of Records*), made one of the most famous and dramatic of all sports announcements. 'Ladies and gentlemen,' he intoned, 'here is the result of event number nine, the one mile: first, number 41, R.G. Bannister, Amateur Athletic Association and formerly of Exeter and Merton Colleges, Oxford, with a time which is a new meeting and track record and which, subject to ratification, will be a new English Native, British National, British All-Comers, European, British Empire and World record. The time was *three* …'

The roar from the spectators drowned out the rest of the announcement. Bannister's time was 3min 59.4s. Bannister, Brasher and Chataway did a joint victory lap. Bannister reflected later that he suddenly felt free of the burden of ambition he had been carrying for years.

It was fitting that he should achieve such a famous feat at the Iffley Road track, which could aptly be called 'The Track that Bannister Built'. It was while Bannister was president of the Oxford University Athletic Club that he'd battled to have the quaint old 1/3-mile track replaced with a six-lane 440-yard track that conformed to international specifications.

Bannister recorded in *First Four Minutes*: 'It was a triumph not only for me, but also for Chris Brasher and Chris Chataway. We shared a place where no man had yet ventured, secure for all time no matter how fast men might run miles in the future.'

These days, with more than a thousand men having gone under four minutes for the mile, people might wonder what all the fuss was about. But in 1954, Bannister's achievement rated far above any golf or tennis feat. Even soccer's World Cup paled by comparison. American magazine *Sports Illustrated* rated Bannister's sub-four-minute mile at Oxford and the ascent of Mt Everest as the two greatest sports achievements of the 20th century.

Landy had arrived in Turku, the former capital of Finland, on 3 May and was sitting in a restaurant when he heard that Bannister had beaten him to the magic milestone. 'I was amazed, really,' he said years later. 'I couldn't believe that

Bannister had managed to lop as much as two seconds off the record in just one race. Back then the four-minute mile was like a barrier, a limit. If the record of 4min 1s was going to be lowered, we thought it would only go down by a tenth of a second or so at a time.

'A lot of people seem to think I must have been devastated, but I wasn't. I was just astonished at how much time he'd taken off the record. Because I thought I was just as good a runner as he was, it gave me a bit of a hurry-up to run a time like that myself. It made me think I really had better pull something out of the hat.'

Landy's first attempt in Europe, on 31 May, resulted in a time of 4min 01.6s, his fastest, but still frustratingly slower than Bannister's. A week later he repeated it. He wondered if he would ever be able to make the step up. Then, on 21 June, 46 days after Bannister's mile at Iffley Road, Landy ran the race of his life in Turku. Against Bannister's wishes, Chataway had travelled from England to take him on, and the extra pace he injected into the race made the difference. Chataway led for the first half-mile. Landy responded by taking over for the last two laps and maintaining the sizzling pace.

He passed the 1500m mark in 3min 41.8s, a second under Wes Santee's world record, then powered home while the Finns cheered him on. He broke the tape in 3min 57.9s (officially rounded up to 3min 58.0s). After two years of chipping away, he had smashed past the four-minute barrier *and* Bannister's record, beating his previous best by 3.7s.

'I was totally amazed,' says Landy. 'I suppose my rhythm had been so good in that race that I didn't have a sense that I was running faster than I ever had in my life.' Though Landy beat Chataway by 40 yards, he said the spur of having Chataway with him at the bell had added urgency to his racing.

Back in London, Bannister was stunned when news of Landy's run came through: 'The margin of 1.4s by which he had broken my record was greater than anything I had feared.'

After Landy's virtuoso effort, attention now turned to the Vancouver Empire Games six weeks later. Everyone was talking about the forthcoming showdown between Landy and Bannister, the Mile of the Century, the Miracle Mile, the meeting between the last two world record-holders and the only two men to run under four minutes.

Landy's world record had a remarkable effect on Bannister. After his epic effort at Oxford, he had lost a little motivation, but now he was spurred into top gear. Bannister later wrote: 'Neither John Landy nor myself – nor the general public – could tolerate the kind of stalemate set up by our two records having been made away from each other. The world seemed almost too small for us and we must meet to settle the score.' Bannister said that while it was lovely to break four minutes at Oxford, his main aim that season was the Empire Games gold medal. Landy summed up his position: 'I wanted a world record and an Empire title for Australia by the end of the year.'

There was huge speculation before their race on the last day of the Vancouver Games. Normally US interest in the Empire (now Commonwealth) Games was muted, but for this race dozens of American journalists were present. It was clearly going to be a famous moment in sport.

Strangely, these two great runners, whose names fitted so comfortably and so often into a single sentence, had never formally met. About a fortnight before the Games began, Landy was working out on the track and ran into Chataway, who introduced him to another distinguished-looking English gentleman. 'John, how are you?' Chataway said. 'May I introduce you to Roger Bannister.'

The three men stood there for 20 minutes, chatting. They complimented each other on their running that summer and then carried on with their training. 'There wasn't much of this thing they call "gamesmanship" back then,' said Landy. 'You met, you raced, you got on with it.' Landy described Bannister as 'a free-flowing runner with a good tactical brain. He didn't compete much but when he did, it mattered to him. I always thought of him as my main rival.'

Bannister, for his part, recalled Landy as 'a modest and unassuming man who had the crucial ability to drive himself on his own'. Bannister also saw in Landy 'a man of steel that was not easily recognised on first acquaintance. I think his upbringing and the English-style grammar school he attended at Geelong was an environment that hid something of his will.'

Both runners had health problems. Bannister had a cold for the week before the race and, perhaps more seriously, Landy had cut his foot on glass from a flashbulb while strolling bare-footed the day before the final. The cut required four stitches. Bannister qualified with a heat time of 4min 08.4s, Landy in 4min 11.4s.

Everyone seemed to have an opinion about who would win the final. The Bannister camp had plenty of backing, especially from British competitors. Bannister often gave the impression of being aloof. His was a sensitive, withdrawn personality, more content rock-climbing or tramping alone than competing in front of thousands. He carried out much of his training in secret, whereas Landy was always happy to train in full view of the world's media. Landy, shorter, stockier, and as bronzed as Bannister was pale, was extremely popular and approachable and was well supported, especially by the New Zealanders and South Africans, as well as his Australian team.

It seemed clear how the race would be run. Landy would take the lead and try to run the legs off Bannister. The Englishman would attempt to hold on as best he could and kick home with his superior sprint.

The day of their race, 7 August 1954, marked the highest point in their rivalry. It had been conducted across oceans, but now the pair were going head to head, to sort out once and for all who was king of the track. There were other good runners in the field. Two young New Zealanders, Murray Halberg and Bill Baillie, would years later become world running figures, but in 1954 Bannister and Landy were several classes above all opposition. The bookmakers had Landy a 4-1 favourite.

Landy duly took the lead early in the first lap and gradually applied increasing pressure, trying to shake off the long-striding Bannister. Landy passed the half-mile in 1min 58.2s, 10 yards ahead of Bannister's 1min 59.4s. Halfway around that second lap, the gap had stretched to 15 yards. Another couple of yards and Landy would have broken contact with his chief pursuer. Landy powered on relentlessly while Bannister, grimly determined, dug deep to stay in touch, then cut the gap.

At the three-quarter mark, Landy was timed at 2min 58.4s and Bannister at 2min 58.7s. This was sensationally fast for the 1950s. Had Landy done enough? Did Bannister have any sting left? Alarm bells were ringing for Landy: 'When he was still there at the bell, I knew I was in trouble. My legs were just starting to feel a bit rubbery.'

Along the back straight, Landy sped up and Bannister struggled to hold on. Around the last turn, more than 20,000 fans yelled and wondered who was stronger. Landy led at the 1500m in 3min 41.9s, only 0.1s slower than his world record. This was the best he had ever finished. Behind him, Bannister was worried. If Landy didn't slow down soon, he would run away with the race.

They went into the final bend, a moment that has become famous in athletics folklore. The crowd was roaring. Athletes on the inside of the track were exhorting greater efforts from their champion. Around the bend, Landy looked over his left shoulder, hoping to see Bannister struggling behind. He saw nothing. And, because of the noise, he heard nothing. He whipped his head to the right just in time to see Bannister drawing alongside. As fate would have it, at the moment Landy looked over his left shoulder, Bannister had attacked on the outside.

Bannister recalled in *First Four Minutes*: 'The moment he looked around he was unprotected against me, and so lost a valuable fraction of a second in his response to my challenge.'

Landy was unable to respond quickly enough. Bannister surged ahead and ran on strongly to win by five yards in 3min 58.8s. Landy was second in 3min

59.6s. It was the first time two runners had broken four minutes in one race. Canadian Bill Ferguson was a long way back in third, in 4min 04.6s.

The most talked-about mile race ever had lived up to every expectation. The world's two fastest milers had both gone under four minutes. Bannister had won again. He was No 1. Some of Landy's friends tried to blame the cut foot for the defeat, but Landy stopped them short. 'There's absolutely nothing wrong with the foot,' he said. 'Bannister was simply the better man.'

Bannister later described the last lap as 'one of the most exciting moments of my life'. He said that Landy was the sort of runner he could never become. 'I admired him for that. Before Vancouver, he achieved a record of solo mile races that I could never have equalled. At Vancouver he had the courage to lead at the same speed in a closely competitive race.'

Landy said there was 'a beautiful symmetry' to the race in Vancouver. 'It was a classic promoter's dream. Just think about it: here's this Brit – he's just run under four minutes for the first time – then along comes this Australian three weeks later and breaks it. You couldn't have dreamt up anything better. It was the closest we'd come to a heavyweight title fight in athletics.'

That race really was the extent of their rivalry. Bannister and Landy were drawn together in the public mind because of the magic of the four-minute mile. They met in one major race, and Bannister won it. Later that season, Bannister won the European 1500m championship, then retired to become a doctor.

Landy retired from running in 1955, but returned for one more year because the 1956 Olympics were in his hometown of Melbourne. He took the oath on behalf of the athletes at the opening ceremony. Though locals hoped for a victory, Landy ran well for third, after having adopted unusual tactics. Instead of taking the lead and attempting to burn off his challengers, he hung back and kicked for home. He could not match Irishman Ron Delany's withering final burst, and German Klaus Richtzenhain pipped him for second, but he finished with surprising speed. Richtzenhain and Landy were timed at 3min 42.0s. It was Landy's last big race. He'd run under four minutes for the mile six times.

Already a hero to the Australian public, Landy had gained even more popularity at the Australian nationals in Melbourne earlier that year. Midway through the third lap of the one-mile final, national junior mile champion Ron Clarke fell. Landy, considering he might have been at fault, turned and went back to help Clarke to his feet – then took off after the leaders and still managed to win the race in 4min 4.2s. Onlookers felt his chivalrous action cost him a world record. His spontaneous act of generosity was ample evidence of what a fine sportsman he was.

But Landy was always like that. Before the final in Melbourne, he'd said to Delany: 'I think you can win this one, Ron.' After the race, when he saw Delany on his knees and thought he was ill, he rushed across to comfort him, not realising that Delany was deep in prayer.

It was a curious twist of fate that the veteran Landy and the teenage Clarke should be linked as runners because of an incident near the end of one career and the beginning of another. Landy and Clarke were similar sorts of athletes. They were superb front-runners who performed brilliantly against the clock and set swags of records, but were unable to win gold medals at major meets.

Bannister himself made a thoughtful gesture at the 1956 Olympics. By this time, 10 runners had broken four minutes for the mile. All 10 were in Melbourne. Six – Delany, Gunnar Nielsen, Istvan Rozsavolgyi, Laszlo Tabori, Brian Hewson and Landy – were competing. The other four – Chataway, Derek Ibbotson, Jim Bailey and Bannister – were in the stands. Bannister presented each of his successors with a black silk tie with a monogram of a silver 4 and two gold Ms within a gold laurel wreath.

Both Bannister and Landy have built distinguished careers away from the track. Bannister, knighted in 1975, enjoyed a fine medical career in which he combined research with a clinical practice as a neurologist. He was Chairman of the Sports Council from 1971–74 and served for many years as Master of Pembroke College, Oxford. He then became the director of the National Hospital for Nervous Diseases in London.

Landy, who was also a good Australian Rules footballer in his university days, spent 21 years working in agricultural research for ICI Australia Ltd. A committed conservationist, he has been involved with many agricultural groups and organisations and has served on various athletics committees, plus serving as a director of the Australian Institute of Sport. He was awarded an MBE in 1955 and in 2001 the Companion of the Order of Australia. Also in 2001, he became Governor of Victoria. Landy married Lynne Fisher in 1971. They have two adult children.

Bannister is a good speaker and has been in demand for half a century to attend various athletics gatherings and write forewords for books on running. I got the impression talking to him one day that he was perhaps slightly miffed at all the attention he had earned by being the first man to break four minutes for the mile. Asked whether he'd rather have done what he did at Oxford that day in May 1954, or won an Olympic gold medal, he said without hesitation: 'There's no question about that. I'd take the Olympic gold any day.'

That surprised me. It is true that gold medals remain in the books forever, whereas world records last only until the next great runner comes along. But the four-minute mile was special. It was a barrier that had defied the best runners for decades. 'Experts' had written long articles proving it was impossible to run that fast.

Regardless, the four-minute mile and the magic around it created a rivalry that crossed continents and endured for two years. It also meant that the names Bannister and Landy would forever be linked.

	Roger Gilbert Bannister	John Michael Landy
Born	23 March 1929, Harrow, London	12 April 1930, Hawthorn, Victoria
World records	One mile: 3min 59.4s, Iffley Road, Oxford, on 6 May 1954.	1500m: 3min 41.8s, Turku, on 21 June 1954.
	4 x 1 mile relay (with Chris Chataway, Bill Nankeville and Don Seaman); the Great Britain team's record of 16min 41.0s was set at London, on 1 August 1953.	One mile: 3min 57.9s (officially 3 min 58.0s), Turku, on 21 June 1954.
Olympic Games	Helsinki, 1952: fourth in 1500m (3min 46.0s).	Helsinki, 1952: 5th in 1500m heat (3min 57.13s); did not qualify. 10th in 5000m heat (14min 56.4s); did not qualify.
		Melbourne, 1956: 3rd in 1500m final (3min 42.03s). Selected for 5000m, but did not start.
European Championships	Brussels, 1950: third in 800m (1 min 50.7s). Berne, 1954: won 1500m (3min 43.8s).	
Empire Games	Vancouver, 1954: won one mile (3min 58.8s).	Vancouver, 1954: 2nd in one mile (3min 59.6s).

John McEnroe serving during the fifth set of his dramatic 1980 Wimbledon final against Bjorn Borg, arguably the greatest tennis match ever played. PHOTOSPORT

The day the reign ended. Bjorn Borg on his way to defeat at the hands of John McEnroe in the 1981 Wimbledon final. It was Borg's first loss at Wimbledon since 1975. PHOTOSPORT

Happy after all these years. John McEnroe (left) and Bjorn Borg age gracefully. PHOTOSPORT

A seminal moment in athletics history. Roger Bannister crashes through the four-minute barrier for the mile at Oxford in May 1954.

Costly error. John Landy looks to his left and Roger Bannister passes on his right as they enter the final straight during the Empire Games one mile race at Vancouver in 1954.

A different era. Even rivals helped each other in the 1950s. Here John Landy does time-keeping duty for Roger Bannister during training before the 1954 European championships at Berne.

3 Showtime Comes to the NBA

Larry Bird v Magic Johnson

Magic Johnson and Larry Bird hung on just long enough to be part of the 1992 US Olympic basketball team – the real Dream Team. There have been several imitations since, but the 12 players the United States sent to Barcelona in 1992 did indeed form the greatest line-up of basketball talent ever assembled in one team.

The team was co-captained by Bird and Johnson. The other members were David Robinson, Patrick Ewing, Scottie Pippen, Michael Jordan, Clyde Drexler, Karl Malone, John Stockton, Chris Mullen, Charles Barkley and the token college player, Christian Laettner. Coach Chuck Daly, who never called a timeout during the tournament, said it was like travelling with a team of rock stars.

After the International Amateur Basketball Federation ruled in April 1989 that NBA players could participate in the Olympics, there was much speculation about who the United States would send to Barcelona. The team would obviously be exceptionally strong, but who would have guessed it would contain so many superstars?

The millionaire American sportsmen were rapturously received at the Olympics. No, they didn't stay in the Olympic village, preferring the luxury of one of Barcelona's finest hotels. And yes, there were some fraught moments – not all the NBA stars were the best of mates. Then there was the fuss over the thorny issue of sponsorship. The American team was sponsored by Reebok, which didn't suit some, notably Michael Jordan, Nike's pride and joy. In the end, Jordan solved the problem by draping a flag over his shoulder, cleverly covering the offending Reebok logo at the medal ceremony. Tickets for the Dream Team's matches were extraordinarily hard to come by, and there was frantic black-market trading during the 10-day tournament.

Johnson and Bird, who had first locked horns in an historic college final in 1979, were at the ends of their careers by 1992. Bird's back had given out and he had to nurse himself very carefully to get to the Olympics. And by 1992, Johnson had stunned the sports world by announcing he was HIV positive. He had departed pro basketball, but agreed to play at the Olympics.

The Dream Team qualified for Barcelona by winning the Tournament of the Americas. Its first opponent in the qualifying event was Cuba, whose players set the tone by delaying the start so they could have their photographs taken with the US stars. At Barcelona it was the same. The Americans ran into Angola first. Naturally the Angolans were hopelessly outclassed, but they couldn't have been happier. They asked photographers to snap them with the Americans and afterwards sought autographs.

The US scored more than 100 points in every game and averaged a record 117 1/4 points. Its closest matches were against silver medallist Croatia (whose ranks included Jordan's Chicago Bulls team-mate Toni Kukoč), and it won those encounters 103-70 and 117-85. Charles Barkley and Michael Jordan led the team in scoring, Moses Malone and Patrick Ewing were the main rebounders, and Scottie Pippen and Magic Johnson had most assists. Jordan made 37 steals during the tournament.

Johnson and Bird generally took things quietly. There was no need for heroics, not with a bench like that. Now and then Bird showed his class by sinking a long-distance basket or by firing a bullet-like pass to an unmarked team-mate, but in truth he looked a little bored by the one-sided victories. Johnson hustled and supported and played a central role in building his team's attacks.

Though it was the Olympics, the Americans played the event like an exhibition tournament. As Jordan said afterwards: 'The greatest basketball I was involved in was in Monte Carlo [before the Olympics]. That's where the Dream Team scrimmaged among themselves.'

The Olympics turned out to be a good way for Bird and Johnson to signal their departure from the big stage. The pair had galvanised the NBA throughout the 1980s, Bird and his Celtics team ruling in the east and Johnson and the Lakers equally dominant out west. They'd met in three NBA Finals, eagerly awaited showdowns that swept up the basketball world. Through the 1980s, either the Lakers or the Celtics (or both) had appeared in every NBA Final. In another aspect of the rivalry, Bird and Johnson had also opposed each other in 10 All-Star games, Bird's eastern team winning seven.

It was odd then that their superlative professional careers should be bookended by two events that had nothing to do with the NBA. At the finish, it was the Olympics, and they were team-mates at last, after all those years of trying to make each other's lives on court a misery. And at the start, there was their famous college clash in the NCAA final, Bird's Indiana State Sycamores, 32-0 for the year, versus Johnson's Michigan State Spartans. The final took place on 26 March 1979, in the Special Events Center at the University of Utah. It was the most eagerly awaited college match ever and drew what is still the largest college basketball television audience – 40 million. Suddenly the rest of the United States got the chance to see what all the fuss was about and why basketball followers were licking their lips in anticipation of these two brilliant youngsters joining the NBA. The Bird-Magic showdown was a turning point for the NCAA Tournament, which became one of sport's hottest properties. CBS, which now broadcasts the tournament, spent $6 billion on its latest 11-year deal.

The fact that neither Indiana State nor Michigan State had any history of reaching the Final Four made the 1979 clash even more appealing. Both teams were there principally on the backs of their superstars. Bird, a 6ft 9in forward, had averaged 28.6 points per game and led an unbeaten Indiana State to the national title game. Johnson, the flashy, gregarious 6ft 9in point guard from urban Lansing, brought a taste of glitz and glamour to his team.

Johnson's Michigan team was too solid all-round for Indiana State and won 75-64. Bird was not able to impose himself. 'Coach gave us a job to do on Larry Bird and we got it done,' said Johnson, who made eight of 15 shots and scored 24 points. Bird was heavily marked all night and limited to just 19 points.

Reflecting years later, Bird said: 'I thought we'd win, because we hadn't lost all year, but after about 35 minutes I knew they had the better team. For us to win, I had to have an extremely great game and I didn't do that.' Johnson has watched tapes of the game frequently and knows it almost play by play. Bird says he has never watched a replay.

Moments after Michigan's victory, photographer Ira Strickstein captured a devastated Bird on film as he wept into a towel. The moment wasn't lost on Johnson. 'When I saw him after the game, crying and mad – what I would have done if they had beaten us – I knew this guy had a passion for the game and a passion for winning,' Johnson said. 'I thought, "Oh boy, I'm going to see this guy a lot more."'

Basketball fans were enthralled by the contrast between the two players. Bird tended to be laconic. He was business-like, and loath to talk about himself. He kept his own counsel, though he thought deeply about the game and was always popular. The ever-smiling Johnson, on the other hand, had an infectious, bubbly personality, a beatific manner and terrific PR skills.

Officially, Johnson was a guard and Bird a forward, but because they possessed such flair and skill they redefined their positions – in fact, they had roving commissions. Magic (his real name was Earvin, but was there ever a more apt nickname?) was at his most brilliant with the ball in the frontcourt. He would glide through defences, feeding team-mates or finding his own way to the hoop. When the Lakers required it, he could play anywhere on the court. He could do everything – pass, shoot, post-up, rebound and even take the vital shot in the dying seconds.

Bird, an assiduous practiser, was not especially fleet of foot, but used angles and a quickish first step to get where he needed to be. He was a deadly shooter from anywhere, passed with precision, rebounded uncompromisingly and played strong defence. He was stronger than he looked, and he had such vision that Celtics coach Bill Fitch nicknamed him Kodak for his ability to merely glance at the floor and know where all nine men were. Bird had 140 double-figure assist games. But, like Bill Russell, a Boston Celtic of a generation earlier, Bird was never about statistics and records. He used to say they were meaningless: 'I could get a triple-double every night if I wanted to, but it doesn't always help the team win.'

The other thing about Bird was that he was ferociously competitive, as Johnson had noted after that NCAA final. Bird was at his best in times of crisis – he finished his career with 11 game-winning shots (in the last five seconds) and nine game-tying shots. On two occasions he had both an overtime-forcing shot *and* a winning shot.

Their individual basketball rivalry moved from one level to the next astonishingly quickly. Bird merely swapped his light blue Sycamores jersey for the green of Celtics. Johnson went from the green and white of the Spartans to the yellow and purple of Lakers.

Bird was born at French Lick, Indiana in 1956. He made the Springs Valley freshman team and four years later turned up at Indiana University. He found the huge Bloomington campus overwhelming, and, after some time out, transferred to Indiana State, where his basketball flourished. In three years, his Sycamores compiled an 81-13 record.

Johnson was born in Lansing, Michigan in 1959. As a freshman he led Michigan State to its first Big 10 title in 19 years. A season later, its record was 26-6 and Michigan State won the NCAA tournament. Johnson was the Final Four Most Valuable Player.

The pair took the NBA by storm during 1979-80, their rookie year. To be truthful, the NBA needed them badly. There were great players about, including Kareem Abdul-Jabbar, Elvin Hayes, Moses Malone, Julius Erving and Rick

Barry, but the league had a flat look about it. When Magic and Bird entered the league in 1979, the NBA Finals were broadcast on a tape-delayed basis. You had to stay up until 11.30 pm to watch the game. The league was dogged by drug problems and attendance was sagging. It needed some glamour and tension, and that's what Bird and Johnson provided.

Bird was white, and played for conservative Boston. Johnson was black, and played for anything-goes Los Angeles. They become pivotal figures in franchises with proud histories, and the central figures in some stirring battles, during the 1980s. They remained loyal to their teams throughout their careers, and that counted with the fans. Their rivalry electrified basketball followers and took the NBA to a higher level.

It's not that they were one-man shows. The Lakers had Kareem Abdul-Jabbar, Bob McAdoo and Norman Nixon, and the Celtics had Nate Archibald, Cedric Maxwell, Kevin McHale, Rick Robey and Robert Parish. All were outstanding players. But the public gaze settled on Magic and Larry. They had the X-factor.

The debate over who was the better player raged among media, fans and even other NBA players. Magic started fast with his NCAA final win. Bird beat him for NBA Rookie of the Year in 1980. It was the start of a tit-for-tat, 'anything you can do I can do better' rivalry that endured for more than a decade. It was personal, too. Johnson told how he would tune in his car radio for the sports news to see how the Celtics, and Bird in particular, had fared on the east coast. Similarly, Bird always kept an eye on what Johnson was up to.

Here's how the rivalry played out:

1979–80
Never have two rookies had such an effect in the same year in the NBA. Bird's arrival galvanised the struggling Celtics. The previous season, Boston had finished bottom of the Eastern Conference's Atlantic Division with a disastrous 29-53 record. With Bird on board and settling in straight away, the Celtics swung to a 61-21 record, the biggest one-season turnaround in NBA history. Bird was named Rookie of the Year (an award that takes no account of play-off matches), shading Johnson for the honour.

Johnson was at least as effective for the Lakers. Not only did he play outstandingly, but he brought out the best in Abdul-Jabbar and his other illustrious team-mates and helped the Lakers develop a signature fastbreak based as much on quick passing as raw speed.

Even with Bird flying, though, the Celtics couldn't get past Philadelphia in the Eastern Conference Finals. The Lakers went all the way, surviving a dramatic NBA Finals with Julius Erving's Philadelphia 76ers. Those Finals showcased Johnson's talents perfectly.

Games were split 2-2 when Abdul-Jabbar hurt his ankle in the fifth game. He helped the Lakers to a 108-103 win, but couldn't play the sixth game. So Johnson, the team's point guard (and still in his rookie season, let's not forget), was moved to centre, and played wonderfully, scoring 42 points and making 15 rebounds and 7 assists in helping the Lakers sew up the title. He was the first Rookie to be MVP for the Finals.

1980–81

Bird completed the previous season's unfinished business, leading Boston to the NBA title, its first in 15 years. Johnson was injured early in the season and got back on court for the Lakers only for the play-offs.

Bird was brilliant individually and in the way he helped Boston gel as a team, recalling the franchise's glory days of the 1960s. Though Boston won the NBA Finals comfortably over Moses Malone's Houston Rockets, it was pushed all the way in the Eastern Conference Finals, winning the sixth and seventh games 100-98 and 91-90 to squeak by Philadelphia.

1981–82

Boston had a tremendous time of it in the regular season, finishing with a 63-19 record, but was turned back 4-3 by Philadelphia, led by Maurice Cheeks and Dr J (Julius Erving) in the Eastern Conference Finals. It was the third consecutive year since Bird's arrival that Boston had improved its regular-season record. The Lakers dominated that year in the Western Conference, whitewashing Phoenix and San Antonio in the play-offs and then beating Philadelphia 4-2 in the Finals.

In the individual statistics Bird, with 1761 points at 22.9 a game, increased his goal-scoring dramatically. But Johnson showed out, too, leading in steals and being second in assists.

Johnson encountered something unusual this season – he was booed by the fans, even at The Forum, the Lakers' home patch. He and Lakers coach Paul Westhead had locked horns. Westhead wanted more discipline from him, while Johnson complained that Westhead wasn't allowing the Lakers free rein to run (this was ironic, considering Westhead later developed an open fastbreak style). In November 1981, Westhead was fired, essentially at Magic's insistence. This caused much ill-feeling at the time, but was a blessing for the Lakers. New coach Pat Riley revelled in the job and was immediately effective.

1982–83
This was a quieter year in the Johnson-Bird rivalry, with the NBA title going to Philadelphia, who whitewashed the Lakers 4-0 in the Finals. Boston suffered a shut-out, too, losing 4-0 to Sidney Moncrief's Milwaukee in the Eastern Conference semi-finals.

1983–84
The Celtics and the Lakers, the two franchises with the greatest NBA tradition, met in a classic Finals. It was the Celtics' 16th Finals, the Lakers' 19th. The Celtics won a thrilling series 4-3, giving Bird his second NBA Championship ring. The Celtics beat Washington 3-1, New York 4-3, Milwaukee 4-1, and Los Angeles (winning two overtime games in the Finals).

Bird was the dominant figure in the Finals, averaging 27.4 points and 14 rebounds through the seven matches to win the Finals MVP. As he'd also won the regular-season MVP, it was very much his season. He was seventh in points-scoring overall, and first from the free-throw line, where he was such a threat throughout his career. Johnson did his job well, leading in assists and being fifth in steals, but for this year at least, Bird was a clear winner.

1984–85
Michael Jordan arrived on the scene and immediately made an impression, but still Bird won his second straight MVP award, taking his game to a higher level. He attempted 218 more shots than the previous season and averaged 28.7 points to finish second in the league in scoring. With 10.5 rebounds a game (8th), 882 from the free-throw line (6th) and .427 from three-point range (2nd), he was a huge force.

Even with Bird firing on all cylinders, the Lakers became champions, beating the Celtics 4-2 in another much-awaited Final. For the Lakers, Abdul-Jabbar and Johnson produced consistently high-class basketball. Abdul-Jabbar, who had initially been uncomfortable with Johnson's exuberance, had eventually been won over by this quality. 'All he wants to do is get the ball to somebody else and let them score. If you're a big man, it's hard not to like somebody like that,' said Abdul-Jabbar.

1985–86
For the third consecutive year, Bird won the MVP award. Only Bill Russell and Wilt Chamberlain had won the award three times before, and Bird was the first non-centre to achieve the feat. Bird led the Celtics to a 67-15 record for a winning percentage of .817 and finished in the top 10 in five categories – points

(4th), rebounds (7th), steals (9th), free-throw percentage (1st) and three-point percentage (4th). He also led the Celtics in assists.

He rounded off a spectacular season by leading the Celtics to NBA glory. He was named MVP of the Finals after a 4-2 win over Houston, led by Akeem Olajuwon and Ralph Sampson. He was dominant individually, but remained as ever the consummate team player.

Johnsons's Lakers lost 4-1 to Houston in the Western Conference Finals. Johnson led the NBA in assists.

1986–87

The Lakers stormed back this season and much of the credit for the improvement went to Johnson, who began to assert himself more as a points-scorer. He averaged a career-high 23.9 points and led the league in assists. He won the MVP award for the first time and continued his brilliant form into the Finals, where the Lakers beat the Celtics 4-2, averaging 26.2 points and 13 assists to win the Finals MVP. A game-winning hook shot in the lane that beat the Celtics in Game 4 is still remembered. As Lakers coach Pat Riley said: 'He's the best. His performance proves that. We wouldn't be anywhere without him.'

Bird had a good season, finishing fourth in points, but had to bow to his West Coast rival this time.

1987–88

Los Angeles defied history by becoming the first team for two decades to repeat NBA Finals victories, but was pushed right to the wire, beating Utah 4-3, Dallas 4-3 and Detroit 4-3. With his cool head and amazing vision, Johnson was a pivotal figure, though James Worthy won the Finals MVP award and Michael Jordan was the regular-season MVP.

Bird was nearly as effective as ever, especially as a points-scorer, but couldn't lift Boston past Isiah Thomas's Detroit in the Eastern Conference Finals. Before the Finals, good buddies Johnson and Thomas exchanged a friendly peck that really set tongues wagging.

1988–89

The Johnson-Bird one-on-one rivalry was fading. Johnson had a wonderful regular-season, and won his second MVP in three years, edging out the incredible Michael Jordan. But in the NBA Finals he suffered a hamstring injury and was not a factor.

Bird played just six games this season. He underwent surgery to remove bone spurs on each heel and did not make it back on court. In his absence the

Celtics faltered. With Bird, Boston had averaged 61 regular-season victories in the previous nine years. Without him, it was 42-40, and was eliminated 3-0 by Detroit in the first round of the play-offs.

1989–90

With no Abdul-Jabbar in the league for the first time in 20 years, much more responsibility at the Lakers fell on Johnson's shoulders – and he responded well. He averaged more than 22 points a game and 11.5 assists (second in the league to John Stockton) as the Lakers stormed through the regular season with a 63-19 record. Johnson was named the league's MVP for the third time. However, the Lakers came unstuck in their Western Conference semi-final against Phoenix, losing 4-1.

While the Celtics struggled to recapture former glory, Bird bounced back to near his best, scoring 1820 points at 24.3 a game, as well as managing 7.5 assists a game and 9.5 rebounds.

1990–91

Michael Jordan, the season's MVP, and his Chicago Bulls began their decade of domination, while Johnson and Bird had solid individual seasons. Los Angeles won the Western Division with a 58-24 record and progressed through the play-offs until Jordan's improving Bulls outfit outplayed it 4-1 in the NBA Finals. In the Eastern Conference play-offs, Boston lost 4-2 to Detroit in the semi-finals.

Johnson was extremely effective in a team whose emphasis had changed to defence, and during the season passed Oscar Robertson's record for the most assists in the NBA. Bird's time as an NBA player was clearly winding down as he struggled with worsening back problems.

1991–92

Johnson shocked the world – not just the sports world – on 7 November 1991 when he announced he was HIV positive. Rumours to that effect had been gathering momentum for a day or two before he called a press conference to confirm the news. No, Johnson said, he hadn't picked up the disease through drug use or homosexual activity, but through unprotected heterosexual sex. It was stunning: one of the world's most famous sportsmen, one of American sport's favourite sons, announcing he had the AIDS virus. Johnson announced his immediate retirement and would, he said, work to educate the public about HIV and AIDS. With Johnson gone, the Lakers lost to Portland in the first round of the play-offs.

It just wasn't the same at The Forum without Magic. For years Jack Nicholson and other Hollywood celebrities had religiously attended Lakers games, adding their own magic to the occasion. In fact, Nicholson was such a Lakers fan he even went on the road with the team. At The Forum Jack was always in the front row, but Celtic didn't revere him to the same degree. At the Boston stadium he was sometimes to be found in the nose-bleeders – the back row of the top deck.

Bird, in constant pain, played just 45 games for a scoring average of 20.2 and managed a respectable .406 success rate in three point throws. His last few years in the NBA had been bedevilled with injury – back, elbow, double heel surgery, back again. Boston lost 4-3 to Cleveland in the Eastern Conference semi-finals and Bird announced his retirement. At the time he held or shared 27 Celtics records. His No 33 jersey was retired.

Basketball experts outdid each other in praising Bird. Bob Cousy, a famous Celtic of an earlier era, said: 'Before I used to vacillate. But Larry Bird came along with all the skills, all the things a basketballer has to do. I think he's the greatest.' Jerry West said: 'He's nearly as perfect as you can get in every phase.' Red Auerbach, who adored Bill Russell, said of Bird: 'He's the greatest ballplayer who ever played the game.'

So Bird and Johnson, who'd entered the NBA together, departed at the same time. But they remained in the news. What effect would the virus have on Johnson? Would he soon be sick and ailing? Though he had retired from pro basketball, he was still a wonderful player and felt as good as ever. He returned by request from the other players for the 1992 All-Star game and, of course, won an Olympic gold medal that year with the Dream Team. Johnson did some basketball commentary work for NBC for a couple of years and in 1994 had a notably unsuccessful (5-13) stint as Lakers coach. Then in 1995–96, he made a comeback and played 32 games for the Lakers. But there were rumblings from some pros about his illness placing them in danger, so he quit the NBA for good.

Bird became head coach of the Indiana Pacers and made the elusive transition from great player to great coach. However, he'd said on taking over the team that he would do the coaching job for only three years, and he stuck to his word. He was named NBA Coach of the Year in 1998 after a 58-24 season. In 2000 he led Indiana to its first NBA Finals. On 11 July 2003, Bird was named Indiana Pacers President of Basketball Operations.

Johnson has since turned his focus to business. He seems ever on the move, as CEO of Magic Johnson Enterprises, his own promotional firm. He continued playing after departing the NBA, taking his hand-picked team to various spots around the globe and charming the locals with his skill on the court and his personality off it. He is a highly successful businessman, having opened a chain of movie theatres, restaurants and coffee bars, and has considered a career in Los Angeles politics. In addition, he became a Lakers team vice-president and minority owner in 1994, and in that capacity enjoyed one more triumph over his old adversary in 2000 when the Lakers, spearheaded by Shaquille O'Neal and Kobe Bryant, beat Bird's Pacers in the NBA Finals.

Bird and Johnson linked again in 2002 when Johnson was inducted into the NBA Hall of Fame. Bird had been inducted in 1998, but Johnson's entry was delayed because of his short-lived 1996 return to the NBA, the Hall of Fame having a mandatory five-year stand-down period between retirement and induction. Johnson's turn came in 2002 and, as is the custom, he was asked to select a Hall of Famer to present him. He chose Bird, an acknowledgement of how intertwined their careers had been. Some years earlier, when Bird was writing his autobiography, he asked Johnson to write the foreword. ('Larry is the only one I really fear,' wrote Johnson.)

The induction ceremony was extremely emotional. Johnson had once said of Bird: 'It's hard to look at a white man and see black, but when I looked at Larry, that's what I saw. I saw myself.'

Johnson said he worried he wouldn't be able to attend – when he tested positive for the AIDS virus, it was thought the diagnosis was a virtual death sentence. 'The thing I'm most happy about,' he said, 'is that I'm actually here – in person, myself – to accept the award, that I'm living, that I get to see this day come … I'm doing very well, like I have been for the last 11 years. It's still laying asleep in my body. So the medicine is doing its job. I'm doing my job. And God is doing his.'

Then he turned his thoughts to Bird. 'Larry and I seemed to be linked ever since that NCAA final. Every time, even today, it's "Bird, Magic, Bird, Magic". He helped me get here and he's probably the biggest reason I'm here. Larry pushed me and made me a better basketball player and made me reach for the stars. Why I wanted Larry here is because I wouldn't be here if there was no Larry Bird.' Asked about what made him and Bird the players they were, Johnson said it was their innate feel for the game. 'We were the slowest two guys in the game,' he joked.

Bird used the occasion to thank Johnson for pushing him for all those years. 'I was going to speak from my heart,' Bird said. 'But, man, he broke my heart so many times, do I have anything left? He played the game like I always wanted to play the game. Over the years, we've sort of grown together. We played against each other a lot of times in great meaningful games, and it has been a long career and a long span. I'm honoured to be presenting a person I have admired and looked up to during my whole career.

'The great thing about our relationship is that we got along pretty well and we're friends, but once we stepped out on the basketball court, believe me, we were enemies. We didn't like each other; there was no question about it. He was a Laker and I was a Celtic. I always knew when I got under his skin a little bit.'

	Earvin (Magic) Johnson	Larry Joe Bird
Born	14 August 1959, Lansing, Michigan	7 December 1956, French Lick, Indiana
NBA career	(Los Angeles Lakers): 1979–91, 1995–96	(Boston Celtics): 1979–92
NBA titles	1980, 1982, 1985, 1987, 1988	1981, 1984, 1986
Records and honours	NCAA title (Michigan State): 1979. MVP: 1987, 1989, 1990. NBA Finals MVP: 1980, 1982, 1987. All-NBA First Team nine times (1983, 1984, 1985, 1986, 1987, 1988, 1989, 1990, 1991). NBA All-Star twelve times (1980, 1982–1992). Made 10,141 assists (the most until John Stockton broke the record). Assists per game 11.2 (the record). Made 6559 rebounds. Rebounds per game: 7.2. Made 1,724 steals. Led league in steals in 1980–81 and 1981–82.	NCAA Player of the Year: 1978. NBA Rookie of the Year: 1980. MVP: 1984, 1985, 1986. NBA Finals MVP: 1984, 1986. All-NBA First Team nine times (1980, 1981, 1982, 1983, 1984, 1985, 1986, 1987, 1988). NBA All-Star twelve times (1980–88, 1990–92). Scored 21,791 points (20th all-time). Points average: 24.3. Scored career-high 60 points against Atlanta in 1985. Led league in three-point shots in 1986 and 1987. Led the NBA in free-throw shooting in 1984, 1986, 1990. Rebound average: 10.0. Assists: 5695. Average assists: 6.3. Steals: 1556.
	Olympic gold medal: 1992. J. Walter Kennedy Citizenship Award for exemplary community service (1992). Vice President, Los Angeles Lakers since 1994–95.	Olympic gold medal: 1992. NBA 50th Anniversary All-Time Team (1996). Coached NBA Indiana Pacers (1997–2000), 147-67 (.687).

4 Chalk and Cheese

Margaret Court v Billie Jean King

The intense and enduring rivalry between tennis legends Margaret Court and Billie Jean King is best defined by their fantastic Wimbledon singles final on 3 July 1970.

It was that rare moment, when two giants of the game meet at their peak and produce a match to honour the occasion. King was in her prime. She'd won Wimbledon in 1967 and 1968 and would win it again in 1972, 1973 and 1975. Court was supreme in 1970 and Wimbledon was the third step towards her Grand Slam that year. Their Wimbledon final, when they were the tournament first and second seeds, was the high point of a rivalry that stretched well over a decade.

What a match they played! Court won 14-12, 11-9 (no tiebreakers in those days). It remains the longest women's singles final ever played at Wimbledon, beating the previous record of 44 games set in 1919 by Suzanne Lenglen and Dorothea Lambert Chambers. When great women's matches are discussed, several stand out, from Lambert Chambers v Lenglen to Capriati v Henin-Hardenne at the 2003 US Open. Many opt for Court v King, Wimbledon 1970, as the greatest of all.

Up to 8-8 in the first set, half the games went against the server, and this in a match involving two of the most effective servers in women's tennis. In the first half of that set there were 22 deuces and 18 break points, eight against King, 10 against Court. It is the longest set played in a Wimbledon final by men or women.

The second set, though shorter, was even more dramatic. At 7-6 Court had match point, which King saved with a forehand volley down the line. In the next game, King had two break points, but could not convert them. On they went until King, serving at 9-10, found herself down 15-40, double match point. That final game was a thriller. From 15-40 King drew on the dregs of her stamina and spirit, saving four match points before succumbing. The 46 games took 2h 26min.

Court had been suffering from a tendon injury in her ankle and had to be given pain-killing injections before her semi-final and final, while King was struggling with knee problems – not that anyone would have guessed from the way they played.

Besides the quality of the tennis, what made the match so memorable was the absolute contrast between the players. A fiction writer scripting their rivalry would have been accused of over-egging the omelette, of making the two principals such wildly different characters that the bounds of credibility were stretched. Yet this was one rivalry where fact outdid any fiction that could have been created.

For more than a dozen years, stretching from the conservative early 1960s, through the years of rebellion and protest into the emancipated 1970s, Court and King battled each other all over the world. They were brilliant tennis players, who still rank among at least the top 10 in history. Both built marvellous, long-standing records at Grand Slam events in singles, doubles and mixed doubles, and picked up scores of lesser titles. They were leaders in their styles of play and in the amount of prizemoney they earned.

But there was more to their rivalry than simply swatting backhands and forehands at each other. They admired the quality of each other's tennis but, despite years together on the world circuit, were never friends; in fact, they were hardly more than nodding acquaintances. The closest they got was shaking hands at the net after another titanic contest.

As Court told Grace Lichenstein in *Behind the Scenes in Women's Pro Tennis*: 'I don't know her [King]. We don't go out to dinner together, we don't go shopping together, we don't think alike. The only thing Billie Jean and I have in common is tennis.'

Court was a shy, introverted girl from Albury, New South Wales. She married when she was 25 and she and husband Barry raised four children. Always deeply religious, Court became a Christian minister after her retirement from tennis.

King grew up in free-wheeling California and was entirely different. She was born to be a leader, loved to compete and had plenty to say on most subjects. She, too, married young, but though she and husband Larry remained married, it was not a marriage in the traditional sense. During the 1970s, King had an abortion and at least one extra-marital affair with a woman, Marilyn Barnett, who sued her unsuccessfully in a well-publicised 'palimony' case in 1981.

Court, tall and long-limbed, had a regal bearing. 'My femininity is something I have always tried to preserve in this dog-eat-dog game,' she once said. Off the court, she preferred to remain private. King, short, stocky and bespectacled, was the centre of attention and was aptly named Madam Butterfly by one of the characters of tennis, fashion designer Teddy Tinling. She was always making a noise, whether leading the charge for more prizemoney for women's tennis, setting up the women's players union, bickering with tournament officials or sticking up for women's rights in general.

Court thought King was brash and lacking class. King suggested Court was happy to take the rewards that came from the efforts of those working for women's rights, without making a stand herself.

Women's tennis, striving to establish an identity and be portrayed as a sport played by serious athletes, was lucky to have two such great players. There were other supporting actors – Maria Bueno and Ann Jones in the early days, Evonne Goolagong and Chris Evert near the end – but King and Court, in their own unique and oh-so-different ways, were the torchbearers for women's tennis.

Born 16 months apart, it was Court, or Margaret Smith as she was before she married, who first made an impression on the world tennis stage. In 1960, aged just 17, she caused a sensation by winning the Australian national title in Brisbane. Maria Bueno was the top seed and Smith was rated just seventh. But Smith stunned the world's top player 7-5, 3-6, 6-4 in the quarter-finals. In the semis she beat defending champion Mary Carter Meitano in three sets. And in the final she completed an amazing week by beating Jan Lehane 7-5, 6-2. She became the youngest winner of the Australian title and progressed from being a promising junior to a world-class player within days. It was the start of a spectacular run of success for Smith, who won the title 11 times in 14 years.

In the early 1960s, tennis was deep in its amateur age. A few Australian men, such as Frank Sedgman, Ken Rosewall and Lew Hoad, had turned pro, but it was a precarious business. Women were not sufficiently big drawcards to entice American tennis entrepreneur Jack Kramer to sign them for the pro ranks. In fact, in 1960, when Kramer's professional troupe arrived in Melbourne, Margaret Smith, Australian champion, was a ballgirl for their exhibition matches.

So in 1960, Smith stayed home. It's difficult to conceive of a Grand Slam tournament winner not playing any overseas tournaments, but such was the case in 1960. The following year, Smith won the Australian title again, and this time travelled to Europe as part of the official Australian women's team, managed by the autocratic Nell Hopman, wife of famous Davis Cup captain Harry Hopman.

The start of an enduring rivalry. Larry Bird powers away from Magic Johnson (left) during the eagerly-awaited 1979 NCAA final. Johnson's Michigan State Spartans beat Bird's Indiana State Sycamores 75-64. The match drew a television audience of 40 million. PHOTOSPORT

Plenty to talk about after all these years – Magic Johnson (left) and Larry Bird. FOTOPRESS

Right from when she emerged as a world-class player in the early 1960s, Billie Jean King gave fans full value because of her exuberance, energy and athleticism. FOTOPRESS

Margaret Court is honoured at Wimbledon in 2000. PHOTOSPORT

Billie Jean King, US Olympic tennis team captain and Fed Cup captain. FOTOPRESS

Smith didn't win any other Grand Slam singles titles in 1961, but hinted at what was to come. She reached the quarter-finals of the French Open, where she handled the unfamiliar clay courts of Roland Garros well, the quarter-finals at Wimbledon (where, as second seed, she beat leading American Nancy Richey 3-6, 6-3, 6-4 in the first round) and the semi-finals of the US Nationals at Forest Hills. She picked up her first Grand Slam title outside Australia in 1961, winning the US mixed doubles with fellow Aussie Bob Mark.

By 1962, Smith and Brazilian Maria Bueno were vying for the status of world No 1. Smith, encouraged by Sedgman, embarked on a fitness and training programme devised by Keith Rogers and Stan Nicholes that would have daunted any other female player. She ran, skipped, lifted weights and spent countless hours on court, developing a power game that would overwhelm most opposition for the next 14 years.

She began 1962 well, picking up the Australian title at Lehane's expense again. In Paris, she took the French crown, winning a nip-and-tuck encounter with fellow Aussie Lesley Turner 7-5 in the third. Turner was always a tough customer on clay – she won the French title the following year. After her victories in Paris and in the Italian championships, Smith headed to London, tipped to claim her first Wimbledon crown.

She was made top seed, but was dismayed to find that for the second successive year she had drawn an extremely difficult first match. This time she was to play bouncing Billie Jean Moffitt. They'd met in the Wimbledon doubles final the previous year, but this singles meeting in 1962 was where the Smith–Moffitt (later Court–King) rivalry really began.

Moffitt was just 18 and didn't have the performances in singles at big events that Smith could boast. But she was an accomplished player even then. She'd grown up on the hard courts of California and had developed a serve-and-volley game that is foreign to nearly every woman player today. Moffitt was short and didn't have the power to win long, baseline slugging duels. She liked to camp on the net and her game was perfectly suited to Wimbledon's grass courts, as she was to show over the next 20 years.

She'd first travelled to Wimbledon in 1961, when she and another Californian teenager, Karen Hantze (later Susman), had surprised everyone, even themselves, by winning the doubles. In the final, they'd beaten Smith and Lehane. At a time when there was not much depth in the women's field, Smith v Moffitt in an early round at Wimbledon represented a tough draw for both.

Moffitt won 1-6, 6-3, 7-5. This was the first time the women's top seed had been eliminated so early (Steffi Graf and Martina Hingis later achieved unwanted membership of this club). Moffitt went on to reach the quarter-finals, where she was despatched by Ann Haydon. It was fitting that the first instalment of a famous rivalry was played out on tennis's grandest stage.

Both women enjoyed such tremendous success that it would be wrong to claim one established dominance over the other. If there had been no King, Court's Grand Slam record would have been mind-boggling. But if Court hadn't been around, King would have created a matchless record. Even with the pair of them, there were enough pickings for both to feast liberally.

Court won a total of 62 Grand Slam titles which, despite the best efforts of Martina Navratilova, remains the record. Included were 26 singles crowns. King's record is inferior, but still mighty impressive. She won 39 Grand Slam titles, including 12 in singles. In head-to-head confrontations, Court had the better of King. At the end of Court's career, it was estimated – though early records are difficult to come by – that they'd met in singles 34 times, and Court had won 21 of them. (Court was also dominant against Maria Bueno. They played 23 times and Bueno won just six.)

Court had a tremendous physical presence. Her arms were three inches longer than was usual for a person of her height (Rosie Casals nicknamed her The Arm, though most players called her Mag or Maggie) and that gave her a massive wingspan at the net, where she was incredibly hard to pass. She had a big serve, which made her a potent force in mixed doubles. Court was arguably the first woman who played mixed doubles like a man – no man ever tried to shield her from the net or take smashes off her. Consequently, her mixed doubles record is supremely good. She achieved two mixed doubles Grand Slams – in 1963 with Ken Fletcher and in 1965 with Fletcher, John Newcombe and Fred Stolle. Court and Any Leading Male Player was the best mixed doubles team around.

She generated great power with her slapped forehand. Her backhand was primarily a slice. It floated to a good depth and allowed her to approach the net, where she dominated. Many people, including Don Budge, advised her to develop a rolled backhand, but she never mastered this stroke. Her volleying was outstanding. And, above all, there was her athleticism. On tour, she'd often train with the top Aussie men – Newcombe, Roche and company – and keep pace with any of them.

King didn't have the power or physical advantages of Court, but nevertheless had a formidable game. She gave her serve a good clip and employed a variety of spins that made it difficult to attack. She was extremely agile about the net and, though she didn't favour rallying from the baseline, had reasonable groundstrokes that included a top-spin backhand. She was never the force on clay courts that Court was, one reason why tennis historians tend to place Court higher.

Over the years there were suggestions that Court was too nervy and was liable to succumb to pressure, especially at Wimbledon. 'Once you're branded, you start to doubt yourself,' Court explained. 'It's not fun when you drive around London and see billboards saying, "Will she be nervous this time?"' King often referred to Court as a 'front-runner', suggesting she was not as good when she trailed because she was apt to become tense.

While there was a degree of truth in the assessments of Court's temperament, the theory was overdone. She won three Wimbledon singles titles, including the 1970 epic, and certainly won her share of close matches elsewhere around the world. How can you win 62 Grand Slam titles, 26 in singles, with a shaky temperament? Further, playing in the cauldron of Federation Cup – the women's equivalent of the Davis Cup – Court built an impeccable record. She led Australia to victory four times and never lost a singles match. That does not really suggest a fragile temperament.

Outside the Grand Slams, Court was even more dominant. When King beat her in the final of the 1966 South African championship, it ended Court's spell of 14 straight singles wins in their private battles.

By 1966 Court had won every big title worth winning and become bored by the hurly-burly of the tennis circuit. In mid-1966, she retired and settled in Perth to run a clothes boutique called The Peephole. This was when she met Barry Court, whom she married in 1967. Soon afterwards they decided Margaret would make a tennis comeback. (Later in her career, she twice took a year off to have a baby. Always she returned seemingly as good as ever.)

At times Court's superiority was astounding. In 1970 she achieved the Grand Slam, winning the Australian, French, Wimbledon and US women's crowns in the same year. Only Maureen Connolly, in 1953, had done this before, and only Steffi Graf, in 1988, has done so since. In four other years she won three of the big four. Court had a quiet confidence. She didn't shout about it, but it was obvious that she had genuine self-belief and the sort of steely determination champions must possess.

King had a magnificent temperament. She would scold herself, berate linesmen and umpires, glare at her opponent and do everything possible to get herself into a match. She played her best at times of crisis. She was able to gear herself for a big match. She was so ferociously competitive and had such a dominant personality that some of her friends, even Rosie Casals, seemed beaten before their matches began.

What lent some weight to claims that King was rock-solid temperamentally whereas Court was brittle was the contrasting ways they fared in their showdowns with Bobby Riggs in 1973. At the time Court was the world No 1.

Riggs, a 55-year-old hustler who'd been triple champion at Wimbledon way back in 1939, challenged her to a match. Riggs was well known for gambling on his matches. He'd do anything for a bet. He'd play while holding an umbrella, or with chairs dotted about his side of the court. He'd give his opponent the tramlines. He'd restrict himself to just one serve … anything for money. And he usually won, because he played well for money whereas most of his opponents froze.

Riggs thought challenging the world's No 1 woman in a Battle of the Sexes would be a good way to drum up publicity and, more importantly, make some handy cash. He wanted to play King, but she would have none of it. She had bigger things on her mind, like fighting for better prizemoney for women and forming the Women's Tennis Association, and didn't want to bother with this self-styled Male Chauvinist.

Describing himself as a 'washed-up middle-aged has-been', Riggs then challenged Court, offering her a $10,000 winner-take-all stake after she had won 12 straight tournaments through the first part of 1973. Despite her claims to the contrary, Court was never shy about chasing a bit of money, and accepted the challenge. Unfortunately, she had no idea what she was getting into. In *Court on Court*, one of her three autobiographies, she admitted:

> I considered the match to be just a brief interlude, a breather for me on the women's tour. I had no idea it would capture people's imaginations all around the world. It mushroomed into a major sports happening. Much of this ballyhoo was due to Riggs' genius for publicising himself. He was in the newspapers and on TV every day plugging the Match of the Century.

They played in San Diego on 13 May, Mother's Day. Court, fed up with the publicity, was not in the best frame of mind. Still, she thought she would win the match easily: 'I was taking it very casually, convinced that I was playing so well I had nothing to worry about from an over-aged character who hadn't played big-time tournament tennis in a quarter of a century.'

The game became known as the Mother's Day Massacre. Court was unable to handle Riggs' mixture of dinks and pushes. She was surprised by how softly he hit the ball, and played a shocker, losing 6-2, 6-1. 'That match will haunt me forever,' said Court many years later. 'It is the biggest regret of my tennis life. I wasn't ready for the showbiz side of it, which I would have been if I'd played Team Tennis by then. I was used to playing at places like Wimbledon, where you could hear a pin drop.'

Riggs lapped it up. He'd given Court a thrashing, and his challenge to King was renewed. But after the Court fiasco, it became a much bigger deal. Riggs taunted King at every opportunity, deriding women's tennis. Finally, just after Wimbledon in 1973, King announced she had accepted the challenge – she would play Riggs at the Houston Astrodome on 20 September 1973, for $100,000. 'Margaret opened the door. Now I'm gonna shut it,' she vowed.

The match, which, let's face it, was rather meaningless, assumed monumental national importance. Riggs was an old man in tennis terms, and not a fit old man at that. He made that a virtue, hyping up the showdown at every opportunity as he gulped down hundreds of vitamin pills for the cameras. King was on a mission. Backed by many fellow players, she became more determined to win the Riggs match than she ever was even for a Grand Slam final.

People got swept up by it all. Not just tennis followers, but everyone. 'I hope she beats his brains out,' the woman at the checkout/the rental car agent/the nurse/the mother would say. 'I hope he puts her in her place,' men would respond. It all sounds far-fetched and ridiculous now, but that's how it was in 1973. Riggs v King was the year's biggest sports event.

National television got involved and the Battle of the Sexes assumed a life of its own, just like a big heavyweight boxing match. Anyone who was anyone travelled to Houston for the night. The ABC broadcast the match to a television audience of 50 million. When the network wanted Jack Kramer to commentate, King threatened to withdraw. She had fought Kramer for years, disgusted by his unwillingness to pay women's players what she felt they deserved.

It was a night of glitz and glamour, showbiz plus tennis. Midgets dressed as dancing bears performed for the 30,472 spectators, still the biggest crowd to watch a tennis match. A band thumped out 'Jesus Christ Superstar', there were cheerleaders, a champagne bar and carving board at courtside. King was carried into the arena on a platform held aloft by bare-chested musclemen. Riggs was wheeled in on a rickshaw pulled by a group of scantily dressed women known as Bobby's Bosom Buddies. King smiled and hammed it up, but her smile masked a ferocious resolve. Riggs might have won Wimbledon and played Budge and Kramer, but he never faced anyone more determined than King was that night.

Court would have been embarrassed by the carry-on. The razzamatazz and glitz just wasn't her. She'd have wanted to play her game, then slip off quietly for a beer – like so many Aussies she enjoyed a beer after a game. But King thrived on being the centre of attention, and was advancing the cause of women's tennis – heck, of women – by taking on the world's proudest Male Chauvinist Pig. There were nerves, of course, but more importantly, there was a burning desire to get Riggs on the court and beat his brains out.

And that's what she did. It was a reversal of the usual man v woman scenario. King was the aggressor, serving and volleying, prowling about the net looking to assert herself. Riggs played the dinks and lobs, and scurried along the baseline. And as in most man v woman match-ups, power and athleticism won through, only it was King who supplied those attributes. She won 6-4, 6-3, 6-3. Riggs gallantly leapt the net and kissed her after the match. King entered into the spirit of it, but she knew she'd done the causes she espoused immeasurable good. It was the biggest match of her life, although in terms of tennis it proved nothing.

King was always adept at gathering headlines. Court was at times unbeatable, but her feats interested just tennis followers. She preferred to stay low-key and never polarised casual onlookers. Not like King, who was – take your pick – a rabid feminist, a brilliant and charismatic personality, an inspiring leader or a show-off.

King had incredible energy. Apart from being a top player – in 1971 she became the first woman to earn $100,000 in prizemoney in a year – she found time to play leading roles in the formation of the Virginia Slims circuit (a series of professional tournaments for women funded by the cigarette company of the same name) and the Women's Tennis Association. She and husband Larry were the prime movers behind the formation of Team Tennis in the United States. She was in huge demand for interviews. Journalists sought her views on every subject under the sun, knowing she would have a forceful opinion on virtually anything. She was on a treadmill, and sometimes professed to be resentful about the loss of her private life. On the other hand, there was never a person more suited to an interview situation. But don't get the impression she was a shoot-from-the-hip fool who made an idiot of herself with absurd public utterances. King thought deeply and made telling points, and she was a pioneer. King and the feminist movement were made for each other. The timing was perfect.

Aside from their off-court diversions – for Court brief retirement, marriage and the birth of her children; for King the causes she stood for and various ventures in the politics and organisation of tennis – the pair found time to play a succession of classic matches. They met everywhere – in cold halls in the middle of the American winter, in the blazing heat of Australia, on clay courts and grass. But their rivalry was defined by their meetings on the really important occasions – the Grand Slams and the Federation Cup (these days called the Fed Cup). Court had the edge. At Wimbledon, she won three of their five singles clashes. At the US Open it was 1-1 and in Australia it was 2-1 to Court. In the Fed Cup, Court won both times they played singles. This gave her an 8-4 record in major meetings.

In *Billie Jean King*, co-written with Frank Deford, King pays tribute to Court the player:

> What a champion she was! What an athlete! She was naturally a left-hander who simply picked up playing right-handed because it was convenient. She was so fast and strong that I often heard about a pick-up race she had against Betty Cuthbert, who had been the Olympic gold medallist in 1956 in the 100m and 200m. By the finish Cuthbert was barely a step in front …
>
> In most respects, Margaret was old-fashioned, just a big, pleasant, thrifty, easy-going, religious farm girl, but in her training she was incredibly sophisticated, far ahead of her time. Looking back to the 1960s, she was the only one of us who had any real sense of physical fitness …
>
> She was such a superb physical specimen she didn't have to extend herself on court. Margaret never bothered to learn to come over her backhand, being content to slice it, but she really drove through her forehand. And she had as good a first serve as I ever faced.

Court closed her career early in 1977. She'd made three comebacks and was preparing to return again, at the age of nearly 35, when she discovered she was pregnant once more and retired for good.

She underwent a personal crisis in the late 1970s. 'I became very sick,' she recalled recently. 'I had a torn heart valve, was suffering from depression and my life became a mess, particularly when my four children were all small. Because of the heart condition, they said I'd have to be on medication for the rest of my life, but I was totally healed through the power of knowing God's word and renewing my mind to it.'

Court, who was raised a Roman Catholic, had remained a regular church-goer even during the major championships, and says a service she attended in France in about 1970 was the start of a chain of events that led to her being ordained as a Christian minister in 1991. She founded the Victory Life Church in Perth. Reverend Court, as she is now, tours Australia in a mobile ministry, as well as ministering overseas.

Over the years, Court's religious beliefs led her into conflict with some other top players. She publicly criticised Martina Navratilova, saying that because she was gay she was not a good role model for tennis. Navratilova said in early 2004:

'She bashed me for being gay. Her line is that it's in the Bible, against God's wishes. So I'm a good player, but parents should not have their children try to emulate me because of my homosexuality. She hardly spoke three words to me in my life.' As many leading women's tennis players down the years have been gay or bisexual (including, of course, King), this must have caused quite a conflict in Court's dealings with them.

King, having been on the circuit for over 10 years, was nicknamed the Old Lady while still in her late 20s. She went on to justify the tag, playing world-class tennis into her 40s. She teamed with Martina Navratilova to win the Wimbledon women's doubles title in 1979 at the age of 36, giving her a record 20 Wimbledon crowns, a mark which Navratilova eventually equalled in 2003, at the age of 46.

King continued to play on the women's tour until the mid-1980s. She was good enough in 1982 and 1983 to reach the Wimbledon semis. Her last Grand Slam title was the 1980 US Open doubles, with Navratilova. She remained closely involved in tennis, captaining the US Olympic women's team in 1996 and 2000 and the US Fed Cup team in 1995–96 and from 1998–2003. She played on the Virginia Slims Legends tour from 1995–97. She did television work for HBO, CTV, ABC, CBS and NBC – people generally wanted to hear what she had to say.

Tennis officials have been at pains to recognise King's immense contribution. The winner's trophy for the WTA's season-ending championship is named after her. She was the association's inaugural president in 1973–75, and served again in 1980–81. In 1995 King received the Sarah Palfrey Danzig Award, the US's highest honour for sportsmanship and contribution to the game. She was No 5 on *Sport's Illustrated*'s Top 40 Athletes list, named in its 40th anniversary year (1994) for significantly altering or elevating sports over four decades. She received the WTA Honorary Membership award in 1986 and the WTA David Gray Special Service Award in 1993. *Racquet* magazine ranked her sixth on its most powerful people in tennis list in 1995. She became the first woman to coach a co-ed pro sports team, the Philadelphia Freedoms, in the Team Tennis competition. Sadly, over the past few years she has had to battle a skin disorder that affects her when she is exposed to sunlight.

Both King and Court have been inducted into the International Tennis Hall of Fame, Court in 1979, King in 1987. They meet occasionally at special occasions, such as Wimbledon's 2000 Parade of Champions. In a book on tennis, both would feature prominently. For all King's longevity and skill, perhaps Court would be one notch higher. But the difference is that Court's name will be found mainly in books on tennis.

King's influence, by virtue of her personality and energy, went way beyond tennis. Books with titles such as *Great Figures of the 20th Century* will always include King. In 1997 the Women's Sports Foundation honoured her with the Flo Hyman Award, given annually to a female athlete who exemplifies dignity in sport and commitment to excellence. *Life* magazine named her one of the 100 most important Americans of the 20th century.

	Margaret Court (nee Smith)	Billie Jean King (nee Moffitt)
Born	16 July 1942, Albury, New South Wales	22 November 1943, Long Beach, California
Titles	WTA Tour (since Open era began in 1968): 92 singles, 48 doubles. Grand Slams: 62 (24 singles, 19 doubles, 19 mixed). Federation Cup (Australia): 1963–70: 35-5 (20-0 singles, 15-5 doubles).	WTA Tour (since the Open era began in 1968): 67 singles, 101 doubles. Grand Slams: 39 (12 singles, 16 doubles, 11 mixed). Federation Cup (US): 1963–79: 52-4 (26-3 singles, 26-1 doubles).

HEAD TO HEAD

Australian Open	1965: Court beat King 6-1, 8-6 1968: King beat Court 6-1, 6-2 1969: Court beat King 6-4, 6-1
Wimbledon	1962: King beat Court 1-6, 6-3, 7-5 1963: Court beat King 6-3, 6-4 1964: Court beat King 6-3, 6-4 1966: King beat Court 6-3, 6-3 1970: Court beat King 12-10, 11-9
US Open	1965: Court beat King 8-6, 7-6 1972: King beat Court 6-4, 6-4
Federation Cup	1964, Philadelphia: Court beat King 6-2, 6-3 1965, Melbourne: Court beat King 6-4, 8-6
Result: Court 8, King 4	

5 'We Need Muscles Like Yours to Beat Germany'

Joe Louis v Max Schmeling

'Joe, we need muscles like yours to beat Germany.' So said US President Franklin D. Roosevelt in 1938 before the much-awaited grudge rematch between heavyweight boxers Joe Louis and Max Schmeling. The fact that even the US President got involved is indicative of the importance of this fight. It transcended sport.

This was a clash not just of countries but also of ideologies. It was Nazi Germany, represented by former heavyweight champion Schmeling, against American freedom and democracy, for which current heavyweight king Louis was holding the banner. Roosevelt invited Louis to the White House in early 1938 and during a conversation asked him if he could feel his muscles. Then he indicated to the heavyweight champ that he was fighting not just for the title, but for his country.

There were any number of ironies and inaccuracies in this simplistic view of the fight. For a start, Schmeling was never really a supporter of Nazi Germany. He had met Hitler, and while winning fights was a Hitler favourite, Schmeling was no Nazi apologist. Hitler was using him as a political tool – not that Americans would have believed that in 1938.

And Louis was a curious person for Americans, from the President down, to embrace. Louis was black. He reached the top of the heavyweight ranks only because he made a point of never upsetting white America. His managers set clear rules for him:

- Never have a picture taken with a white woman.
- Never go into a nightclub alone.
- There would be no 'soft' fights.
- There would be no fixed fights.

- Never gloat over a fallen opponent.
- Keep a 'deadpan' image in front of the cameras.
- Live and fight clean.

Louis said little about race relations or politics. He behaved impeccably in public. In private, he was a serious womaniser – he had affairs with stars such as Lana Turner, Sonja Heine and Lena Horne – and spent money like it was confetti. But in public he kept his nose clean.

He had to – before Louis, the only previous black heavyweight champion was Jack Johnson, who ruled from 1908 to 1915. Johnson, outspoken and flashy, was reviled by white America. He openly consorted with white women and boasted that no white man could beat him. Such was the hatred of Johnson that a Great White Hope campaign was launched to find a white man to take his title. That day finally arrived on 5 April 1915, when giant Jess Willard outlasted an ageing and undertrained Johnson over 26 rounds in the broiling sun of Havana. Johnson later claimed he'd thrown the fight.

Once Willard became champion, no black fighter was permitted to fight for the heavyweight crown for two decades. Even brilliant Harry Wills was denied a crack at Jack Dempsey's title in the 1920s. Then along came Louis: humble, quietly spoken, sincere, careful not to offend. And a fantastic boxer with dynamite in both hands.

This was the man Americans were relying on to crush the symbol of Nazi Germany. Never mind that many black people in the United States were not permitted to vote. Never mind that in the US armed forces there was a clear dividing line between blacks and whites, with the menial tasks going to the blacks. And never mind that until Louis stepped into the ring for his return match against Schmeling, he had been a hero only of black America. Now he was being held up as representing the good of the United States against the evil of Germany.

That's how Americans, and many others around the world, saw the fight. For the boxers themselves, it was different. The political overtones meant far less to them than what went on in the ring.

Schmeling had been world champion from 1930, when he won the title on a disputed foul, to 1932. His ambition for the rest of the 1930s was to become the first man to regain the title. When he signed to meet Louis in 1938, he believed he could create boxing history. After all, he'd already beaten Louis once. They'd met in 1936 and Schmeling had floored the previously unbeaten American, pummelled him mercilessly and knocked him out in the twelfth. It was one of the biggest upsets in boxing history.

Louis, for his part, had to beat Schmeling before he could regard himself as a true champion. It didn't matter that he had already knocked out former champions Primo Carnera, Max Baer, Jack Sharkey and James Braddock. Or that he'd won the title decisively by knocking out Braddock in the eighth round. Or that he had already defended it successfully three times. For Louis, talk of Germany and Hitler's concept of Aryan supremacy was not a motivating factor. He wanted to beat Schmeling because he wanted to prove he was the world's best heavyweight boxer.

It all happened a long time ago, and it's easy these days to downplay the intense feelings of the time. After all, Germany was defeated in World War II and is now a strong ally of the United States. The huge hold Nazism had over Europe belongs in the history books. Similarly, race relations are different in the United States. Decades ago, blacks were given the vote there. Black sportsmen are the highest paid sports stars in the country – just think of Tiger Woods, Serena and Venus Williams, and any number of basketballers, baseballers and footballers. In the 1930s, every leading heavyweight boxer except Louis was white; now top American white heavyweight fighters are rare. It's a different world, and to comprehend the significance of the Louis-Schmeling rivalry, we have to take our mindset back to the 1930s.

Louis, born Joseph Louis Barrow, grew up in Alabama, the seventh of nine children of Monroe and Lily Barrow. As the son of an impoverished sharecropper, he lived in a ramshackle cabin and had minimal schooling. His mother moved her family to Detroit in 1924 after her husband was committed to a mental institution. Before long, Louis, muscular and athletic, was attracting attention as an amateur boxer.

He won the US Amateur Athletic Union 175lb championship in 1934 and turned professional immediately. He already had a formidable reputation, having lost just four decisions in 54 amateur bouts. Especially during the Depression, the money a professional boxer could earn was immeasurably greater than what could be made at the Ford car factory, where Louis worked.

A set of happy coincidences meant Louis had a strong management team supporting him. His managers were two wealthy, well-connected black men, John Roxburgh and Julian Black. Roxburgh, a warm, friendly figure, had made his money on the numbers and was an influential figure in black gambling circles. He came from an accomplished family – his brother was a senator. Black, a cold, clinically business-minded operator, owned a popular speakeasy in Chicago. Though in 1943 Roxburgh was to be jailed for two years for his involvement in a numbers racket, he and Black looked after Louis well. They ensured his image was little short of angelic. Louis became the most poker-faced, taciturn sportsman imaginable.

Their best decision was to bring in as trainer former lightweight champion Jack Blackburn. Initially Blackburn, who had been schooled in life's hard knocks, wouldn't take a share of Louis's earnings. He wanted a guaranteed salary because he felt no black heavyweight would ever be given the chance to fight for really big money, not after the outrage Jack Johnson had caused three decades earlier. But Blackburn, a master ring technician, coached Louis brilliantly, teaching him how to generate power, how to move as little as possible for maximum effect, how to punch in combinations.

Under Blackburn's tutelage, Louis, tagged the Brown Bomber, improved dramatically. He would shuffle forward behind a formidable left jab and when he saw the first glimpse of an opening would knock out an opponent with any of an array of punches or combinations. Only six months after turning pro, he met and knocked out Lee Ramage, a top-rated heavyweight, in Chicago. The following year, such big names as Natie Brown, Carnera, King Levinsky, Max Baer and Paolino Uzcudun were all whipped by the sensation from Detroit.

The Carnera fight was crucial. It was the first time Louis had fought in New York and he was up against a man-mountain who had previously held the world title. Louis cut him to ribbons, battering him brutally and knocking him out in six rounds. When, three months later, he smashed Baer, another former champion, in four rounds, many boxing followers felt that Louis was already the best in the world. The champion at the time was a former wharfie named James J. Braddock, but it seemed Louis needed only to get Braddock into the ring to claim the title. In the meantime, he would continue battering his way past anyone who dared to face him.

Like Mike Tyson in the 1980s, Louis had a fearsome reputation. In a way, he was more forbidding than Tyson. Whereas Tyson exuded obvious menace as he sneered and chased his man, Louis was ice cold. It was an executioner's calm. Louis knew, the opponent knew, and everyone watching knew, that when he caught up with his man he would knock him out – such was the power of his punching.

On 19 June 1936, Louis, a prohibitive 10-1 favourite, stepped into the ring at Yankee Stadium to face Schmeling. Virtually everyone predicted Schmeling would go the way of the other big names who had taken on Louis and would become the Brown Bomber's 28th straight victim. But Schmeling didn't see it that way. He was nearly 31 years old. He'd done a lot of boxing and was underrated. He was somewhat methodical in his approach, but had power and courage and was a good ring technician.

The beetle-browed Schmeling was born in Brandenburg in 1905. He looked astonishingly like American boxing idol Jack Dempsey, which helped his marketability when he arrived in the United States in 1928. Before that he had built a solid career in Europe – two years as an amateur, four as a professional – winning various national and European light-heavyweight and heavyweight titles. He became a German sports hero during the glitter and glamour of Berlin's Golden Twenties.

In the United States, canny, quotable Joe Jacobs managed Schmeling. (This association was later to cause Schmeling much anguish. Jacobs, while indispensable as a manager, was Jewish, which hardly endeared Schmeling to the Nazi regime.) Schmeling met with immediate success in America, several quick knockouts and a 15-round decision over Uzcudun earning him a fight with Jack Sharkey for the heavyweight title that Gene Tunney had vacated in 1928.

The Schmeling-Sharkey bout, at Yankee Stadium in New York on 12 June 1930, was a farce. Sharkey was leading comfortably when, in the fourth round, Schmeling toppled to the canvas, apparently in agony from (so he claimed) a low blow. Chaos reigned. Jacobs, from Schmeling's corner, began shouting: 'Foul! Foul!' He yelled at Schmeling not to get up. Spectators screamed and abused Schmeling, who writhed on the canvas while referee Jimmy Crowley began his count. At 'five', the bell rang. Schmeling, on Jacobs' advice, wouldn't resume the fight after the break and a confused Crowley, having spoken to several influential newspaper reporters nearby, awarded him the fight on a foul. Sharkey was nonplussed, though ironically his career record shows he several times benefited through foul victories. The decision did not go down well with the 80,000 spectators and severely dented Schmeling's popularity.

So Schmeling became the first European heavyweight champion (excluding Cornwall-born Bob Fitzsimmons, who learned his boxing in New Zealand) and had won the world title while lying on the canvas. He didn't have a memorable reign. In 1932, after one unimpressive defence, he was outpointed by Sharkey in a dubious split decision at Long Island. Jacobs famously claimed: 'We wuz robbed!' when he heard the verdict.

Over the next few years, Schmeling compiled a spotty record. He became a good name for up-and-coming fighters to try to get on their CVs. (His knockout by Max Baer, a Jew, plus the fact that he was still managed by Jacobs, caused him to be viewed with a certain contempt by the Hitler regime for a time.)

But Schmeling kept his wits about him. After he watched Louis outpoint Uzcudun, he said in his heavily accented English: 'I see something.' It transpired he had correctly detected that Louis dropped his left after throwing a punch with that hand, and was therefore vulnerable to a right, Schmeling's specialty.

Schmeling's defeat of Louis at Yankee Stadium in 1936 shattered the black American community. Many of Louis' supporters had bet their life's earnings on him, as they had done in all his recent fights. They felt terrible – for Louis and themselves – when he was beaten. To be so utterly outclassed, and then knocked out … it was devastating.

Although outpointed early in the fight, Schmeling produced a right in the fourth round that sent an over-confident Louis to the floor for the first time in his pro career. Louis never recovered, though he fought on instinct for another eight rounds. In the twelfth he took another huge right and was knocked out. Afterwards, Hitler's Propaganda Minister, Josef Goebbels, claimed Schmeling was an Aryan superman.

It was Schmeling's win over Louis that tied him to Hitler and Nazism in the public mind. Hitler cabled him after the fight: 'Most cordial felicitations on your splendid victory.' He sent flowers to Schmeling's wife, movie actress Annie Ondra. Goebbels cabled: 'I know that you have fought for Germany. Your victory is a German victory.'

The captain of the German zeppelin *Hindenburg* gave Schmeling a special berth for the return journey home. Hitler greeted him on his return and feted him like a conquering hero. Films of the bout were shown across Germany. Worse, soon afterwards, Hitler made insulting remarks about Negroes at the 1936 Berlin Olympics and sought to use the Games as blatant propaganda for Nazism. Schmeling was present at the Olympics opening ceremony.

Some American writers, especially from the south, used Schmeling's victory as a chance to deride Louis. O.B. Keeler of the *Atlanta Journal* wrote how the 'Brown Bomber' had become the 'Pet Pickaninny'. Ben Wahrman of the *Richmond Times-Dispatch* scoffed at the 'Brown Bummer'. It was, many sports reporters wrote, a victory for the Nazi over the Negro. In 1936 such remarks were made without too much thought. Within two years, the term 'Nazi' would have far more sinister connotations. By then, Louis would be portrayed as the hero, Schmeling the villain.

Schmeling's win should have set him up for a crack at Braddock's world title, but key promoter Mike Jacobs was reluctant to go ahead with the fight. For a start, the major drawcard remained Louis, who showed he had bounced back from his walloping by knocking out Sharkey just two months later. Louis–Braddock would be a much bigger drawcard than Schmeling–Braddock.

With the political climate the way it was, Mike Jacobs and many other

American boxing officials also felt that if Schmeling beat Braddock he would grab the championship belt and sail back to Germany, where the title might remain for years. So although the New York State Boxing Commission matched Schmeling and Braddock, and Schmeling even weighed in for the contest, it never took place. Jacobs then bribed Braddock to defend against Louis. As a carrot he offered him 10 per cent of the money he would earn from Louis's championship fights over the next 10 years.

Schmeling himself had quashed any thoughts of a rematch with Louis, saying he was interested only in fighting Braddock, that he had already shown his superiority over Louis. Normally amiable and laidback, Louis fumed. He wanted desperately to get Schmeling back inside the ropes. After every win, he would sit in the locker room and say: 'I wish it was Schmelin'.'

In the event, Louis duly fought and comprehensively beat Braddock in eight rounds. But he did not seem overly elated. He told reporters he wouldn't feel like a champion until he beat Schmeling. Even when he successfully defended his title three times, he kept imploring Jacobs to get him Schmeling.

The rematch was finally set for Yankee Stadium on 22 June 1938, by which time Schmeling was nearly 33. Since their first fight, the world had changed. Germany was now clearly identified as the enemy. Even though World War II wouldn't begin for another year, and American entry into the conflict was several years away, Nazism was reviled throughout the United States. Jewish lobby groups threatened to boycott the fight, and protesters demonstrated on Schmeling's arrival in New York, then outside his hotel, at his training camp and before the fight. When Schmeling walked along the street, people would raise their right arms in contemptuous Nazi salutes.

'It gave me a bad feeling because I always thought I was liked in America,' said Schmeling in *Joe Louis: The Brown Bomber*, a book co-written by Barbara Munder and Louis's son Joe. 'I found out later that the propaganda wasn't against Max Schmeling, the fighter, but Max Schmeling, the German.'

Schmeling wrote in his memoirs:

I was desperate. It was only two years since the same city had congratulated me so enthusiastically … now I began to realise it was no longer a matter of business. The goal that united all of them, promoters, editors and boxing functionaries, was of a political nature: they had accepted a German champion in 1930, but a world champion that came from Hitler Germany was unacceptable.

[I could understand the reaction, but] the American people blamed me for the congratulatory telegrams of the Nazi leaders and the

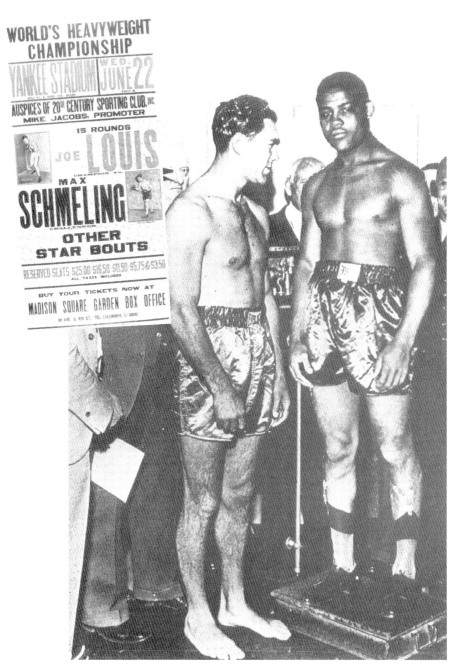

Joe Louis, surprisingly wearing street shoes, weighs in before his second bout with Max Schmeling.

Schmeling's triumph: Joe Louis is knocked out in the 12th round of the first fight.

Louis's triumph: Max Schmeling is knocked out in the first round of the return fight.

A triumphant Ayrton Senna salutes fans after another of his 41 Formula One Grand Prix victories. PHOTOSPORT

Discussion was often serious and tense when Alain Prost (left) and Ayrton Senna were McLaren-Honda team-mates. FOTOPRESS

Since retiring as a Formula One driver, Alain Prost has often worked as a television commentator. PHOTOSPORT

occasional contact with them. Roosevelt had also invited Joe Louis to the White House before the fight. The politicisation of sport, which was pushed so hard by the Third Reich, found a sort of echo on the other side of the Atlantic. The one group came to emulate the other one, and this was bad for sport.

It was as if Schmeling and Louis were to fight the war in advance.

On his way into the ring, a cordon of 20 people surrounded Schmeling, who had a towel over his head to protect him from the cigarette boxes, banana peels and paper cups that were thrown at him. As is still the case today, the big heavyweight fight drew all manner of celebrities. Among those present were Hollywood's Clark Gable, Gary Cooper, Bob Hope, Douglas Fairbanks, many senior government officials, governors and high-fliers of New York society. Louis was a 2-1 favourite.

Although it lasted less than one round, the Louis–Schmeling rematch – a genuine grudge fight – became one of the most talked-about events in ring history. 'I've waited two years for this chance and now my time has come,' said Louis. 'I'm out for revenge. All I ask of Schmeling is that he stand up and fight without quitting.'

It has been said that Louis hated Schmeling, but that seems unlikely. Louis's professional pride had been pricked and he was desperate to even the score. And, of course, there was the politicisation of the fight. But Louis was not the sort of person who fought on hate. 'I was mad after he knocked me out in the first fight because he said something about me being a foul fighter,' Louis told British boxing commentator Harry Carpenter one time. 'When I went into the ring against him the second time, I wanted to knock him out as a man who was in there trying to knock me out. But to hate him, that's another matter. I don't hate that easy. Hating is something that comes deep. I never learned to do that.'

Before the fight, Schmeling took a phone call from Hitler, who wished him well.

As to the fight itself … well, it was not so much a fight as a massacre. It's doubtful if there has ever been a better heavyweight fighting machine than the Joe Louis who stepped into the ring that night. The 70,000 spectators were spellbound by the fury he unleashed.

The normally shuffling Louis was absent – a raging tiger paced the ring, eager to confront Schmeling. Within moments, Louis rocked the German with a succession of jolting left jabs, then buckled his knees with a right to the jaw. Schmeling bounced off the ropes into a wicked right to the body. His scream of agony could be heard several rows back as the punch broke several of his ribs.

Down went the German. He dragged himself to his feet and took another hail of hammer blows. Once more he toppled over. At this point, back in Germany, officials following the fight on radio cut the transmission. They didn't want their people to hear a member of Hitler's supposed master race being thrashed.

Schmeling got up a second time, and was immediately floored again. He staggered drunkenly to his feet, but another right to the jaw sent him down yet again. A white towel was thrown from his corner, but referee Arthur Donovan ignored it and kept counting. Finally, Schmeling was counted out after 2min 4s. During that short time, Louis had landed 14 clean right-hand blows. It was the second shortest championship fight in heavyweight history. Schmeling spent 10 days in a New York hospital and another six weeks in hospital in Germany.

The German always said that on that night Louis was unbeatable: 'He was prepared. On that day there was nobody who could have beaten him, not even Jack Dempsey in his prime. Joe quickly took control. I was just a target for him.'

Schmeling was regarded by the Nazi regime as a fallen hero after his defeat. Many years later, it was revealed that in late 1938, Schmeling risked his life by hiding the two teenage sons of a Jewish friend, David Lewin. He kept the boys, Henry and Werner, in his apartment at Berlin's Excelsior Hotel, leaving word at the desk that he was ill and that no one was to visit him. Later, he helped them flee the country to safety. They travelled to the United States, where Henry became a prominent hotel owner. In 1989, Henry invited Schmeling to Las Vegas to thank him for saving his life with actions that could have cost him his own.

By 1941 Schmeling, unwilling to be used for Nazi propaganda purposes, was drafted into active service, serving as a paratrooper. After injuring a leg escaping from the British in Crete, he was given a desk job. He remained anti-Nazi throughout the war, and after it was over frequently visited American troops, giving away signed photos and having his photo taken with them.

Schmeling made a comeback to boxing in 1947, but gave it away after a year, retiring a comparatively wealthy man. In 1957, he bought a Coca-Cola dealership in Hamburg-Wandsbek and expanded it successfully, remaining closely involved in the business until his old age. The Coca-Cola deal, plus other business interests, made Schmeling extremely rich and he became one of the most generous philanthropists in Germany. Schmeling's long career, and his brushes with Louis, never affected his health. He became the oldest surviving heavyweight champion on Jack Sharkey's death in 1992 and in 2004, aged 98, was still in good health.

Louis became champion at the age of 22 and defended his title regularly. At one point he boxed every month and his opponents were said to belong to the Bum of the Month Club, though some were far from bums. Besides many quick knockouts, Louis had some tremendous fights when defending his title. Welshman Tommy Farr, Billy Conn, Tony Galento, Chilean Arturo Godoy, Bob Pastor, Buddy Baer and Jersey Joe Walcott all worried him, though in any rematch, Louis was always demonstrably better.

Before he took on former light-heavyweight champion Conn the first time, some felt Louis wouldn't be fast enough to catch the Irish-American. Conn boasted about how he would stay on his toes and keep away from Louis's lethal punches. When this suggestion was put to Louis, he said, in what has become one of sport's most famous quotes: 'He can run, but he can't hide.' (It was true. Conn, leading comfortably after 12 rounds, was knocked out in the 13th.)

During his reign, Louis's popularity kept growing. The way he comported himself, plus his sensational ability, made him everyone's favourite. He became a pivotal figure for black sportsmen, a contemporary and friend of Jesse Owens and a predecessor of Jackie Robinson. Louis said little about racial equality, but his ability and record in the ring spoke eloquently enough for his many fans.

During World War II, when he would have been in his boxing prime, Louis served in the US Army. Twice he put his world title on the line and donated his purse to the naval and army relief funds. He became a sergeant instructor and toured the world, speaking to troops and fighting exhibition bouts in front of thousands of troops.

After the war, Louis returned to the ring, though heavier and slower. He held on to the title, but he was past his best. On 1 March 1949 he retired. He had been champion for 11 years, 252 days, the longest continuous reign as heavyweight champion. He had defended his crown a record 25 times. This was more defences than the previous eight champions combined had managed. There had never been a more loved heavyweight champion. Louis had provided thrills in the ring, and been humble and unassuming out of it. His retirement would have been the perfect way to end his career. If only …

A legend in the ring, Louis became a pitiful figure out of it. Always a heavy gambler and big spender, by the time he retired he owed alimony to his first wife, was in debt to Mike Jacobs and to his management, and was being chased by the Internal Revenue Service for hundreds of thousands of dollars in back taxes. His supporters chastised the government for its greed – after all, Louis had risked his title and donated his purses to the US war effort. It wasn't fair.

Now old for a boxer, and creaky, Louis's money problems forced him to make a comeback in 1950. It was a miserable episode. He was outpointed by Ezzard Charles and then knocked out by a young Rocky Marciano. The image of the greying, balding, 36-year-old Louis lying slumped against the ropes after the pounding inflicted by Marciano left many Americans sports fans deeply saddened.

Louis's life spun into decline. He could not extricate himself from his debts. He tried professional wrestling, he boxed exhibitions, he refereed. There were marriage problems (he was married four times, including twice to the same woman), heart problems, addiction to drugs and drink, mental disorder. He smoked heavily. He was never particularly articulate, so his efforts to become a boxing commentator were largely unsuccessful. By the time the US government announced in the early 1960s that it was no longer pursuing him for back taxes (which had mushroomed to more than $1 million), the once-proud champion was a shell of his former self.

But he stayed around boxing, for a time assisting former champion Sonny Liston (he was one of the pallbearers at Liston's funeral). He sometimes visited Muhammad Ali's training camps. Louis and Ali, often cited as the two greatest heavyweights, were about as different as two people could be. One was quiet, softly spoken, measured, the other loud and outrageous. Yet there was a bond between them. Ali sometimes offered Louis assistant trainer roles, in essence a way of giving him some cash, of keeping him involved. Snatches of their conversations have been repeated many times: in 1976, Ali said, 'It's a funny thing, Joe. I dreamed last night we had a fight. I knocked you out.' 'Don't even dream it,' Louis replied.

In the end, Louis was given a job as a 'greeter' at Caesar's Palace in Las Vegas, where tourists and boxing aficionados would shake hands with the Champ and have their photos taken with him.

The contrasting fortunes of Louis and Schmeling after their retirements from boxing had a happy side, for Schmeling, a millionaire many times over, kept in touch. 'I never had a bad feeling about being beaten by Joe Louis. Sport is sport. It has nothing to do with hate,' he said. The two men met several times, once sharing a meal in the Archway Lounge in Chicago where, Schmeling recalled, he was the only white man in the restaurant. 'It was the start of our friendship.'

Schmeling was later a feature guest on a *This Is Your Life* television programme about Louis, his appearance on the show both shocking and delighting Louis. In 1966, Louis travelled to Hamburg and as Schmeling's guest watched the world title fight between Ali and German Karl Mildenberger.

Although many of Louis's 'friends' drifted away after the money had dried up, Schmeling showed his true colours. He assisted with some of Louis's financial problems, and helped cover the hospital and medical bills of his last years, when he was wheelchair-bound after suffering a stroke. When Louis died in 1981, Schmeling paid for the funeral arrangements. Jesse Jackson delivered a moving eulogy.

	Joe Louis Barrow	Maximilian Adolph Otto Siegfried Schmeling
Born	13 May 1914, Lafayette, Alabama Died: 12 April 1981, Las Vegas	28 September 1905, Brandenburg, Germany
Professional Career	1934–51 71 fights, 68 wins, 3 losses. World heavyweight champion: 1937–49 (25 successful defences). Elected to Boxing Hall of Fame, 1954.	1924–48 70 fights, 56 wins, 4 draws, 10 losses. World heavyweight champion: 1930–32 (1 successful defence). Elected to Boxing Hall of Fame, 1970.
Note: In 2001, HBO produced a film about Schmeling and Louis, called *Max and Joe*.		

6 Dicing with Death

Alain Prost v Ayrton Senna

Ayrton Senna was a great Formula One motor racing driver whose legend has been enhanced by his tragically premature death. The Brazilian, three times a world champion, died on 1 May 1994 after a crash during the San Marino Grand Prix. He had just turned 34. His death, following that of Roland Ratzenberger during qualifying the previous day, stunned the world of sport, and particularly of motor racing. They were Formula One's first fatalities for 12 years.

Because he died while at the peak of his considerable powers, Senna remains fixed in our minds as an all-time great. He never grew old, his driving skills never waned. He is like Jimi Hendrix, James Dean, John F. Kennedy, Janis Joplin, Marilyn Monroe, Princess Diana – in our memories they remain young and vital.

While Senna was a brilliant driver, his death seems to have skewed the perception of his rivalry with Frenchman Alain Prost. Senna and Prost, Prost and Senna – the outstanding drivers of their time. Their rivalry was the most intense in Formula One history.

Senna was colourful, dramatic and charismatic, deeply religious, a brave, romantic hero who touched the lives of millions. He drove at blinding speed. He was unyielding, ruthless and obsessive. He took Formula One motor racing to a new audience, but at the same time was responsible for some on-track behaviour that went beyond the pale.

The softly spoken Prost, aptly nicknamed The Professor, was more calculating and controlled. He guided his car around a circuit, placing it in the best position, driving like an artist, with touch and mechanical sympathy. Off the track he was a sensitive person who spoke his mind, a trait that caused both Renault and Ferrari to sever relations with him during his career.

These brief summaries do neither full justice. Senna would not have won three world crowns, 41 Grands Prix and earned a record 65 pole positions if he hadn't known about driving the percentages. He was an astoundingly good wet-weather driver. And Prost wouldn't have won four world crowns and a then record 51 Grand Prix victories without being able to drive at incredible speed.

But memory plays funny tricks, especially when the sentiment and tragedy of death is factored in. In time Prost may achieve the full recognition his incredible record merits. But in the meantime he remains overshadowed by Senna, despite having a marginally better record. At the time of his retirement, Prost had recorded the most Formula One wins and the most points in Formula One racing (798.5). Not only a master tactician and a cool, rational driver, he also had a fine mechanical understanding of his cars.

The Prost–Senna rivalry went beyond passionate. It was bitter. Formula One followers referred to it as World War III. Reflecting on it in recent years, Prost said, 'Metaphorically, Senna wanted to destroy me.' Until the final few months of Senna's life, when there was a rapprochement, the two drivers couldn't stand the sight of one another, which made the fact that for two years they were team-mates at McLaren all the more ironic. Never have team-mates less wanted to help their partners.

There were brief moments when the bitterness disappeared. On one occasion in Hungary the two sat down in the Elf motorhome and had a long talk, perhaps realising they were more alike than their public profiles suggested. But they were never friends. They were too competitive and needed to be too aggressive for a friendship to develop, at least while they were still driving.

In 1988 they had a serious disagreement at Estoril. At the end of the first lap, Prost whisked out of Senna's slipstream passing the pits. Senna swung wide and tried to force Prost into the pit wall. Prost kept his nerve, slammed the throttle to the floor and squeezed past. Onlookers said that less than 15 centimetres separated them from potential tragedy that day. Afterwards the row between them degenerated to within a whisker of a punch-up. While in the McLaren motorhome discussing the race, Prost said very calmly and quietly: 'Ayrton, I didn't realise you wanted the championship that badly.' Throughout the remainder of the year, Prost complained of how stressful it was being in the same team as Senna, whom he did not trust. Senna, by contrast, seemed to thrive on the acrimony.

Their rivalry was epitomised by their efforts at Suzuka in the 1989 and 1990 Japanese Grands Prix. By 1989, their second year together at McLaren, their relationship was at an all-time low. At San Marino, Senna suggested that in the interests of harmony and safety the team should adopt a no-overtaking rule for the initial laps. He got away to an early lead, but the race was red-flagged after the seventh lap. At the restart Prost was away quicker, but Senna nipped by going into the Tosa hairpin. Prost understandably considered this to be contrary to the pre-race agreement. McLaren boss Ron Dennis tried to act as an intermediary and Senna was asked to apologise.

The 1989 season wound its way towards Suzuka, with the two drivers not talking and Prost preparing to move to Ferrari the following year. At Suzuka, both men qualified on the front row. Prost got away surprisingly quickly and grabbed the lead. Senna dogged the Frenchman all the way. It was a marvellous display of aggressive driving, but Prost hung on. With just six laps remaining, Senna sped into the fast left-hand bend just before the pit chicane. Prost, determined not to allow the Brazilian the slightest glimmer of hope, closed the door on him and the two McLarens slid to a halt in the middle of the track, their wheels locked together.

Prost climbed out of the cockpit believing the championship was his. Senna sought assistance from the marshals, then resumed the race. However, he rejoined at the wrong place and though he went on to win the race was subsequently disqualified.

At the appeal afterwards, Senna was hammered. He was fined $100,000 and received a suspended six-month ban. Prost won the world title and Senna fumed, believing that Frenchman Jean-Marie Balestre, the president of the FIA, had acted to ensure his countryman became world champion.

The feud grew even more bitter through 1990 and Senna left no doubt that at some point he would extract revenge for what had happened at Suzuka in 1989. And so he did, though he had to wait until the championship reached Suzuka again for the opportunity. On the morning of the race, Senna said ominously: 'If he gets to the first corner ahead of me, he'd better not turn in because he's not going to make it.' Sure enough, on finding Prost ahead of him at the turn, Senna rammed him off the track, taking both cars out of the race. Senna became the world champion. In a logic-defying decision, the stewards called it a 'racing incident' and the FIA took no action. Senna at first vehemently denied he had crashed deliberately, though later he recanted that version.

The sight of two brilliant drivers crashing in successive years at Suzuka spoke volumes for the extent of their rivalry. Formula One drivers will do anything not to crash – the list of drivers killed in action is too long to be ignored. Drivers operate at incredible speed and know that the slightest touch can lead to tragedy. Yet here were Senna and Prost, so embittered that they twice appeared to crash deliberately.

In any discussion on great Formula One drivers, Prost and Senna belong in the highest company. There's Juan-Manuel Fangio of the 1950s, and Michael Schumacher of the modern era. Scotsman Jim Clark has his supporters. Maybe Stirling Moss, though he never did win a world title. And there are Prost and Senna. Just as Ali and Frazier dragged the best out of each other, so Prost and Senna both seemed better drivers for having the other to compete against. After Senna's death, Prost never drove in a Formula One race again. Perhaps the fire was extinguished once the challenge of Senna had been removed.

The United States produces so many sports greats that it's difficult for one to stand out. For every Babe Ruth there's a Bobby Jones, for every Pete Sampras there's a Carl Lewis, for every Mary-Lou Retton there's a Venus or Serena Williams. But in smaller countries, superstar sportsmen enjoy cult status for life. Brazil, of course, is football mad. Pele is a god and others are not far below him. Ayrton Senna enjoyed that sort of celebrity.

Senna's death had a massive impact in his home country. The Brazilian government declared three days of mourning as his body lay in state. He was given a state funeral and drivers from around the world, including Prost, served as pallbearers. When the Brazilian soccer team won the World Cup later in 1994, the players solemnly unfurled a banner paying homage to Senna. Senna books were churned out.

Ayrton Senna da Silva was born in Sao Paulo in 1960 (he dropped the da Silva in 1982, taking his mother's maiden name). His wealthy father put him into a racing kart when he was only four and he raced successfully throughout his teenage years. From 1979 to 1981, he finished second twice, and fourth once, in the world karting championships. In 1981 he dropped out of university and had a full season of British Formula Ford racing, driving for the Van Diemen team for 13 wins from 18 starts and winning the championship.

In 1982 he upgraded to the Formula Ford 2000 group, driving for Rushen Green Racing. It was another successful year – 22 wins from 28 drives – with British and European titles. By 1983 he was driving in Formula Three for West Surrey Racing and took the British championship after a torrid battle with Martin Brundle.

The following year he made his Formula One debut, driving a little-fancied Toleman-Hart (later Benetton) and taking a championship point on his second outing. He was second at Monaco in his first real skirmish with Prost. The Frenchman was leading, but Senna reeled him in quickly after being 13th on the grid, only for the race to be ended prematurely by steward Jacky Ickx because of rain. Seeking a better car, Senna signed for Lotus in 1985. His departure from Toleman was testy and their contractual difficulties took a good deal of sorting out.

By 1985, Senna had the experience, the ability and the car to make an impact on the Formula One scene. The man he was targeting was Prost, who'd been runner-up in the world championship in 1983 and 1984 and was regarded as the next great driver.

Prost, born in St Chamond in 1955, was a natural. He won the world junior karting title in 1973. In 1976 and 1977 he won Formula Renault French and European titles. He moved into the European Formula Three scene in 1978 and, after initial problems with his Martini Renault, stormed to a succession of victories the following year, taking the European and French titles and the prestigious Monaco Formula Three race. Setting his sights on Formula One, Prost recorded some startling times in a McLaren Formula One test drive during the winter of 1979–80. This earned him the McLaren No 2 seat alongside John Watson for the 1980 season.

There was to be no Formula One teething period for Prost. He was 12th on the grid for his Grand Prix debut in Argentina, and finished sixth. He scored world championship points in his first two Grands Prix and was stymied only because the McLaren team of 1980 was in disarray.

Renault, who knew talent when they saw it, offered Prost a team place in 1981. It was to be a mixed year, with Prost retiring in nine of the 15 races. He did win three Grands Prix, however – at Dijon-Prenois, Zandvoort and Monza – and finished fifth in the championship. It was the same story in 1982, when he finished fourth in the championship. In 1983 he jumped to second behind Brazilian Nelson Piquet.

An improved McLaren team lured him back in 1984 when he equalled the record set by Jim Clark in 1963 with seven Grand Prix victories, yet lost the world title to his resurgent team-mate Niki Lauda by just half a point. By the end of 1984, the McLarens were humming and Formula One experts regarded Prost as the man to beat. However, he would need to contend with the daring driving of the magnetic young Brazilian Senna.

Over the next nine years Prost and Senna dominated Formula One driving. They kept a wary eye on each other and the rest of the motor racing world was awed by their skill and their rivalry. Here's how they fared in those years:

1985

Prost at 30 was more established and experienced than his 25-year-old South American rival. Senna had his triumphs, including his first Grand Prix win, at Estoril, in treacherous conditions. Later he won at Spa-Francorchamps, and there were four other podium finishes. Senna ended the season in fourth place in the drivers' championship, having scored two Grand Prix wins and claimed seven pole positions.

Prost, though, was the king in 1985, collecting the world title he'd so barely missed the year before. He began by winning the Brazilian Grand Prix and never looked back. He eventually won five times and stood on the podium 11 times.

1986

Senna made a significant advance, though still finishing only fourth in the championship. He again won twice, and had six other top-three placings. Eight times he earned pole position. It was a tight championship and Senna's 55 points meant he was only 17 behind the champion, Prost.

For the Frenchman, it was a close-run thing. With four races remaining, Senna, Prost, Nigel Mansell and Nelson Piquet were all in with a chance, but Prost held on and sealed the title by winning the Australian Grand Prix in Adelaide. Mansell needed only a third placing in Adelaide to claim the crown, but had a blow-out and retired.

Prost became the first driver since Jack Brabham in 1959–60 to win back-to-back world crowns. Considering his McLaren-TAG Porsche did not have the firepower of the Williams-Hondas driven by Mansell and Piquet, it was a brilliant achievement. But a look at the statistics reveals how far Senna had closed the gap. Prost had four victories to two, but earned just one pole position to Senna's eight. Prost had triumphed because of his calmness and greater consistency.

1987

With a new team-mate, Satoru Nakajima, and a new engine (a Honda Turbo), this was an exciting season for Senna, who helped develop his team's pioneering work with computer-controlled 'active' suspension. Senna won Grands Prix at Monte Carlo and Detroit and had six other podium finishes. His 57 points placed him third in the championship.

Prost slid considerably, despite wins in Brazil, Belgium and Portugal, and totalled just 46 championship points for fourth, the first time he'd finished behind Senna. Piquet won the world championship.

1988

In the off-season, Senna moved to McLaren-Honda and became Prost's team-mate. It was always an uneasy alliance and things deteriorated rapidly until it became a tinderbox situation. Nonetheless, the season was a triumph for the red and white McLaren-Honda cars, which scored 15 wins from 16 starts and broke all sorts of records.

Senna finished the season as world champion because of the peculiarity in the scoring where drivers counted their best 11 finishes. Senna, who had a record eight Grand Prix wins and three second placings, totalled 94 points. Prost, who won seven times and had seven second placings, totalled 105 points. Yet Senna's best 11 finishes gave him 90 points, enough to carry off the championship by three points. Prost always spoke of the 1988 title as the one that was stolen from him because of the rules. It's safe to say that though his team-mate became world champion for the first time, Prost gleaned no satisfaction from that fact.

The motor racing world paid tribute to the extraordinary Senna. The incomparable Fangio said: 'He is an absolutely extraordinary driver, simply born to race. He is quick and sensitive.' Niki Lauda: 'Whoever wants to beat him has to completely re-invent racing.'

1989

Senna and Prost were team-mates again, but antipathy soon turned to outright hostility, ending with the outrageous crash at Suzuka near the end of the season. Prost began with three second placings, and later won four times. When the judges' decision at Suzuka went in his favour he became world champion, despite refusing to continue in the final race, at Adelaide, because of rain.

Senna, the team-mate from hell this year, finished behind in the championship, despite six victories. He was involved in four collisions, including brushes with Mansell, Prost and Brundle in three of the last four races. His inability to stay out of trouble ended up costing him the championship, though at his best most felt he was the fastest driver around.

1990

Though Prost had been with McLaren in 1980, and then again after 1984, he moved to Ferrari for the 1990 season. The thought of having to remain in the same team as Senna was just too much. Gerhard Berger, who replaced Prost at McLaren, got on really well with Senna, however.

This was a season of fantastic racing as the two rivals battled each other all around the world. Prost won in Brazil, Mexico, France, Britain and Spain. Senna replied with victories in the United States, Monaco, Canada, Germany, Belgium and Italy. The season built to a fantastic climax with only the Japanese and Australian Grands Prix remaining.

At Suzuka 200,000 fans waited eagerly for the fireworks. They came, but not in the way most had hoped. Prost's Ferrari was shunted by Senna's McLaren at the first corner – a move many felt was Senna's way of repaying Prost for the previous year's incident at the same track. Both drivers retired from the race. Senna escaped censure and took a championship-winning lead. At Adelaide he crashed, and Prost was third. It wasn't enough, though – Senna finished with 78 points to Prost's 71.

1991

Senna was clearly the best driver this year. He had seven wins (including the rain-shortened Adelaide Grand Prix) and earned eight pole positions. Prost never won a race or started from pole position. His best efforts were three second placings, and he slipped to fifth in the championship after a season that involved repeated off-track arguments with the Ferrari bosses. Senna's closest challenger was Mansell in a Williams. This may have been Senna's greatest performance, because the McLaren was a declining force by 1991 and it required brilliant driving to take the title.

1992

Prost, disillusioned by the political machinations of 1991, sat out 1992, doing Formula One commentary for French television.

Senna's McLaren-Honda car was significantly out-powered this year by Mansell's Williams-Renault. Mansell won the first five races and that virtually decided the championship. Obviously not happy at McLaren, Senna had talks with Ferrari and Williams. Frank Williams told Senna his fee was too high, which left Senna in an awkward position. He pondered the alternatives, contemplating following Prost's example and sitting out a year. He even tested an IndyCar for Emerson Fittipaldi, but in the end stayed with McLaren.

1993

With Prost back, and driving for Williams, Senna was obviously going to struggle. (Prost had made it a condition of his signing for Williams that Senna not be a team-mate.) Senna was now driving for McLaren on a race-by-race contract and began squeezing team boss Ron Dennis for ever more money, reportedly demanding $1 million for each race. Yet he drove superbly, winning five races and placing second in the South African and Spanish Grands Prix. He knew he was the underdog, driving an uncompetitive car, and it brought out a mellower side in him. He said at the end of the season: 'Not being in a position to win was very difficult. I find it quite hard to cope with that. But I am learning to make myself a better driver and a better human being. I have better self-control and show my emotions less.' He even began to get along slightly better with Prost, saying: 'Beating Alain Prost is no longer part of my motivational set-up.'

Prost won seven races and earned no less than 13 pole positions in 16 races. He was a clear winner of the championship with 99 points to Senna's 73. Senna enjoyed one memorable triumph, however. In the final race, at Adelaide, the Williams of Prost and Damon Hill were lapping 0.6s faster than Senna's McLaren. But they weren't able to maintain their consistency and Senna ended up winning the race from Prost.

There was an unforgettable scene on the podium, when Senna pulled Prost onto the top step beside him, offering a respectful hand of friendship. They embraced amicably. Prost was the world champion, but was honest enough to acknowledge Senna's outstanding work on this day. Senna's actions showed that perhaps he was maturing. In the light of the tragedy that was just around the corner, these scenes after Prost's final Grand Prix race, and Senna's last Grand Prix victory, took on extra poignancy.

1994

Senna had said often enough he wanted to drive a Williams, and got his wish in 1994 – which led to Prost sitting out the season, not wanting to be Senna's team-mate ever again. Having compiled a fabulous record of titles, wins and pole positions, and with his long-time rival again on sabbatical, or possibly retiring, Senna was asked why he was continuing. 'Bigger numbers,' he replied. The fire still burned.

Even before his fatal crash, it was not a happy season for Senna. He found the Williams car difficult to handle. At the Brazilian Grand Prix, in front of his adoring home fans, Senna led the race for 21 laps until he pulled into the pits for fuel. Michael Schumacher scooted in front and won the race. Senna pushed too hard to regain contact and spun off with 16 laps remaining. Three weeks later, in the Pacific Grand Prix at Aida, Japan, Senna was hit by Mika Hakkinen and forced to retire on the opening lap.

Then came Imola, and tragedy. On the Friday afternoon, Senna was close to tears when his friend and countryman Rubens Barrichello was taken to hospital following an horrific crash during qualifying. On the Saturday, Austrian Roland Ratzenberger ran off the road and was killed after smashing into a concrete wall at the Villeneuve Corner before Tosa. Senna locked himself in his motorhome and did not appear for several hours.

That Saturday evening, Senna and Prost, ferocious rivals for all those years, made peace. Prost was at Imola in his capacity as a television commentator. Observers saw signs of old wounds being healed. Prost felt Senna had become less intense.

Did Senna have a premonition of what might happen? Some of his pit crew have suggested so. His personal trainer, Joseph Leberer, said Senna was unusually uneasy and quiet on Sunday morning. He was leading the race when he crashed on the fifth lap. There has been speculation about the cause of the crash. Possibly the car's steering column sheared or perhaps a bumpy track surface was to blame. Whatever the cause, Senna was helpless as his Williams hurtled into the concrete wall at Tamburello. Senna was officially pronounced dead in a Bologna hospital later that afternoon.

Prost stayed close to motor racing. He joined McLaren in a test and advisory capacity in 1995, then took on a huge challenge in buying the Ligier team, which was renamed Prost Grand Prix before the 1997 season. It was a risky business. Previously only two top Grand Prix drivers, Jack Brabham and Bruce McLaren, had run their own teams with any long-lasting success. Prost overhauled the struggling Ligier outfit, moving its base from Magny Cours to the outskirts of Paris, but the strain of running a Formula One team took its toll. Prost didn't have the entrepreneurial skills of a Ron Dennis or Frank Williams. In 2002 his team foundered.

In seeking to judge whether Senna or Prost was the superior driver, it's necessary to acknowledge that Formula One is seldom a level playing field. Some teams, and some cars, are vastly superior. Even a great driver will not win the world title if his car is significantly inferior. Having said that, by my reading, statistics point to a slight supremacy for Prost. There is little doubt that Senna was unmatched in qualifying – he claimed pole position twice as often as Prost (65 to 33). But it's the race that counts and Prost set the fastest lap time more than twice as often as Senna.

In the two years (1988–89) that Senna and Prost drove together at McLaren – the best opportunity to compare them as drivers – Prost came out marginally ahead, scoring 186 championship points to Senna's 154. He had three fewer wins than Senna, but 24 first or second placings compared to Senna's 18.

While Senna had incredible raw speed, analysis of their Grand Prix victories points to Prost being better able to win from behind. Prost won just 56.86 per cent of his races from the front row compared to Senna's 82.92 per cent. But when starting from the second row or worse, Prost won 43.14 per cent of his races compared to just 17.08 per cent for Senna.

Senna was always a man who stirred incredible emotion. I don't expect his millions of fans all around the world to concede on his behalf to Prost. This is one debate that will rage for years.

	Alain Marie Pascal Prost	**Ayrton Senna da Silva**
Born	24 February 1955, St Chamond, France	21 March 1960, Sao Paulo, Brazil Died: 1 May 1994, Imola, Italy
Professional Career	Made Grand Prix debut aged 24 years, 323 days. Registered first pole position in his 16th race start. Won first Grand Prix at 26 years, 131 days, at his 19th attempt. Put together one sequence of four successive victories (Canada, France, Britain and Germany, 1993) and twice achieved three victories in a row. Grand Prix career ran 13 years, 298 days (13 January 1980–7 November 1993). Average points per race: 4.01. World champion: 1985, 1986, 1989, 1993.	Made Grand Prix debut aged 24 years, 4 days. Registered first pole position in his 16th race start. Won first Grand Prix at 25 years, 31 days, at his 16th attempt. Twice achieved four wins in a row (Britain, Germany, Hungary, Belgium, 1988 and US, Brazil, San Marino and Monaco, 1991) and once achieved three in a row. Grand Prix career ran 10 years, 37 days (25 March 1984–1 May 1994). Average points per race: 3.81. World champion: 1988, 1990, 1991.

HEAD TO HEAD

Prost started 57 races before Senna made his debut. Senna raced three times after Prost retired.

Prost won Senna's first race (Brazil, 1984) and Senna won Prost's last race (Australia, 1993).

Of the 140 times Prost and Senna raced each other, Prost finished on the road ahead of Senna 37 times and Senna headed Prost 41 times. In the remaining 62 races, either or both drivers did not finish.

Starting		
	Prost	**Senna**
Pole	33	65
Second place	53	22
% starts on front row	43.21	54.03
Starts won	25.62%	25.46%

Progression		
Races	**Victories**	
	Prost	**Senna**
First 50	7	5
First 100	23	23
First 150	39	39

Career comparison

	Starts	1st	2nd	3rd	4th	5th	6th	Pole	Fastest lap	Pts
Prost	199	51	35	20	10	5	7	33	41	798.5
Senna	161	41	23	16	7	6	3	65	19	614

With each other in the same race

	Starts	1st	2nd	3rd	4th	5th	6th	Pole	Fastest lap	Pts
Prost	140	41	29	18	8	3	3	23	33	650.5
Senna	140	36	22	13	7	5	3	59	18	544

Prost won 29.28% of his starts with Senna in the race.
Senna won 25.71% of his starts with Prost in the race.

Without each other in the same race

	Starts	1st	2nd	3rd	4th	5th	6th	Pole	Fastest lap	Pts
Prost	59	10	6	2	2	2	4	10	8	148
Senna	21	5	1	3	0	1	0	6	1	70

Prost won 16.94% of his starts when Senna was not in the race.
Senna won 23.80 % of his starts when Prost was not in the race.

At McLaren

Here's how Prost and Senna went in the two years they drove together for McLaren:

	Starts	1st	2nd	3rd	4th	5th	6th	Pole	Fastest lap	Pts
Prost	32	11	13	1	1	1	0	4	12	186
Senna	32	14	4	0	1	0	1	26	6	154

Prost won 34.37% of his starts with Senna as a McLaren team-mate.
Senna won 43.75% of his starts with Prost as a McLaren team-mate.

Grand Prix wins		
	Prost	**Senna**
Australia	2	2
Austria	3	0
Belgium	2	5
Brazil	6	2
Britain	5	1
Canada	1	2
Holland	2	0
Europe	1	1
France	6	0
Germany	2	3
Hungary	0	3
Italy	3	2
Japan	0	2
Mexico	2	1
Monaco	4	6
Portugal	3	1
San Marino	3	3
South Africa	2	0
Spain	3	2
United States	1	5
	51	**41**

World championship finishing positions				
	Prost		Senna	
	Wins	Position	Wins	Position
1980	0	15th eq.	DNE	DNE
1981	3	5th	DNE	DNE
1982	2	4th	DNE	DNE
1983	4	2nd	DNE	DNE
1984	7	2nd	0	9th eq.
1985	5	1st	2	4th
1986	4	1st	2	4th
1987	3	4th	2	3rd
1988	7	2nd	8	1st
1989	4	1st	6	2nd
1990	5	2nd	6	1st
1991	0	5th	7	1st
1992	DNE	DNE	3	4th
1993	7	1st	5	2nd
1994	DNE	DNE	0	—

Wins from grid positions

	Pole	2nd	3rd	4th	5th	6th	Other
Prost	18	11	6	5	7	3	13th
Senna	29	5	5	1	1	0	0

Prost won 35.29% of his races from pole position and 56.86% from the front row.
Senna won 70.73% of his races from pole position and 82.92% from the front row.

Prost won 43.14% of his races when starting from the second row or worse.
Senna won 17.08% of his races when starting from the second row or worse.

Hat-tricks (pole position, fastest lap during race, winning Grand Prix)

Prost	8
Senna	7

7 The Old Firm

Celtic v Rangers

Q: How do you get a Celtic fan to stand up?
A: Say: 'Will the defendant please rise.'

Q: What do you have when 100 Rangers fans are buried up to their necks in sand?
A: Not enough sand.

Q: What do Rangers fans use for birth control?
A: Their personalities.

Q: What do you call a Celtic fan with a bottle of champagne at the end of the season?
A: A waiter.

They're the sorts of jokes football club fans the world over use to rib their opposition. But in the case of Glasgow teams Celtic and Rangers – the Old Firm, as they're known – the jokes mask a deeper, more intense rivalry, one with its roots in religion, class and nationality.

Football rivalries evolve. For decades, Tottenham Hotspur and Arsenal were hostile rivals. Their north London derbies were each club's biggest matches of the season. But over the past decade or so, as Tottenham has fallen off the pace slightly, Arsenal's major rival has become Manchester United, and the two clubs have vied for the league title and other honours. Similarly, Manchester United and Manchester City had a ferocious rivalry, but as United has grown ever stronger, the club has left City behind somewhat, and Arsenal is now their prime focus in England. It doesn't mean Tottenham v Arsenal and Manchester City v Manchester United games lack edge, but there's no doubt rivalries can change over time.

In December 2003 an online survey into rivalry among British football fans produced 2800 responses. Among the conclusions:

- More than 45 per cent of fans say rivalry is tradition; 35 per cent say it's geographic.
- More than 75 per cent of fans would rather thrash their rivals than win a last-minute thriller.
- Is rivalry healthy? About 37 per cent of fans say rivalry is a significant part of football violence, but 71 per cent still feel the positives outweigh the negatives.

Among British football rivalries, Everton and Liverpool emerged as the most amicable. The fiercest? Well, that was no contest. It was, by some distance, Glasgow Celtic v Glasgow Rangers. Glasgow, once known as the second city of the Empire, has always had a reputation as a tough, gritty, violent town. As with the town, so with the supporters of its two principal football clubs.

Rangers and Celtic are massive financial concerns. A Deloitte & Touche survey a few years back ranked Rangers the sixth and Celtic the tenth richest British clubs. At world level, Rangers was 16th richest and Celtic 21st. Both clubs have won vast numbers of trophies and enjoyed periods of immense success.

In the period 1966–74, Celtic established a record of nine successive league titles. Rangers equalled that mark when it ruled from 1989–97. Celtic became the first British club to win the European Cup when it beat Inter Milan 2-1 one famous evening at Lisbon in 1967. That Celtic team, every one of whom was born within 30 miles of Celtic Park, thereafter was known as the Lisbon Lions. Rangers' moment of European glory came in 1972 when, having twice been runner-up, it won the Cup Winners Cup by beating Moscow Dynamo 3-2 in Barcelona.

Celtic has had famous players like Charlie Shaw, Alex McNair, Joe Dodds, Jimmy McGrory, Jimmy Delaney, Jimmy McMenemy, Jimmy Quinn, Patsy Gallagher, Bobby Murdoch, Bobby Evans, Billy McNeill, Steve Chalmers, Bobby Lennox, Jimmy Johnstone, Kenny Dalglish, David Hay, Danny McGrain, Charlie Nicholas, Paul McStay and Henrik Larsson.

Rangers stars have included Nick Smith, Jock Drummond, Alec Smith, Neilly Gibson, Jacky Robertson, Alec Bennett, Sam English, Alan Morton,

Andy Cunningham, David Meiklejohn, Bob McPhail, George Brown, Dougie Gray, Jerry Dawson, George Young, Jock Shaw, Willie Woodburn, Willie Waddell, Willie Thornton, Jim Baxter, Eric Caldow, Ian McMillan, Willie Henderson, John Greig, Derek Johnstone and Ally McCoist.

Celtic had a legendary early figure in Willie Maley, a dominant figure at the club from 1888 until 1939. His Rangers equivalent was William Struth, the club's trainer/manager for the years 1920–54. These men ruled ruthlessly and produced champion teams. More recently, each club, when in grave financial difficulty, has been rescued by a guardian angel, Fergus McCann (Celtic) and David Murray (Rangers).

Celtic has had low moments – none worse than during the Depression years between the two World Wars, and in the immediate post-World War II era when, for the only time, it faced relegation from the top division. It has also enjoyed golden eras, such as in the early 1900s and the 1960s–1970s. Rangers' fortunes soared at the turn of the 20th century, then during the 1920s and again in the 1990s, but it tasted a succession of defeats at Celtic's hands in the 1960s and 1970s.

This chapter does not purport to cover all the marvellous football played by Rangers and Celtic, the memorable moments, wonderful players, trophies won. Other books have done that job superbly. The focus here is the rivalry – why it developed, what it has meant and how it has changed.

Celtic's first official match was against Rangers on 28 May 1888, beginning a rivalry that still burns. They have battled each other for supremacy in Glasgow, in Scotland, and to make the biggest impression in Europe. They draw their fan bases not just from Glasgow, but from all over Scotland, from Ireland and from many other parts of the world. Glasgow is one of those cities – like Manchester and Liverpool – with two major football teams, but the Glaswegian rivalry has been much more vicious over a sustained period than in other football towns. As the two major football teams for more than a century in not only Glasgow but Scotland, they have faced each other up to 10 times a year. That has only added to the enmity.

This is not to say that Celtic v Rangers is necessarily the biggest football rivalry in the world. After all, there are titanic rivalries in many countries – just think of Real Madrid v FC Barcelona in Spain, Internazionale Milan v AC Milan in Italy, Fluminese v Flamingo in Brazil, Olympiakos v Panathinaikos in Greece. But for intensity of feeling and repercussions outside football, it's difficult to go past Celtic-Rangers. The tribal loyalties of the two clubs have been built on religious gang warfare and Ulster politics, not merely on football, and have resulted in a literally deadly rivalry.

Almost all the record crowd figures in Scottish football are the result of Old Firm clashes. In 1898, a league record attendance of 44,968 was set at Celtic Park when the home team took on Rangers. In 1928 there were 118,115 present when Rangers beat Celtic 4-0. The current league record of 118,567 was set on 2 January 1939, again in a Celtic v Rangers clash. Since those heady times, league attendances have fallen owing to the impact of televised football and the replacement of terraces with grandstand seating. But Celtic-Rangers still outdraws other matches and gets packed houses. Black-market tickets can cost £250 or more.

The colour and noise at Old Firm matches has to be experienced to be believed. One side of the ground is a sea of green and white, sprinkled with the tricolours of the Irish Republic; the other is red, white and blue and bedecked with Union Jacks. Celtic is identified with the green that represents Catholics and the Irish Free State, Rangers with the blue of Scotland and Ulster. Fans hammer out songs. Rangers supporters will have a go at the Pope and the IRA (even though Celtic as a club has not strongly sided with Irish nationalism since 1921, and hardly at all since the troubles of the 1960s). Celtic fans sing 'Hail Glorious St Patrick', 'God Save Ireland', 'Slievenamon', 'The Soldier's Song', 'There is a Happy Land' and, especially, 'Keep the Green Flag Flying'.

The rivalry was at its fiercest, and most destructive, between the two World Wars. Brakes (supporters clubs) became a menace to the game. Their members were not just fervent, but rabid, and acts of violence and thuggery became common, especially after their team had lost. Interestingly, English clubs like Millwall, Chelsea and Manchester United experienced similar problems with their more obsessive supporters in the 1970s.

Celtic was formed in 1887 by the large immigrant Irish population in the east end of Glasgow to raise money for Catholic charities, and also out of a desire for Catholics to play together on one ground. Much of the Irish community was crowded into slums and discriminated against by the mainly Protestant native Glaswegians, partly because of its 'foreign' status and partly because of the Irish willingness to work for low pay. A 'them and us' mentality quickly arose.

With this large fan base and players grabbed from Edinburgh's Hibernian club (formed in 1875, with its constitution stating that players had to be Catholic), Celtic was immediately successful. The club galvanised opposition by ignoring the rules of amateurism then existing in Scotland and openly poaching leading players, including defender Dan Doyle from professional Everton. In its first year Celtic reached the Scottish Cup final.

The Catholic links were obvious. The *Glasgow Observer*, the official paper of the Catholic community, championed the Celtic cause ceaselessly. The first Celtic patron was the Archbishop of Glasgow, Archbishop Eyre. Other archbishops followed him. (Clergy, nearly all Catholic, are still ever-present at Celtic games and have traditionally received free admission.) In 1893 Celtic won the Scottish, Glasgow and Charity Cups. Committeeman Ned McGinn wired to Rome: 'We've won three Cups Your Holiness.' Celtic has donated to a wide number of Catholic causes and many open-air masses have been held on the club's home ground.

Rangers was formed in 1873 by a group of lads from the Grairloch area of west Scotland. It played first on Fleshers' Haugh on Glasgow Green, then moved to Burnbank and Kinning Park before settling at Ibrox in 1899. The club struggled until the 1880s when Celtic's arrival roused it. In pre Celtic days, Queen's Park was the significant Scottish football club. In 1890–91, Rangers shared the first Scottish league championship with Dumbarton, but didn't win it again until 1899. (It made a good job of it that year, winning all 18 matches, still the only team to complete a 100 per cent record in the league.) Rangers didn't win its first Scottish Cup until 1894, 20 years after that event began.

While Celtic didn't begin as Catholic-only, the club's formation divided football into pro- and anti-Catholic, and Rangers was the leading club to take up the anti-Catholic baton. It must be said, though, that there was a strong anti-Catholic sentiment in Scotland generally at the time, not just in football. Rangers' staunch 'no Catholics' policy, even when it hindered the club by depriving it of outstanding players and able administrators, has taken more than a century to break. While today the club has no problem signing Catholic players, there still seems to be a reluctance to sign Scottish Catholics.

Celtic was initially called The Irishmen, an indication that the strength of the club was derived from Irish Nationalists. Rangers, on the other hand, was royalist. It has always strongly supported the monarchy, and even in modern times the team carried a photograph of the Queen to away games.

Early on, Old Firm matches were billed as Scot v Celt and were treated as internationals. Then Celtic v Rangers became a clash between Catholics and Freemasons. More, in the first half of the 20th century, when Orangeism (anti-Catholicism) was at its most flourishing, Rangers had many officials, fans and even players with Orange links. Ibrox was for decades offered as a venue for Orange Order and other non-Catholic organisations like Boys Brigade. Rangers would play fund-raisers in Ulster. The Orange Order is no longer such a force outside Ireland, but even so, some recent Rangers players have visited Northern Ireland, perhaps partly in demonstration of their political sympathies.

The differences between the clubs could be seen in countless areas. Until the past couple of decades, some Celtic fans were IRA supporters and Celtic was associated with the fight for Home Rule. The club is viewed as anti-establishment. By contrast, some Rangers fans were Ulster Defence Association supporters. Rangers is the flag-bearer of the Protestant monarchist tradition and supports the Union Jack. The majority of Celtic fans vote Labour. Just one-third of Rangers fans vote Labour; most vote Conservative. Rangers is the club with the largest Tory support in Scotland. Celtic has the largest Labour support in Scotland. Rangers is right wing, Celtic left wing.

Football followers speak and write of Celtic's 'spirit' and Rangers' 'tradition', which isn't to say that Celtic has no tradition and Rangers no spirit. It's just the way the clubs have been pigeonholed – Celtic players have individual flair and are cheeky; Rangers have relentless teamwork, organisation and defence.

Celtic was, especially until the past quarter-century, the poorer club, and the more frugal. Even into the 1980s, when the club had become a massive financial concern, Celtic was labelled as a millionaire club being run out of a biscuit tin. The first Celtic board was made up of six publicans and a builder. Rangers' first board comprised two rich employers, white-collar workers and a skilled tradesman (a fitter). Rangers' first patron was the well-to-do Sir John Ure Primrose.

Of all the points of contention between the clubs, the one that has caused most acrimony has been religion. There has always been an important distinction between the clubs in the way religious affiliations are viewed, however. Celtic, though a Catholic club, has always been willing to employ Protestants. Indeed, the club's most successful manager, Jock Stein, was a Protestant. Stein was made manager in 1965 and led Celtic not only to domestic football glory, but to its famous 1967 European Cup victory. Many Celtic fans are Protestants. Kenny Dalglish, a Protestant, was a Rangers fan, but was signed by Celtic. Danny McGrain, the great Celtic and Scotland skipper, was a Protestant. (Rangers scouts believed, because of his surname and the school he attended, that he was a Catholic – a terrible blunder.)

There were six Protestants in the 1980 Celtic Cup-winning team. Celtic club directors, especially in the early years, were nearly all Catholics. But in 1895 a motion to restrict the board to no more than three Protestants was lost. Catholics are still proud of Celtic but the Catholic bonds have weakened as the harsh realities of big business have taken over.

By contrast, Rangers adopted a no-Catholic stance from the beginning. From the 1890s, no Rangers board member was a Catholic, and certainly no manager. Even low-level staff were dismissed if they were discovered to be Catholic. Players who became involved with Catholic women came under club pressure. Nevertheless, for decades Rangers officials insisted the club did not have a sectarian policy. These were hollow claims, and now and then the truth slipped out. In 1967, during a visit to Canada, Rangers vice-chairman Matt Taylor was asked about the club's refusal to sign Catholics and replied: 'It is part of our tradition. We were founded in 1873 as a Presbyterian Boys club. To change now would lose us considerable support.' In the mid-1970s, club manager Willie Waddell created headlines by stating that Rangers could now sign a Catholic (thereby admitting a change to a rule the club had for decades insisted did not exist).

But though Rangers was loath to admit its sectarian policies, the public knew. Way back in 1965, former Rangers player Ralph Brand criticised the club for its 100 per cent Protestant policy. In 1980, another former Rangers player, Graham Fyfe, spoke in a television interview of the religious bigotry at the club.

Rangers happily signed Americans, Icelanders, South Africans, players from all over Europe, but ignored Catholics. There were almost no exceptions. Archie Kyle, lured from Celtic in 1904, played for Rangers till 1908. He was the only long-term Catholic in the top team until the 1980s, when Maurice (Mo) Johnston became a *cause célèbre* by signing ... but more of that later. There were other pre-World War I Catholics in Willie Kivlichan, Colin Mainds and Tom Murray, but they were not at the club long and made little impact. Between the wars, Rangers fielded just two Catholics – Don Kichenbrand, a South African and not a practising Catholic (an important consideration), and Laurie Blyth, whose signing was a mistake and who was quickly released.

There was little movement from Celtic to Rangers. It was as if once a player had signed for Celtic, he was tainted. Tully Craig went from Celtic to Alloa to Rangers in 1923. The next example wasn't for another 54 years, when Alfie Conn went from Celtic to Spurs to Rangers in 1977.

Rangers' anti-Catholic stance surfaced in other ways. For example, even in the 'more enlightened' modern times, it was unthinkable for any Catholic player in the Rangers team to make the sign of the cross on the field. It wasn't until 1998 that the ban was officially lifted (though the practice is still unofficially frowned upon), when Gabriel Amato crossed himself. Yet the following year, Claudio Reyna, a Catholic player from the United States, was warned not to wear a green shirt to training and told that the club discouraged players from crossing themselves in view of their supporters.

Even so, since the mid-1980s there has been an undeniable chipping away at the anti-Catholic stance. It has been a case of business ahead of bigotry.

Rangers manager Graeme Souness eventually broke the mould. When he joined the club as player-manager in 1986, Souness announced he would not be bound by a century of bigotry. His job was to produce a winning team. On the field, Souness was a tough, no-nonsense player who sometimes appeared to go out of his way to provoke his opposition. He had success immediately. In his first season, Rangers won the league and the league cup. He never shied away from physical confrontation and seemed to approach his managerial responsibilities the same way.

In 1987, Souness signed Mark Walters, a black player from Aston Villa. Staunch Rangers supporters gulped on receiving the news that a black player had been signed, but came to accept him.

Perhaps encouraged by his success with Walters, the pragmatic Souness turned his sights to breaking down other barriers. Feeling that the club was a prisoner of its own prejudice, he wanted to sign a Catholic player. Names mentioned included Ray Houghton, John Collins, Liam Brady, Ian Rush, Derek Statham and John Sheridan. The big breakthrough came on 10 July 1989 when, to the chagrin of supporters, Rangers signed former Celtic star Mo Johnston for £1.5 million. He was, in effect, the first Catholic signed by Rangers since World War I, certainly the first deliberate signing. Johnston had said that Rangers was a club he'd have nothing to do with, so his signing could not have been more sensational. The biggest surprise was that the breakthrough player was a Scottish Catholic.

The red-haired Johnston, who had left Celtic to go to Nantes in 1987, seemed the ideal player to break the mould. The son of a Protestant father and a Catholic mother, he was not a staunch Catholic. But he had gone to a Catholic school.

Rangers fans were stunned by Johnston's signing. Many ripped up their season tickets, and club shirts and scarves were burned, along with effigies of Souness. A wreath was delivered to the club and on the gate a sign appeared: 'Traitor's Gate'. Within a few hours, graffiti appeared on the streets of Glasgow's east end. Among the messages: 'Wanted Dead or Alive Maurice Johnston the Turncoat', 'Souness You Roman Bastard' and, more frighteningly, 'Collaborators Can't Play Without Kneecaps'. Celtic fans tagged Johnston *le petite merde* – 'the little shit' – a reference to his time with the French club.

On 4 November 1989, Johnston scored the vital winner with two minutes to go against Celtic, which helped his cause immensely – he might have been Catholic scum, but at least he helped Rangers win vital games against the old enemy!

In 1991 Johnston left Ibrox, as did Souness. The manager had never been particularly popular, but in hindsight was one of the most influential figures in Rangers history. His era is often called the Souness Revolution. He bought big, including star English players Terry Butcher, Chris Woods, Trevor Steven and Gary Stevens, plus Ray Wilkins from Paris St Germain, and Richard Gough, the Spurs captain who became the first Scottish 'million pound' player. Souness never seemed at great pains to foster talent from within, but his signings did help start the club on its winning run. The expensive signings tested fans' loyalty, however, as they led to much higher ticket prices. After he'd departed Rangers, Souness referred to 'bigotry that never sat easily on my shoulders, a bigotry that will always be at Ibrox'.

One of the results of signing so many English players was that the atmosphere at Ibrox changed. The cross of St George was seen in the stands, and songs like 'Rule Britannia' were heard. Some Rangers fans switched their national team support to England. (With so many Celtic fans supporting Ireland, that didn't leave many supporters of the Old Firm backing Scotland!)

In the 1990s Rangers signed a number of foreign Catholics, including Lorenzo Amoruso (its first Catholic captain), plus Basile Boli, a black French player who was a republican Catholic (imagine that a few decades earlier). In 1998 Neil McCann became the next Scottish Catholic after Johnston to be signed. That same year, Bob Brannan became the first Catholic to be appointed to a top-level post at Rangers.

It's one thing to officially change a policy, but it's another to change people's beliefs and perceptions. There's little doubt a bigoted streak still runs through Rangers. This was perhaps exemplified by the example of vice-chairman Donald Findlay QC, who on 29 May 1999 was videoed at a private party singing sectarian songs after Rangers had beaten Celtic 1-0 in the Scottish Cup final. The tape of this performance was sold to the *Daily Record*. In the fallout, Findlay resigned from Rangers, was fined £3500 by the Dean of Faculties and turned down for an honorary degree by the University of St Andrews.

In view of the rancour so evident over more than a century of rivalry, it seems surprising that Celtic and Rangers initially got on well. During the late 1880s and early 1890s, players from the two clubs socialised and there was much goodwill. But that quickly changed when Celtic became the leading club in Scotland virtually overnight. The Scottish league was formed in 1890 and Celtic first won it in 1893. (That was also the year that Rangers scored its first win over Celtic.) In 1894 the first New Year's Day match between the clubs took place. This has become a traditional fixture, drawing overflow crowds and often resulting in violence off the pitch among warring fans.

By 1896 the first signs of acrimony arose. *Scottish Sport* warned that 'bad blood crept in'. Two years later, the New Year's Day match was abandoned 1-1, in response to the first example of brawling between supporters. *Scottish Sport* referred to the crowd as 'the scum of the city, drunken and brutal in their behaviour and language'. Since the 1898 fracas, there have been explosions of fan misbehaviour every few years. Sometimes the brawls have taken place at the ground, sometimes elsewhere. It's been rightly said that Old Firm games are not over until hours after the final whistle. In recent times, the New Year's Day match has been pushed back a day or two in an effort to avoid some of the trouble.

There have been many other bad moments. In 1902, controversial refereeing decisions and misbehaviour by players incited the crowd. Sandy McMahon, a Celtic favourite, tripped the referee and was sent off, which sent his club's supporters over the edge. In 1905 there were two pitch invasions, the first occurring during the New Year's Day match at Ibrox. The second, on 2 March, was much more serious. Rangers was leading 2-0 with eight minutes remaining in its Scottish Cup semi-final at Parkhead when Jimmy Quinn, the great Celtic centre forward, became involved in a tussle with Rangers fullback Alec Craig. Quinn kicked out at Craig and was ordered from the field. The game had to be abandoned when spectators broke through with iron-spiked palings and attacked the referee.

In April 1909 there was a terrible fans v police brawl during a Scottish Cup replay, which caused the Cup to be withheld for the year. The scheduled Cup final, a draw, attracted 70,000 fans. The replay, also a draw, attracted 61,000. When the second replay also looked to be heading for a draw, tempers were aroused. A riot ensued, and pay-boxes were wrecked, goalposts and nets burnt and hose pipes cut, preventing firemen putting out fires. The rioting resulted in 100 injuries, including police and firemen.

There was a tragedy during an Old Firm match in 1931 when Celtic goalie John Thomson died after diving at the feet of Rangers' Sam English. Rangers skipper Davie Meiklejohn, once he realised Thomson's injury was serious, begged the baying Rangers supporters to stop singing, indicating it was a serious moment. Hostilities between the two sets of supporters were put on temporary hold, the event actually bringing sections of the Old Firm fans together, united in grief. The match continued, but with neither side intent on playing to its full capacity. In film footage of the incident you can see both Rangers and Celtic players helping as Thomson is stretchered off the pitch – an example of humanity overcoming rivalry, perhaps.

The 1940 Charity Cup semi-final at Ibrox drew 30,000 fans. Alex Venters of Rangers kicked the ball away in disgust at one refereeing decision and refused to collect it when told to do so by the referee, walking off the field to be showered with stones by Celtic fans. The next year, Celtic's Jimmy Delaney and

John Crum were stretchered off during a violent match. When the referee made no move to punish the culprits, bottles pelted the field. Celtic's ground was closed for a month after this incident.

There was a riot during a 1952 fixture. Rangers was winning when unhappy Celtic fans began causing trouble. This disturbance led to an inquiry by Glasgow magistrates into Old Firm troubles. They recommended an end to the New Year's Day game, crowd limits, all-ticket games, no flags at games. This resulted in 'the Great Flag Flutter' after the Scottish FA Referee Committee told the two clubs to remove from their grounds 'any flag or emblem that has no association with the country or the sport', an edict aimed especially at the Irish flag that flew at Celtic's ground.

Celtic and Rangers fans united in grief following the tragedy of 2 January 1971 at Ibrox, when 66 people died and 145 were injured after the derby match. A fatal crush had developed on Stairway 13 when the huge crowd poured off the terraces at the Rangers end. Sadly, the tragedy did not bring about a long-term rapprochement.

In May 1980 there was unprecedented violence with a riot on the pitch after the Scottish Cup final at Hampden Park. Ecstatic Celtic fans surged on to the ground, cavorting and whooping. They faced a hail of fists, boots and bottles from angry and drunken Rangers fans and the fracas developed into arguably the worst Old Firm riot since 1909. Both clubs were fined £20,000.

One of the most bizarre incidents of Old Firm rivalry occurred on 17 October 1987, when a bitter match at Ibrox finished in a 2-2 draw. As a result of the police report on 'acts of violence and deliberate provocation [by the players] on the field', Rangers goalkeeper Chris Woods and team-mates Terry Butcher and Graham Roberts, plus Celtic's Frank McAvennie, were charged with 'conduct likely to provoke a breach of the peace among spectators'. Butcher was found guilty and fined £250. Woods was found guilty and fined £500. The charges against Roberts and McAvennie were not proven.

When Celtic lost a league match 3-0 to its arch-rival in 1999, it meant the championship went to Rangers. Celtic fans revolted, pelting (and injuring) referee Hugh Dallas with a hail of coins. Some Celtic fans rushed on to the pitch to attack Dallas, but were intercepted by security guards. More than 100 were arrested.

A 21-year-old Rangers fan, David Hutton, was sentenced to life in jail for murdering a teenage Celtic supporter after the 1999 Scottish Cup final, won 1-0 by Rangers. Hutton and another Rangers fan, 21-year-old Peter Rushford, attacked McFadden after the three had argued over which was the better team. Rushford was found guilty of assault and sentenced to one year in prison.

It would be wrong, however, to paint a picture of Scottish football where only Old Firm matches resulted in disasters. At Ibrox in 1902, 26 people were killed and nearly 1000 injured when part of the West Stand collapsed during a Scotland–England international. When Celtic met Dundee in 1920, there was a terrible fracas at Celtic Park, which was then closed for four weeks. In 1922, the Celtic–Morton match at Cappielow Park was marred by ugly clashes between fans during and after the game.

Things have changed at both Rangers and Celtic over the past decade or so. Money now rules. Decisions are made with the bottom line in mind, and often cut across club traditions. Celtic has looked overseas and bought big, as in the case of Pierre van Hooijdonk, lured at great expense from Breda in Holland, Paolo Di Canio from Italy and Jorge Cadete from Portugal. None proved especially successful. Neither were high-profile managers like Liam Brady and Kenny Dalglish. There have been board coups, takeovers, and a share issue that raised £13.5 million towards building a new 60,000-seat stadium.

But Celtic's spending has been restrained compared to that at Rangers. David Murray bought up large in an attempt to help Rangers beat Celtic's nine-in-a-row record. Even after Rangers failed to land a record tenth straight title, new manager Dick Advocaat spent more than £100 million in less than four years. The result: Rangers, one of Britain's glamour clubs, is in a parlous financial state. The club has landed some big names, but at what price? Brian Laudrup arrived from Fiorentina, the troubled Paul Gascoigne from Lazio, several Italians were bought at great expense, plus Frenchman Basile Boli and German Jorg Albertz. At the end of 2003, it was announced that Rangers manager Alex McLeish had agreed a five-year deal with French international Jean-Alain Boumsong, who would earn £45,000 a week, making him the highest paid player in Scottish football. As at Celtic, there were all sorts of comings and goings in the Rangers boardroom as the club tried to balance mounting debt with the requirements of paying huge wage bills.

There was a time when Celtic and Rangers were merely two great football clubs. Now, at least to the people running them, they are two massive businesses, and their business happens to be football. And what about the fans, who seem to have been taken for granted by the moguls making the decisions? There is still a lot more to a Celtic v Rangers match than mere football, and after all these years, and with so much turbulent history behind them, it is difficult to imagine a time when Rangers and Celtic will not be ferocious rivals.

	Glasgow Rangers	Glasgow Celtic
	founded 1873	founded 1887
	Both joined league in 1890 and were division one founder members.	
Scottish league division one (later premier division) champions	(50): 1891, 1899, 1900, 1901, 1902, 1911, 1912, 1913, 1918, 1920, 1921, 1923, 1924, 1925, 1927, 1928, 1929, 1930, 1931, 1933, 1934, 1935, 1937, 1939, 1947, 1949, 1950, 1953, 1956, 1957, 1959, 1961, 1963, 1964, 1975, 1976, 1978, 1987, 1989, 1990, 1991, 1992, 1993, 1994, 1995, 1996, 1997, 1999, 2000, 2003.	(39): 1893, 1894, 1896, 1898, 1905, 1906, 1907, 1908, 1909, 1910, 1914, 1915, 1916, 1917, 1919, 1922, 1926, 1936, 1938, 1954, 1966, 1967, 1968, 1969, 1970, 1971, 1972, 1973, 1974, 1977, 1979, 1981, 1982, 1986, 1988, 1998, 2001, 2002, 2004.
	Since the league began in 1890–91, it has been contested 107 times and either Rangers or Celtic has won the title 89 times. The next highest after Rangers' 50 and Celtic's 39 titles are Aberdeen, Hearts and Hibernian, each with four.	
Scottish Cup	(31): 1894, 1897, 1898, 1903, 1928, 1930, 1932, 1934, 1935, 1936, 1948, 1949, 1950, 1953, 1960, 1962, 1963, 1964, 1966, 1973, 1976, 1978, 1979, 1981, 1992, 1993, 1996, 1999, 2000, 2002, 2003.	(32): 1892, 1899, 1900, 1904, 1907, 1908, 1911, 1912, 1914, 1923, 1925, 1927, 1931, 1933, 1937, 1951, 1954, 1965, 1967, 1969, 1971, 1972, 1974, 1975, 1977, 1980, 1985, 1988, 1989, 1995, 2001, 2004.

Scottish Cup finals between Rangers and Celtic		
	1894	Rangers won 3-1
	1899	Celtic won 2-0
	1904	Celtic won 3-2
	1909	Game abandoned and cup withheld after riot in third match after two draws
	1928	Rangers won 4-0
	1963	Rangers won 3-0 (after 1-1 draw)
	1966	Rangers won 1-0 (after 0-0 draw)
	1969	Celtic won 4-0
	1971	Celtic won 2-1 (after 1-1 draw)
	1973	Rangers won 3-2
	1977	Celtic won 1-0
	1980	Celtic won 1-0 (after extra time)
	1989	Celtic won 1-0
	1999	Rangers won 1-0
	2002	Rangers won 3-2

	Glasgow Rangers	Glasgow Celtic
League Cup	(23): 1947, 1949, 1961, 1962, 1964, 1965, 1971, 1976, 1978, 1979, 1982, 1984, 1985, 1987, 1988, 1989, 1991, 1993, 1994, 1997, 1999, 2002, 2003.	(12): 1957, 1958, 1966, 1967, 1968, 1969, 1970, 1975, 1983, 1998, 2000, 2001.
League Cup finals between Rangers and Celtic	1958 Celtic won 7-1 1965 Rangers won 2-1 1966 Celtic won 2-1 1967 Celtic won 1-0 1971 Rangers won 1-0 1976 Rangers won 1-0 1978 Celtic won 2-1 (after extra time) 1983 Celtic won 2-1 1984 Rangers won 3-2 (after extra time) 1987 Rangers won 2-1 1991 Rangers won 2-1 (after extra time) 2003 Rangers won 2-1	
European titles	European Cup Winners Cup, 1972	European Cup, 1967

8 The Rivals Who Wouldn't

Sebastian Coe v Steve Ovett

The Sebastian Coe–Steve Ovett rivalry was the most unsatisfying of any dealt with in this book. It's not that it didn't burn fiercely, or that the two English middle-distance runners weren't brilliant athletes. Rather, Coe and Ovett – 'Covett', as the media called the duo – spent nearly a decade circling around like two old warhorses, and seeming to devote too much energy to ducking each other.

During their prime, from 1976 to 1986, these two track superstars, who lived just a few hundred miles apart, clashed only five times. Outside the Olympic Games, where they were obliged to run if they were at all serious about their sport, they didn't face each other for 11 years after the 1978 European championships in Prague.

They were rivals, of course. They were from the same country, and chased the same titles and glory. They were personalities who made television coverage of athletics compelling. They broke each other's world records and ran fabulous individual races. But they wouldn't meet each other. As competition is the key ingredient of top sport, this is a black mark against them, and should affect the way they are regarded in track and field history.

In earlier rivalries, sports fans were treated to pulsating international competition and the rivals' reputations increased the more they put themselves on the line. Bjorn Borg and John McEnroe, Chris Evert and Martina Narvatilova, Arnold Palmer and Jack Nicklaus … they competed wherever and whenever. In middle-distance running, Australians John Landy and Herb Elliott, and New Zealanders Peter Snell and John Walker, would throw a pair of spikes into their bags at the start of the northern summer, hop on a plane to Europe and take on anyone who wanted to run against them. They thrived on competition and would often run on consecutive days and several times in a week.

By the time Coe and Ovett arrived on the scene, the track and field world had changed. There was big money to be made, at first under the counter and then, once the sport went open, in appearance money and prizemoney. Athletes became fussier about their opposition. Yes, they might run at Koblenz or Oslo or Rome, but they'd need to know who was in the field. Who were the pacemakers? What money was at stake? Who were the promoters and the sponsors? Top athletes, aware that unbeaten records increased their market value, became extremely selective.

Farcical situations arose with mile and 1500m races staged on the same track on the same evening so top runners could avoid each other. Sometimes there would be A and B races over the same distance, both fields containing quality runners who were being kept apart. The European circuit began to resemble a series of exhibition meets, with everything designed to ensure a fast time, but less attention on competitive racing.

As a side-issue, this affected even the best at the Olympics, where they couldn't control every aspect of the race. As great a runner as Hicham El Guerrouj, who looked supreme in dominating specially selected fields, had problems when the race had not been choreographed for him. Despite running dazzling world records the rest of the time, he could not produce the goods at the 1996 or 2000 Olympics, struggling to handle himself in a race as opposed to an exhibition.

Since the Coe–Ovett era, leading milers have generally proved equally gun-shy. Englishman Steve Cram was fairly good about fronting up, at least early in his career, but Said Aouita, Noureddine Morceli, El Guerrouj and Venuste Niyongabo have been reluctant to face each other on the regular Grand Prix circuit.

Every now and then, though, something magical happens. On 16 July 1985, for some unexplained reason, Cram and Aouita ran in the 1500m at Nice. What a race they had. The pair, locked together, sprinted the final 300m and no one knew who would win until Cram thrust out his chest on the line and got there by a centimetre or two. Only then did we look at the clock. Cram had run 3min 29.67s to smash Ovett's world record by more than a second. Aouita, just 0.04s behind, was also way under the old mark. This was a great world record because it resulted from genuine competition, not from an artificially contrived run set up by pacemakers. It resembled the Filbert Bayi-John Walker clash at the 1974 Christchurch Commonwealth Games, when both ran under Jim Ryun's world mark. The Christchurch race was so compelling that the time mattered only later.

Ovett was involved in one similar world record run. At Koblenz on 27 August 1980, he chipped 0.7s off his 1500m world record. As he and German Thomas Wessinghage battled to the finish line, athletes and spectators were oblivious to the time, such was the intensity of the duel. Only afterwards was it realised that Ovett had run 3min 31.36s, a world record. Wessinghage was just 0.22s behind, also under the previous mark, as was third-placed German Harald Hudak.

Greats like Elliott, Snell, Kip Keino and Walker would have handled themselves well even today, against runners who are clearly quicker. They raced so often – in big fields, against front-runners and sitters – that they got used to pushing and shoving, jockeying for position, changing tactics in mid-race. They were true racers.

Ovett and Coe fail to measure up in that critical respect. They spurred each other, but from a distance. Ovett once explained: 'Seb and I would have both been good without each other, but wouldn't have been so good without the incentive provoked by the other. It added a great deal of excitement, of competitiveness.'

Coe had more natural speed, as shown by his fabulous running in the 800m, where he held the world record for more than 18 years. He was small and slight, but had twinkling feet and always seemed to have a higher gear to move into. He set the world record for the 800m in Oslo in July 1979, taking a full second off Cuban Alberto Juantorena's mark. Coe's time, 1min 42.33s (rounded to 1min 42.4s), lasted two years until he bettered it himself with a fantastic 1min 41.73s effort at Florence, on 10 June 1981. This run set such a good world record that it wasn't until 1997 that Kenyan Dane Wilson Kipketer finally beat it. Imagine that – an important track record, not achieved at altitude or through assistance from banned drugs, lasting 16 years.

Given Coe's 800m domination, it is amazing he never won an Olympic gold over the distance. At Moscow in 1980, he ran poorly and finished second to Ovett. In 1984, he was outrun by Brazilian Joaquim Cruz and again had to settle for silver. Coe also never won a world or even a Commonwealth Games 800m title. At European Championship level, he was third in the 800m (behind German Olaf Beyer and Ovett) in 1978, second behind Hans-Peter Ferner in 1982, and finally won the title in 1986.

With his fantastic 800m speed and his ability to hold it over a mile, the 1000m best showcased Coe's talents. He established two world records at the distance. The second, 2min 12.18s, was set at Oslo in 1981. It wasn't broken until Kenyan Ngeny Noah sliced 0.22s off it – 18 years later!

While Coe excelled in the 800m and 1000m, his 1500m and one mile ability drew him the most fame. They are the prestigious races in a track and field meet.

Coe won the Olympic 1500m gold in 1980 (Ovett was third) and retained the title in 1984. No other runner has retained the Olympic 1500m title. In addition, Coe set one world record over the 1500m and three over the mile.

Though small in stature, Coe had a wonderful stride and a finishing kick any runner would fear. He proved to be a superb record-breaker, and won his share of major races, but not as many as he might have, given his almost unequalled talent.

Ovett was even more versatile than Coe – he won major championship titles over three different distances. He took an 800m silver medal as an 18-year-old at the 1974 European championship and competed in the 800m and 1500m at the 1976 Montreal Olympics. In the 800m he was a distant fifth behind Juantorena; in the 1500m he bowed out after being the victim of some rough running in the semi-finals.

As Walker faded, Ovett became the world's pre-eminent 1500m/miler over the next three years. He missed the 1978 Commonwealth Games, but won the European championships 1500m title (and was second in the 800m) that year. By 1980, he had compiled a staggering sequence of consecutive 1500m and mile victories (a streak that eventually totalled 45) and was favoured to win the Olympic gold. In the end he won Coe's specialty, the 800m, but had to settle for third in his own, the 1500m. As keen as Ovett was to win the 1500m gold, he lost the absolute sharp edge of desire when he won the 800m gold. The 1500m crown went to Coe, the finalist who was most desperate for success.

Ovett, injured, bypassed the 1982 Commonwealth Games and at the 1983 world championships, below full fitness, finished fourth in the 1500m, in the shadow of Cram, who won in the grand manner. Though Ovett harboured hopes of it all coming right at the 1984 Los Angeles Olympics, he was hit by bronchial problems and did well even to make the 800m and 1500m finals, having to emerge from a hospital bed to line up for the 1500m. After that, Ovett switched to longer distances, to such effect that he won the 1986 Commonwealth Games 5000m gold medal and was tenth over the same distance in the 1987 world champs.

Ovett initially shied away from world record attempts, but once Coe got into the act, the temptation, and commercial considerations, became too great. He set three world marks in the 1500m and two over the mile.

Even this brief resumé illustrates what fantastic runners Coe and Ovett were. What a pity they devoted so much energy to playing hide-and-not-seek. They first clashed at a low-key meeting in 1972 at the English schools cross-country championship when Ovett finished second and Coe tenth. Who would have guessed at the rivalry that was to grow?

By 1978, when they next raced each other, they were the new generation of England running stars, ready to take over from Brendan Foster and David Bedford. Ovett was tall and strongly built and had an imposing physical presence. Coe, a year younger, had emerged at senior level a couple of years later (after a superb schoolboy athletics career), but in 1977 stamped himself as a high-quality 800m runner.

Already the contrasts were evident. The son of a market trader, Ovett was born and grew up in Brighton. There was a down-to-earth air about him – he was his own man. For instance, Ovett handled his own affairs where possible, whereas Coe signed with the marketing company International Management Group.

Ovett ran with an air of arrogance. It was nothing for him to signal to the spectators that he had a race won while only halfway down the home stretch. On the track, he had beautiful balance. Even at times of utmost stress, he never looked flustered. It seemed incredible, watching him sprint towards the line during some of his world record runs, that he could be anywhere near the required pace, so effortless did he look. There were none of the tortured grimaces of a Zatopek; Ovett flowed. From the age of 16, he was coached by his mentor, Harry Wilson.

Coe, on first appearance, seemed the more serious. He was from Sheffield and placed great store by his academic studies – he attended Loughborough College and earned an economics degree. He was coached by his father, Peter.

Ovett had a curt relationship with the English media and this soon developed into all-out hostility. He generally refused even to talk to the media and was labelled Mr Grumpy for his (non) efforts. The Coes seemed more aware of public relations. Coe, and/or his father, were generally available. They were well spoken and handled public duties well. The media being the media, Coe received a better hearing. He was portrayed as a decent chap, intelligent and popular. Ovett was depicted as hard to get to know and prickly.

Fellow athletes told a different story. They said Coe could be superior and stand-offish, and had a cold streak, whereas Ovett was a good bloke who revelled in the camaraderie of the athletics scene and was a rather gregarious personality.

John Walker said in his autobiography *Champion*:

> I've always got on better with Ovett than with Coe. Not that I have ever exchanged unpleasant words with Coe, it's just that Ovett is more outgoing, more friendly, while Coe tends to be a loner … The delightful side of Ovett is the side few people know. He is a practical joker and often has other athletes in stitches of laughter; he works assiduously around Brighton for handicapped children and shuns any publicity for it,

and is often at Crystal Palace on a weekday helping out promoter Andy Norman working with children from disadvantaged families.

These days Ovett and Coe are at pains to say that they never had problems with each other, that any off-the-track rivalry was a figment of the media's imagination. It's true that the English media did portray an enmity between them, while the runners shied away from making comments about each other. Before 1984, though, they didn't have much time for each other. For instance, in *Ovett*, Ovett recounts the post-race scene at Moscow in 1980 after Coe had won the 1500m:

> His words to me as we shared the dope-testing room rankled. I passed him a drink and he said, 'So you got silver then?'
> 'No, I got bronze,' I replied.
> 'Oh good.'
> Those two words told me more about the man than the race did. I know they had a double meaning, but I have the memory of the way he said it.

Coe responded in his biography *Born to Run:* 'Between 1979 and 1981 … Steve annoyed and irritated me; while what he thought I was as a person maddened him.'

Ovett summed up the media's fascination with the pair like this:

> Seb was projected as the clean-cut young gentleman, the academic who spoke well; on the other hand, there was this vaguely artistic character of less intelligence with rough edges, a natural result of being the son of a man whose livelihood came from a market stall. Add to this a concocted long-running feud between the two of them and you have the ideal ingredients to keep Fleet Street fuelled.

They openly admired each other as runners, however, Ovett describing Coe as the best middle-distance runner he'd met. Coe said that for energy and physical presence, no one he faced approached Ovett: 'He could galvanise the public and convince a group of contemporaries that the race was only for second place.' Certainly they complemented each other. Athletics followers – and all sports lovers – eagerly awaited their battles on the track.

But though they were the world's dominant middle-distance runners in 1979, they contrived never to meet. Coe ran that year at Cosford, Crystal Palace (three times), Loughborough (four times), Cleckheaton (twice), Stretford, Malmo, Meisingset, Oslo (twice), Spalding, Turin, Twin, Viareggio and Zurich. He set 800m, 1500m and mile world records within six weeks.

The same year, Ovett ran track races at Tullyease, Crystal Palace (11 times), Enfield (twice), Bremen, Nijmegen, Dublin, Hendon (twice), Gothenburg, Berlin, Cologne, Brussels, Koblenz and Gateshead.

It can't have been easy to avoid each other, but they managed it. They replaced physical encounters with their 'paper' battles. On 15 August 1979, Coe smashed by more than a second Filbert Bayi's world record for the 1500m, running 3min 32.03s (rounded to 3min 32.1s) at Zurich. Less than three weeks later, Ovett, who had previously shunned record-breaking attempts, set out to beat Coe's mark at the Ivo Van Damme Memorial meeting in Brussels and was timed at 3min 32.11s. 'If at the finishing line, I had breathed in, expanding my chest, then I would probably have become world record-holder,' he reflected later.

In 1980 there was some excuse for the continued jockeying for position. The Moscow Olympics were the focal point of the season and neither was keen to meet his major rival beforehand. Before the Olympics, Ovett ran two fabulous races at Oslo. On 1 July, he nabbed Coe's world one mile record. A few days later he equalled Coe's world 1500m record, running 3min 32.09s (rounded to 3min 32.1s). If he hadn't waved to the crowd in the home straight, Ovett would have broken the world record. Instead, he and Coe became joint holders, further sharpening the rivalry.

At the boycott-weakened Olympics, the Britons contested two dramatic races. The first was the 800m. It was thought Ovett would be an outside shot for a medal, and that Coe would win as he liked. But Ovett ran a smart final, always in prime position. By contrast, Coe slipped back disastrously through the field. In the home straight Ovett sprinted effortlessly for victory. Coe, forced to make up too much ground down the straight, could do no better than second place, half a second adrift.

Then followed a week of waiting as Coe pondered on the gold medal he had frittered away. Ovett became an even heavier favourite in the 1500m (bookmakers gave odds of 11-4 on him to win a second gold). Was he too confident?

In the 1500m final, Coe ran impeccably. He stayed with the front-runners and when he struck for home, no one could get near him. Coe surged into the lead on the final bend, then kicked again for home with a withering burst. Ovett tried to match him, but had to settle for third, behind Jurgen Straub.

So the pair left Moscow with a gold each, pride restored and fans still not really sure who was the better runner.

For the rest of the summer these two athletes, in peak condition, again avoided each other. Coe ran at Crystal Palace, Zurich and Viareggio. Ovett fronted up at Crystal Palace (he ran the 5000m there, Coe the 800m), Budapest, Lausanne, Crystal Palace again, Koblenz and Crystal Palace twice more. Ovett equalled, then beat, the world record for the 1500m and set a world mile record. But he didn't test himself again against the best outside the Olympics.

Into 1981. Surely they would now get down to the serious business of some head-to-head racing. Both ran superbly and had full schedules, but again they steered clear of each other. Coe ran at Cosford (twice), Crystal Palace (six times), Borough Road, Cleckheaton, Gateshead (twice), Florence, Helsinki, Stockholm, Oslo, Leicester, Viareggio, Zagreb, Zurich, Brussels and Rome.

Ovett was seen on the track at Atrim (twice), Crystal Palace (four times), Gateshead (twice), Venice, Oslo (twice), Helsinki, Milan, Lausanne, Budapest, Bergen, Berlin, Koblenz, Ardal, Rome, Rieti and then, four times, in Australia.

Coe's form was amazing. He set four world outdoor records, over 800m, 1000m, and the mile (twice). But Ovett was fairly useful as well, with a world mark over the mile. They competed at the same meet five times. At the Talbot Games at Crystal Palace on 31 July, Coe ran the 800m and Ovett the 1000m. Both won. They might have left Crystal Palace content, but again there was a certain frustration among spectators.

The situation was becoming ridiculous. Their rivalry assumed massive proportions, fuelled by a relentless English media.

On 7 July 1981, Coe ran 3min 31.95s for the 1500m in Stockholm. The following day in Milan, Ovett ran the same distance in precisely the same time, something it would be impossible to do on purpose. The English runners, separated by distance so often, still seemed somehow connected. Then came nine famous days in August. Coe set a world one mile record on 19 August, Ovett broke it on 26 August and Coe broke it again on 28 August.

Finally the runners agreed to a three-race series in 1982: 3000m at Crystal Palace on 17 July, 800m in Nice on 14 August and the mile in Eugene, Oregon on 25 September. It promised to be an amazing season, as both also intended winning Commonwealth Games and European titles.

But they'd waited too long and forces beyond their control took over. Ovett was severely injured in late 1981, ramming his right leg into an iron church railing while on a training run. That cost him months of training, and the Coe-Ovett dream series remained just that, a dream. Ovett finally came right, but by then Coe had suffered a stress fracture and was out of action. By the time Coe had recovered, Ovett had torn a hamstring. Neither got to the Commonwealth Games and only Coe, who also suffered glandular fever during the season, ran at the European championships, where he was below his best.

In 1983, a week after his 1500m world record had been broken by Sydney Maree, Ovett mustered a strong finish to reclaim it with a time of 3 min 30.77s. Despite various illnesses and injuries, Coe and Ovett were nearly as good as ever in 1983, and a match for any other middle-distance runner, even the emerging Cram and Aouita – but they still didn't face each other.

By 1984 the magic of the rivalry remained in the public mind, but other runners had arrived. Cram was the world 1500m champion. Aouita was proving to be brilliantly versatile. Sydney Maree was doing great things over the mile. At the 1984 Olympics, Coe staged his great comeback, taking the 1500m gold and 800m silver and giving the fingers, metaphorically and literally, to the doubting English media. ('Who says I'm finished?' he shouted at the media benches moments after his 1500m triumph.) Ovett, hit by a severe virus infection, was never a factor. He was last in the 800m final and withdrew during the 1500m final, having defied doctor's orders even to start in it.

And that was it. They never met again while they were world-class runners.

Ovett focused on longer distances, his last really major race being a down-the-track finish in the 1987 world championships 5000m. Coe kept his form, but his health varied. He became ill during both the 1986 and 1990 Commonwealth Games, but ran spectacularly well during the 1986 European championships, being first in the 800m and second in the 1500m. He controversially failed to make the British team for the 1500m at the 1988 Olympics (the three chosen were Cram, Peter Elliott and Steve Crabb), though by then he was so much part of the establishment that IOC chief Juan Antonio Samaranch tried all he could to have him included, even suggesting he be offered a 'wild card' entry.

Coe and Ovett did clash once more, in England in 1989. Amazingly, the only time they'd faced each other in England was 17 years previously, when they were schoolboys. In 1989 they contested an invitation 800m race at Birmingham. It was a strange business all round. By then, of course, they weren't the dominant world runners they'd been a decade earlier, but some English papers still tried to beat up their meeting. A *Daily Mirror* headline shouted: 'It's on!' Coe versus Ovett still held a certain appeal, even if it was more nostalgic than athletic.

Coe, in the twilight of his career, was intent on qualifying for the 1990 Auckland Commonwealth Games, and was using the Birmingham race as a step along that path. Ovett was even further past his best, though he was still running competitively. By 1989, a new batch of British middle-distance runners held centre stage. They included Cram, Elliott, Tom McKean and Crabb.

Coe treated the Birmingham race in a straightforward manner, and won in a respectable 1min 46.83s. Ovett, though, was unhappy before and after. He was paid to run and felt he was being used, a pawn in a media and marketing beat-up. After the race, in which he finished ninth (of 10 starters), Ovett broke down in tears during a television interview, trying to explain about payments and inducements. He'd been in no frame of mind to race, and it was a sad way for the Coe–Ovett on-track rivalry to finish.

Coe, aged 33, was sixth in the 800m at the 1990 Commonwealth Games, his international swansong.

They've both remained part of the athletics scene. Ovett did athletics commentaries for some years, mainly for ITV, and was very good. He commentated much as he is – not afraid to offer an opinion and certainly not one to withhold praise.

Coe went into politics, of the sports and political kinds. He was the Conservative MP for Falmouth and Camborne in Cornwall from 1992-97, and then chief aide to the leader of the Opposition, William Hague. On 31 March 2000 he was appointed to the House of Lords, taking the title of Lord Coe of Ranmore. His other posts have included vice-chairmanship of the Sports Council board, membership of the Health Education Council, and Chairman of the Sports Council's Olympic Review. He was the International Olympic Committee's Athletics Commission chairman from 1981–92. In 2000, he was appointed President of the Amateur Athletics Association and three years later won election to the International Amateur Athletics Federation's council.

Coe, now deputy chairman of London's 2012 Olympic bid, has always been a staunch campaigner against drugs in sport. In 1981 he addressed the Olympic Congress (the first athlete to be given that opportunity) and devoted most of his allotted four minutes' speaking time to railing against drugs cheats. In 1987 he wrote a comprehensive report entitled 'Drugs in Sport'. It stressed that drug-testing should be done by an independent group, not a sport's governing body. He has remained outspoken on the subject and the Football Association has sought his help in creating a new and watertight testing system.

Coe has written several books and is in demand as a public speaker. He has remained closely linked with athletics, too, through the media, as a British newspaper columnist, and for television. He began coaching Australian 800m runner Tamsyn Lewis in 2001. His 13-year marriage to former equestrian star Nicola McIrvine ran into trouble in 2000 amid stories of a relationship with Australian Commonwealth Games heptathlete gold medallist Jane Flemming, his business manager. But that relationship foundered after a year or so.

These days Ovett lives in Australia, having been based for some years in Scotland, and seems very content with his relatively laidback lifestyle. Coe rushes about the globe more. Occasionally they meet. They both travelled to Auckland in early 2003 for a John Walker fund-raising dinner, when they were happy to be interviewed together, spoke well and were full of praise for each other.

Ovett contributed the foreword for Coe's biography, writing:

> I was very fortunate indeed to have come into contact with Seb. His mere presence made life more exciting. It would have meant nothing to have dominated without challenge. Nothing to have won everything without defeat. We have, I think, very little in common off the track and yet we are friends. I sometimes think our saga could not have been scripted or acted out any better than fate dictated.

Ovett's opinion must carry weight. But many will not agree with him. What a pity two people who seemed finally to enjoy each other's company, even if they were such different personalities, should have spent so much energy avoiding competing against each other.

Brendan Foster, one of the wise old men of British athletics, said: 'I believe they would agree now they should have raced each other more often. Obviously Olympic titles were important, but there were times when they should have given the opportunity to a wider audience in Britain, to enable dads to take their kids for something to remember, so that instead of taxi drivers in London saying, "I was there when Chataway beat Kuts at White City", they could be saying, "I saw Ovett against Coe".'

Ovett addressed the missed confrontations in *Born To Run*:

> It wasn't as simple as one guy not being willing to run against the other. When you're aiming for peaks, you don't run every weekend, you're not a commodity for public consumption. Situations were created by pressure from promoters, as much as anything. It was all cloak-and-dagger …
>
> I believe we could have organised ourselves better. It was the time when the sport was changing, towards becoming professional. If Seb and I had acted together, it might have forced the sport to make changes that might not have been good for it; the governing bodies might not have coped. The benefits might have been only financial.

So Coe and Ovett helped their sport by not facing each other!

Theirs was a rivalry, no doubt about it. But a rivalry that was never resolved on the track, and therefore an ultimately unsatisfying one.

	Sebastian Newbold Coe	Steven Michael James Ovett
Born	29 September 1956, Chiswick, London	9 October 1955, Brighton, England
Olympic Games	1980: 800m: silver medal 1500m: gold medal 1984: 800m: silver medal 1500m: gold medal (Olympic record time of 3min 32.53s)	1976: 800m: fifth 1500m: fifth in semi-final 1980: 800m: first 1500m: third 1984: 800m: eighth 1500m: did not finish final
Commonwealth Games	1986: 800m: third in semi-finals (did not contest final) 1990: 800m: sixth	1986: 5000m: first
European Championships	1978: 800m: third 1982: 800m: second 1986: 800m: first 1500m: second	1974: 800m: second 1978: 800m: second 1500m: first
World records		
800m:	1min 42.4s, Oslo, 5 July 1979. 1min 41.73s, Florence, 10 June 1981.	
1000m:	2min 13.40s, Oslo, 1 July 1980. 2min 12.18s, Oslo, 11 July 1981.	
1500m:	3min 32.1s, Zurich, 15 August 1979.	3min 32.1s, Oslo, 5 July 1980. 3min 31.36s, Koblenz, 27 August 1980. 3min 30.77s, Rieti, 4 September 1983.
One mile:	3min 49.0s, Oslo, 17 July 1979. 3min 48.53s, Zurich, 19 August 1981. 3min 47.33s, Brussels, 28 August 1981.	3min 48.8s, Oslo, 1 July 1980. 3min 48.40s, Koblenz, 26 August 1981.
Two miles:		8min 13.51s, Crystal Palace, 1978.

Head-to-head meetings

25 March 1972:	English schools cross-country champs, Hillingdon. Ovett 2nd, Coe 10th.
31 August 1978:	European championship 800m, Prague. Ovett 2nd, Coe 3rd.
26 July 1980:	Olympic 800m final, Moscow. Ovett 1st, Coe 2nd.
1 August 1980:	Olympic 1500m final, Moscow. Coe 1st, Ovett 3rd.
6 August 1984:	Olympic 800m final, Los Angeles. Coe 2nd, Ovett 8th.
11 August 1984:	Olympic 1500m final, Los Angeles. Coe 1st, Ovett did not finish.
24 June 1989:	Invitation 800m, Birmingham. Coe 1st, Ovett 9th.

9 Ice Queens

Tonya Harding v Nancy Kerrigan

The rivalry between American figure skaters Nancy Kerrigan and Tonya Harding didn't begin on 6 January 1994 with 'the whack that was heard around the world' – but that's when it turned into a classic case of good versus evil.

The 'good' was represented by Kerrigan, the defending US figure skating champion. Kerrigan came from a well-to-do East Coast family, had a clean, wholesome image and was a favourite of the establishment. The 'evil' came in the form of Harding, who had been raised in a trailer park in Oregon, lacked Kerrigan's social graces and was a talented but rather rough-edged skater – the classic outsider.

These one-dimensional views of the two women suited the media and the public well and, even though not absolutely accurate, were close enough to make for a classic rivalry. The media portrayed Harding as white trash jealous of Kerrigan's money and talent. The way Kerrigan and Harding have conducted their lives since those harrowing times in 1994 has only added to the popular viewpoint.

Their story had every ingredient required for a best-selling novel or a prime-time soap opera: an American sweetheart, a jealous and unprincipled rival, a crime of violence, money, the lure of Olympic fame and glory, the FBI and jail sentences. No wonder their story has been the subject of numerous books and television programmes in the past decade.

On 6 January 1994, after a practice session before the US Olympic figure skating trials in Detroit, Kerrigan was clubbed on the right knee by a burly male wielding a metal bar. The assault forced Kerrigan out of the trials, and placed in grave jeopardy her place in her country's team for the forthcoming Winter Olympics in Lillehammer, Norway. This was sensational enough.

But the juiciest part was yet to come. Over the next weeks and months, it transpired that Harding, Kerrigan's fiercest American rival, was more than merely an unwitting beneficiary of the attack. Her former husband, Jeff Gillooly (they'd married young, divorced in 1993, but still lived together), had organised the assault and, piece by piece, the level of Harding's involvement seemed to escalate.

Rows erupted over whether Harding, who in Kerrigan's absence won the national title in Detroit, should be permitted to represent the United States at the Olympics. And what about Kerrigan? Should she be gifted a spot on the team? A threatened multi-million dollar lawsuit added to the frenzy.

Then there was the drama of the Olympic competition itself. With a background like this, no wonder the figure skating became one of the most watched events in American television history. And after the Olympics, the fallout built up steam with criminal investigations and inquiries by American figure skating authorities.

The tragedy, which ran for years, means that Kerrigan and Harding are as linked in the public mind as Bonnie and Clyde, Laurel and Hardy, Abbott and Costello. That fact may be unpalatable to both women, but it is undeniably so. As Kerrigan said in 1998: 'It will always be there and every time there is an Olympics, it will be brought up.'

How did it ever come to this? How did what appears on the surface to be the refined and cultured sport of figure skating get caught up in activities more suited to the Mafia or back-street muggers?

By 1994, Nancy Kerrigan, from Stoneham, Massachusetts, was 24 years old and her career was heading towards a sharp peak. The Lillehammer Winter Olympics were to be her golden moment. Kerrigan began skating when she was just six years old at a rink near the family home. She became enthralled by the sport and spent hours practising and watching it on television. She was always competitive – being around two older brothers ensured that. She won her first competition when she was nine, at the Boston Open, and by the age of 14 was perfecting the triple-triple combination. She was clearly extremely talented, and enjoyed the support of a large extended family living close by.

Through the mid-1980s, Kerrigan began to establish herself in the junior figure skating ranks, first in New England, then nationally. There were good performances at such events as the national senior championships, the World University Games and the US Olympic Festival. She attended Stoneham High School until 1987 and then gained a business degree from Emmanuel College. In 1990, she finished fourth in the US Nationals. She was now one of the big names in the sport. Over the next few years, she improved steadily. At the 1991

Three pivotal figures in the Celtic-Rangers rivalry. Jock Stein (top left) was the hugely successful Celtic manager of the 1960s and '70s; Graeme Souness (top right) was the Rangers manager who broke through the club's religious prejudices; and Mo Johnston (above) was the first Scottish Catholic of modern times to play for Rangers. PHOTOSPORT

First blood to Steve Ovett (279), winner of the 1980 Moscow Olympic 800m gold medal, ahead of countryman Sebastian Coe (254). PHOTOSPORT

Contrasting fortunes.
Above: Steve Ovett, winner of
the Moscow Olympic 800m,
waves to the crowd during the
medal ceremony. PHOTOSPORT
Right: A week later, after the
1500m, it's Coe on top with
Ovett looking on. PHOTOSPORT

Tonya Harding (left) and Nancy Kerrigan, medallists at the 1991 world figure skating championships in Munich. FOTOPRESS

Harding (left) and Kerrigan practise before the 1994 Winter Olympics at Lillehammer. FOTOPRESS

Tonya Harding (left) is hit by Samantha Browning during their professional boxing bout at Memphis in 2003. Browning won a split decision. FOTOPRESS

Nationals, she was third. The following year she was second. In 1993, she won the title.

Though not yet at her peak, she'd represented the United States at the 1992 Albertville Winter Olympics and come away with a bronze medal. Shortly afterwards, she finished second at the world championships. When she won the US title in 1993, she became an early Olympic gold medal favourite and her training through late 1993 was pointed towards the following year's Games. Kerrigan always handled herself well in public. She did not put a word out of place, she was pretty and she enjoyed a big following. She was America's sweetheart.

Then came the shocking events of January 1994.

Across the other side of the country, another figure skater, cut from a different cloth, was also eyeing the 1994 Olympics. Tonya Harding was born at Portland, Oregon, in 1970. Hers was not a settled childhood – her mother was married seven times. She dropped out of high school in her sophomore year. But she was outstandingly athletic. At one point she was one of only two women (the other was world champion Midori Ito of Japan) who could land a triple axel jump in competition. Harding's natural talent, plus plenty of hard work, took her through a successful junior figure skating career and as soon as she became a senior, she began to win titles. By 1987 she was hinting at future glory by finishing fifth in the US national championships. In 1991, she won the title. She attended the 1992 Winter Olympics at Albertville, where she was shaded by Kerrigan to finish in fourth spot.

The stakes got higher through 1993. Then a plan was hatched to remove her major Olympic rival – Kerrigan – and so greatly boost Harding's chances of Olympic success. With the benefit of hindsight, it seems like an episode from a Keystone Cops movie, so inept was the planning and execution. But at the time it was a serious business.

Harding has never publicly admitted she took part in the planning of the attack on Kerrigan. However, according to the FBI's extensive written report on the assault, Harding was a knowing participant in the conspiracy that began on 28 December 1993, when she agreed to have Gillooly pay bodyguard Shawn Eckardt $2700 to arrange an attack. It was carried out by Eckardt's nephew, Shane Stant, who clubbed Kerrigan above the knee with a baton. Stant's friend Derrick Smith drove the getaway car.

Kerrigan had just finished a practice session at Detroit's Cobo Arena and was talking to a reporter when Stant attacked her. She dropped to the ground and began sobbing and screaming: 'It hurts. It hurts. It hurts so bad. I'm so scared.'

It was a bad time for women's sport. Already two leading figure skaters, Katarina Witt and Harding herself, had been threatened with assault. Harding employed a bodyguard service. And eight months before the business in Detroit, world tennis No 1 Monica Seles had been stabbed by a crazed Steffi Graf fan, Gunther Parche, who figured that if he could take out Seles, then Graf would return to the top of the world tennis rankings. Parche was more successful than the Harding clan, for Seles didn't return to the court for over two years. Her absence enabled Graf to become world No 1 again and to win a succession of Grand Slam titles. But Kerrigan was limping about within a day and was back on the ice after 10 days.

If the attack itself was an astounding story, what followed was mind-boggling. Within three weeks, police had arrested the four men involved. Eckardt told the FBI about the plot that was hatched with Gillooly, and the mystery quickly unravelled. Eckardt later said Harding knew about the plot and that at one point she told him: 'You need to stop screwing around with this and get it done.' Of course, once Gillooly was identified, questions were asked about Harding's connection to the attack. Gillooly implicated Harding, saying she 'gave the go sign'.

Harding duly went on to win the national title, but figure skating officials were left with some awkward decisions. Should Kerrigan, the national champion the previous year, be gifted a spot on the Olympic team? It has been an unshakeable policy of any US Olympic team selection that competitors must qualify at the Olympic trials to be selected. Such brilliant athletes as Harrison Dillard and Carl Lewis at various times missed out on contesting Olympic events because of their slip-ups at Olympic trials.

Eventually American officials found a loophole in their rules and selected Kerrigan for Lillehammer, and what would become known as the Battle of Wounded Knee II began. Then there was the thorny question of what to do about Harding, who had earned a spot on the team by her performances on the ice, but was being drawn ever closer to the scandal. The US Olympic Committee decided to exclude her from the team, but quickly changed its stance when Harding threatened a $20 million lawsuit to prevent her removal. Harding was confirmed as a US team selection after midnight on the first day of the Olympics. At that point she was still totally distancing herself from the attack.

There was one memorable snapshot of a chain-smoking and brazen Harding climbing into a pick-up and vowing to 'kick butt' at the Olympics. A drama of OJ Simpson proportions loomed. Suddenly the Lillehammer Winter Olympics, which for Americans at that time of the year would normally be a pleasant diversion from the more seriously followed sports of ice hockey and basketball, became the major focus of not just American but world sport.

Kerrigan got to Norway a week early and trained happily enough at the Olympic venue. But what would happen when Harding arrived?

Harding arrived in mid-February, accompanied not just by her choreographer, Erika Bakacs, and her coach, Diane Rawlinson, but also by her lawyer, Dennis Rawlinson, and a phalanx of media representatives, including reporter Joel Loy and other employees of the television show *Inside Edition* (Harding was reportedly paid $50,000 for an exclusive contract with the show), CBS anchor Connie Chung and Associated Press representatives. It was like a circus, and the media couldn't get enough of it. Newspapers ran extensive figure skating stories – and not just in their sports sections, but across the front page. Magazines from *Time* to *Sports Illustrated* featured figure skating. The media presence at Lillehammer was suffocating.

The world waited to see how the skaters would greet each other. We must bear in mind that at this stage, Gillooly and the other three men had been arrested, but there had been no direct evidence implicating Harding in the assault.

US Olympic officials were obviously concerned. They requested separate training times on the ice for Kerrigan and Harding, a request that was denied. The two skaters met on 16 February, coming at each other from different directions at the Olympic Village, both with groups of friends. There was a stop for a short conversation – Kerrigan said: 'It's been a tough month for us, huh?' – then they went on their way.

But the air was frosty, and not just in the ice skating arena. They sat at opposite ends for the US Olympic team photo (in a team photo taken in Detroit on 9 January, they'd been seated together). When they did train at the same time, they barely acknowledged each other. Indeed, there was one incident that became much reported when they accidentally bumped into each other. Asked in one interview about the extent of their relationship, Kerrigan replied: 'There isn't a relationship.'

The Olympic figure skating competition was a brilliant event, full of drama. After the opening day's short technical programme, Kerrigan led from world champion Oksana Baiul of Ukraine and France's Surya Bonaly. Harding, who had been out of sorts, was well back in tenth position. Seats for the second and final day (the free skate) went for $1000. Kerrigan again skated brilliantly, but was shaded for the gold medal by the 16-year-old Ukrainian orphan. She lost by the narrowest possible margin, one-tenth of a point on a tiebreaker. Four judges gave their first-place votes to Kerrigan, four others gave theirs to Baiul.

The ninth judge, Germany's Jan Hoffman, split his right down the middle. He awarded Kerrigan a 5.8 for technical merit and a 5.8 for artistic impression. He gave Baiul a 5.7 for technical merit and a 5.9 for artistic impression. The scores were even: 11.6 for Kerrigan, 11.6 for Baiul. How was the tie broken? From Wednesday's technical programme they took the first mark, the technical one. From Friday's free skate they took the second mark, for artistic impression. So Baiul's 5.9 on Hoffman's card beat Kerrigan's 5.8, and that decided the gold medal.

Harding improved marginally to eighth, but her performance was marred when a bootlace broke. About 45 seconds into her routine and sobbing uncontrollably, she went across to the referee's stand to show the lace. She was permitted to restart her performance after a break of about half an hour.

Incredibly, 204 million viewers tuned into the CBS coverage of the Olympics, making Lillehammer the most watched Winter Games ever. The figure skating broadcasts became the highest rated Wednesday and Friday of any network in US television history and were the sixth and eighth most watched broadcasts of all time, not far behind the final episode of *M*A*S*H*, the all-time No 1. The newspaper headline writers had a field day, with efforts such as 'Beauty Crushes the Beast' and 'Few Tears, No Blood as Snow White Beats Poison Dwarf'.

So Kerrigan hadn't won the gold, but people who like happy endings were still pleased. The good girl had finished second; the bad girl eighth and in tears. The media coverage was almost entirely favourable to Kerrigan. Headings such as 'Thin Ice Under Harding Weakens', 'Harding Will be Left Out in the Cold', 'Kerrigan Knocks Out Portland Pretender' and 'Tougher Than She Looks' only served to reinforce the good versus evil nature of the story.

The odd crack appeared in the Kerrigan aura of virtue, but it didn't seem to matter much. She was less than gracious in congratulating Baiul, complaining that the judges hadn't noticed how flawless her own performance had been and that they'd missed Baiul's mistakes. When the medal ceremony was delayed because no one knew the Ukrainian national anthem, Kerrigan said (privately, she thought, but with live microphones nearby): 'I don't know why they're bothering reapplying her makeup. She's only going to start crying again.' And after skipping the closing ceremony to be in a parade at Disney World (her $2 million sponsor), Kerrigan, riding on a fire engine with Mickey Mouse, complained (again without knowing she could be heard): 'This is dumb. I hate it. This is the corniest thing I have ever done.'

When Kerrigan and Harding got back to the United States, they faced vastly different futures. Kerrigan was received like a conquering hero and has gone on to enjoy a hugely successful career based around her figure skating prowess. Sponsors from Reebok to Revlon paid millions of dollars to be associated with her. Three weeks after returning home, Kerrigan hosted *Saturday Night Live* and the show got its highest rating in six years.

Kerrigan had a relationship with her manager, Jerry Solomon of ProServ (who was separated at the time). They married in 1996 and had a son, Matthew, in December that year. Kerrigan successfully combined motherhood with figure skating and she and Solomon jointly produced several shows in which she starred. She travelled with the *Champions on Ice* tour and appeared in shows such as *Divas on Ice*, *Footloose on Ice*, *Ice Capades*, *Grease on Ice* and *Halloween on Ice*. Kerrigan was co-author of *Artistry on Ice*, which was published in 2003.

Kerrigan basically finished competitive skating after the 1994 Olympics, though she returned in 2000 for the Goodwill Games at Lake Placid and showed she'd lost little of her former skill by finishing third. In the intervening years she'd restricted herself mainly to the figure skating spectaculars, or to exhibitions, such as a 1998 challenge match involving other big names like Michelle Kwan at Springfield, Massachusetts, just along the road from her home.

There were other interests, too. Kerrigan, who lives in Lynnfield, Massachusetts, did an increasing amount of watercolour painting on ceramics, becoming so proficient that her work began to sell. She lent her name to the Nancy Kerrigan Foundation, which raises awareness of, and supports, the visually impaired. There are Nancy Kerrigan fundraising pro-celebrity golf tournaments, featuring past and present LPGA stars. She is always a popular guest on television chat shows.

By contrast, Harding had her work cut out staying out of jail. Gillooly was sentenced to two years' jail (he eventually served eight months). In a plea bargain agreement with the Multnomah County Court, Harding pleaded guilty to hindering the investigation of the attack on Kerrigan. The penalties imposed included three years' supervised probation, a $100,000 fine, a $50,000 donation to a fund to benefit the Special Olympics, $10,000 court costs, and 500 hours of community service work. Many who followed the case felt she'd done well to avoid a stint in jail.

The question of whether Harding had planned or agreed to the assault remained a murky area, although the US Figure Skating Association apparently had no doubts. Meeting in Colorado Springs on 29–30 June 1994, the USFSA discussed the Harding case for nine hours. Harding elected not to attend. At the end of that time, a five-member panel stripped her of her 1994 national title and banned her from the organisation for life, having decided she knew about the attack in advance. This was the first time an official body had come to that conclusion. 'By a preponderance of the evidence, the five members of the panel concluded that she had prior knowledge and was involved prior to the incident,' hearing panel chairman William Hybl said. 'This is based on civil standards, not criminal standards.'

The figure skating body ruled that Harding's conduct 'intentionally undermines the concept of sportsmanship and fair play embodied in the USFSA bylaws and rules and amateur sportsmanship in general. Ms Harding's actions as they related to the assault on Nancy Kerrigan evidence a clear disregard for fairness, good sportsmanship and ethical behaviour.' Harding did not appeal the decision.

It left Harding in a difficult position. Her life had been centred around figure skating. It was what she was good at. Now that had been taken away from her. She skated in public only rarely in the years that followed – at the intermission during a minor league hockey game at Reno in 1996, in 1998 as part of a television special, and in 1999 when she finished second in a competition in Huntington, West Virginia.

She has progressed from one disaster to another over the past decade. In 1994 she become involved for a short time with professional wrestling, becoming 'celebrity manager' of Art Barr, who wrestled under the name of The American Love Machine. She tried a career as a singer, backed by a band called The Golden Blades, but gave it up soon after a show in Portland when she was roundly booed and pelted with empty plastic bottles and other missiles.

On 23 December 1995, only a short time after her final break-up with Gillooly, Harding married again, to Michael Smith, in a ceremony on a yacht on the Willamette River. Three and a half months later she filed for divorce, citing irreconcilable difference. In 2002 she was sentenced to 10 days in Clark County Jail (she served eight) for drinking alcohol while on probation in 2000 and hitting her boyfriend, Darren Silver, with a hubcap. To secure her release, she was forced to attend an anger management course and to swear off alcohol.

In October 2001 Harding was a contestant on the US version of the popular British TV quiz show *The Weakest Link* (she was voted out in the second round). And then there has been the professional boxing chapter of her life. It began when she laced on the gloves to face Bill Clinton love-interest Paula Jones in a made-for-television boxing match. The fight, which took place in March 2002, was billed as Tonya 'TNT' Harding versus Paula 'The Pounder' Jones and rated exceptionally well for Fox TV. Harding, a trained athlete, destroyed Jones in three rounds in a tawdry scene that did credit to no one. Encouraged, Harding then pursued a career as a genuine professional boxer.

She made her debut (if we exclude the Jones farce) at Memphis, on 22

February 2003 at the age of 32, when she met American Samantha Browning in one of the undercard fights to a Mike Tyson heavyweight bout. Browning beat her in a split decision over four rounds. Undeterred, Harding pressed on with her boxing career, showing more enthusiasm than talent, and won her next three fights – against Shannon Birmingham, Alejandra Lopez and Emily Gosa – on points decisions, before being knocked out (in 73 seconds) by Melissa Yanas in Dallas in August 2003. She has not fought since then. Only hours before a scheduled fight with Tracy Carlton in Oakland, California on 20 March 2004, she withdrew when she and her manager received death threats.

For her boxing bouts Harding receives US$12,000–$15,000 per fight, a huge amount for a woman, inflated owing to her notoriety. She still skates for enjoyment, using her old sport as part of her boxing training, and has applied to the US Figure Skating Association for reinstatement. In February 2004 she skated for *The Early Show* in New York's Woolman Rink in Central Park.

Over the years Harding has been the subject of many books, and has appeared regularly on the chat show circuit. She was interviewed by Larry King in June 2000, shortly after the infamous hubcap incident. There have been other unsavoury incidents. Gillooly, who renamed himself Jeff Stone on leaving jail, provided a lurid 23-minute videotape of himself and Harding engaging in sex on their wedding night, which was sold through *Penthouse* magazine. It was never made clear whether Harding agreed to the marketing of the tape and received profits, but she did pose for *Penthouse*. In recent years she has been the victim of numerous pornographic forgeries.

As would be expected, the paths of Kerrigan and Harding, who did not move in the same circles even when they were both leading amateur figure skaters, seldom crossed after those tumultuous weeks in early 1994. However, there was one meeting in 1998, when Fox paid each of them $100,000-plus for a two-hour special called *Breaking the Ice*. It was filmed in New York and James Brown conducted the interviews. Kerrigan was first on camera and, when asked about Harding, said: 'I don't regard her. I only think about it when asked. I think it was unnecessary. It shouldn't have happened.'

Harding, looking nervous, then walked into the studio and the pair exchanged a cold and abbreviated greeting. Harding asked for forgiveness. 'I would like to apologise again for being in the wrong place at the wrong time and with the wrong people,' she said. 'If I could have known, I would have done anything to stop it. I say that from the bottom of my heart.'

The apology hardly had Kerrigan bursting out in smiles and leaning across to hug her former rival. She said: 'From all of this, I hope she could learn from that and better her life and not hurt anyone else.' Later: 'I am glad you moved on and I hope that you can find happiness and maybe children can learn from these mistakes.'

Later Harding, in a nauseatingly sweet voice, said: 'I could never hurt anyone. Never.' Then she said she had forgiven herself. For what? 'For being involved with people who were horrible. For being selfish on my part for wanting the gold medal at the Olympics.'

Kerrigan, looking back at Lillehammer, said it was the best performance of her career. 'I was really proud of myself.' And so she should have been. To recover from the physical and mental scars of the attack and skate so brilliantly spoke volumes for her strength of mind and ability.

The oddest thing about the assault, as Kerrigan herself conceded during the Fox interview, was how much it benefited figure skating. The sport had always been popular with television audiences, despite having a somewhat prissy reputation, and stars such as Sonja Heine, Peggy Fleming, Dorothy Hamill, Katarina Witt, John Curry, Scott Hamilton and Robin Cousins were long admired for their skill. But during the 1994 Winter Olympics figure skating became compulsive viewing. Officials from other world sports looked on enviously for a fortnight as figure skating occupied centre stage. 'The attack in a bizarre way helped the sport,' said Kerrigan. 'It brought awareness to the sport.'

	Tonya Maxine Harding	Nancy Ann Kerrigan
Born	12 November 1970, Portland, Oregon	13 October 1969, Woburn, Massachusetts
Winter Olympics	1992, Albertville: 4th 1994, Lillehammer: 8th	1992, Albertville: 3rd 1994, Lillehammer: 2nd
World Championships	1991: 2nd 1992: 3rd	1991: 3rd 1992: 2nd 1993: 5th
US National Championships	1987: 5th 1988: 5th 1989: 3rd 1990: 7th 1991: 1st 1992: 3rd 1993: 4th 1994: 1st (title later withdrawn)	1990: 4th 1991: 3rd 1992: 2nd 1993: 1st 1994: did not compete – injured

1994: Six months that rocked the figure skating world	
January 6	Kerrigan is smashed on the right knee during the US national figure skating championships in Detroit.
January 7	Kerrigan withdraws from the championships, which are doubling as the US Olympic trials.
January 8	Harding wins the US title. Kerrigan and Harding are chosen for the US team for the forthcoming Lillehammer Olympic Games.
January 13	Harding's bodyguard, Shawn Eckardt, is arrested in connection with the assault on Kerrigan.
January 14	Three men are charged with assault.
January 16	Kerrigan skates for first time since the attack.
January 18	Harding meets authorities for the first time about the Kerrigan incident and is quizzed for several hours. She says she has left Gillooly.
January 19	Harding's husband Jeff Gillooly is also charged.
January 27	Harding admits knowing of the plot after the attack.
February 1	Gillooly pleads guilty and says Harding approved the plan.
February 6	Harding threatens a $20 million lawsuit to retain her Olympic team place.
February 12	Harding's position in the Olympic team is confirmed.
February 17	Harding and Kerrigan practise together at the Olympics under tight security.
February 25	Kerrigan finishes second, Harding eighth in the Olympics.
March 16	Harding plea-bargains to avoid a prison sentence.
June 30	Harding is stripped of her 1994 national title and banned for life by US Figure Skating Association.

10 'Nobody Roots for Goliath'

Wilt Chamberlain v Bill Russell

T he 1960s match-up between Wilt Chamberlain and Bill Russell is one of the most celebrated rivalries in sport. Only trouble is, even now no one's sure who came out on top.

It's not that they didn't meet often enough for people to judge. They were the greatest NBA players of their era and fought titanic struggles year after year. When it was all done, Russell's Boston Celtics had scooped most of the major titles, but Chamberlain had compiled the most fabulous array of individual records in basketball history. A common view holds that Chamberlain was the greater individual player, and that fellow centre Russell knew how to win championships. But that doesn't do justice to Russell's skills, particularly on defence, and is mean-spirited towards Chamberlain.

Chamberlain played in good teams – the Philadelphia Warriors, the San Francisco Warriors, the Philadelphia 76ers and, especially, the Los Angeles Lakers of the late 1960s and early 1970s. But he wasn't always surrounded by the depth of talent of Russell's great Celtics teams. Chamberlain supporters claim he'd have won more NBA crowns if he'd not had to carry his teams.

Russell was always a winner. Before he turned pro, he guided his college team to two national titles and led the United States to the 1956 Olympic gold medal. He had that rare ability to turn teams of champions into champion teams.

The late 1950s–early 1960s was a fabulous era for the Celtics, with Bob Cousy, Bill Sharman, John Havlicek, KC Jones and Sam Jones on board. But only Russell was there for all 11 Celtics NBA titles between 1957 and 1969. He was the glue that held it together, bringing out the best in his team-mates in a way that not every great player can. Russell was the supreme team player who blocked shots to team-mates or fired precision outlet passes. He was perfect for the fast-break basketball the Celtics made their trademark. 'I played because I enjoyed it,' he once explained, 'but there's more to it than that. I was part of a team, and dedicated myself to making that team the best.' Yet despite possessing a nifty left-handed hook, Russell never made the top dozen in points-scoring. 'Shooting,' he said, 'is of relatively little importance in a player's overall game.'

Who was greater – Chamberlain or Russell? The debate has smouldered since the early 1970s, when these two towering figures finally bowed out of the NBA. What is unarguable is that Chamberlain and Russell, through their individual brilliance and their rivalry, captured the imagination of the American public and lit up the NBA. There had been previous outstanding figures, notably George Mikan, but Chamberlain and Russell took the NBA to the masses and made it appealing to television, creating the massive pay packets today's stars enjoy.

Chamberlain, with his ever-present headband and wristbands, was a giant, in both physique and personality – he was 7ft 1in and nearly 300lb. He was called Wilt the Stilt, but preferred his other sobriquet, The Big Dipper. He was so imposing and talented that any opponent became the underdog. As Chamberlain said: 'Nobody roots for Goliath.' Was there ever a big man with such ability and athleticism? Russell wasn't exactly Lilliputian either, but was four inches shorter and 50 pounds lighter. In their match-ups, Chamberlain was often viewed as the villain of the piece. When he retired in 1973, Chamberlain held many major NBA records, but basketball aficionados recalled him more for his epic battles against Russell and the Celtics.

Every year these two great centres would test each other physically and mentally. They'd post up under the boards, leaning on each other, nudging, shoving, trying to gain an edge. Then they'd bound to the other end of the court and do it all again.

Statistically, Chamberlain held the edge. He averaged 25.7 points and 28 rebounds in games against Russell while the Celtics centre averaged 14.9 points and 24.7 rebounds. Chamberlain set the records for rebounds in a game, with 55 against Russell on 24 November 1960, and for rebounds in a play-off match with 41, again against Russell, on 5 April 1967. But he'd have traded most of his records for a few of Russell's NBA crowns.

The rivalry began on 7 November 1959, at Boston Garden. Chamberlain outscored Russell 30-22, Russell out-rebounded Chamberlain 35-28, and the Celtics beat the Philadelphia Warriors 115-106. That first meeting about sums up the story of their battles.

A year later, when Chamberlain established the mark for the most rebounds in a game, Philadelphia still lost to the Celtics 132-129. Russell scored 18 points, and made 19 rebounds and 5 assists. Chamberlain's totals were 34 points, 55 rebounds and 4 assists. Chamberlain dominated the statistics, but victory went to Russell.

And yet, and yet … Chamberlain's statistics are so compelling they can't be dismissed with a shrug and an off-hand comment about 'winning's all that matters'. Between 1961 and 1963, Chamberlain scored 50 or more points against Boston six times, and one of those was a 62-point outing. Outspoken, showy and brash, Chamberlain was The Man years before Michael Jordan had been heard of.

Russell was born in 1934, in Monroe, Louisiana. His family moved to Oakland during World War II, and that's when Russell began playing basketball, although he didn't become a starter at McClymond's High School until he was a senior. After graduating in 1952, he trialled for the University of San Francisco Dons. Coach Phil Woolpert was reasonably impressed and gave him a scholarship.

Russell led the Dons to 55 consecutive victories and back-to-back national championships. In 1955, he was named the Most Outstanding Player of the Final Four after grabbing 25 rebounds to spearhead San Francisco's 77-63 victory over La Salle in the final. In 1956, his second straight All-American season, Russell scored 26 points in the Dons' 83-71 title victory over Iowa. This game revealed a pattern that was to be repeated through his career – when the situation demanded, he could step up and score. He excelled in the clutch.

To acquire Russell in 1956, famous Celtics coach Red Auerbach traded two solid players, Ed Macauley and Cliff Hagan, to the St Louis Hawks for the second pick in the draft, then held his breath while the Rochester Royals, picking first, passed on Russell, opting for Sihugo Green, a guard out of Duquesne. (In 1984 Michael Jordan was only the third pick in the draft, behind Akeem Olajuwon and Sam Bowie.) Boston had to wait for Russell until December. After he'd led the United States to a gold medal at the Melbourne Olympics, he signed a one-year, $19,500 contract.

The prototypical defensive centre, Russell established his rebounding credentials right away, averaging 19.6 per game, and helped the Celtics win its first NBA title after a classic Finals series against the Hawks that went into a second overtime period in the seventh game. The Celtics lost to the Hawks in the finals the following year, then won eight NBA crowns in succession. If Russell, the 1957–58 MVP, had not sprained his ankle in the third game of the 1958 Finals, the Celtics might have made it 10 in a row.

In terms of individual statistics, Russell was outstanding; it's just that

Chamberlain was even better. For instance, Russell set an NBA record with 51 rebounds against the Syracuse Nationals on 5 February 1960. Nine months later, Chamberlain bettered it. Russell could have concentrated on putting up more imposing personal statistics, but the team came first. Early in his career with the Celtics, Auerbach promised him that during salary negotiations, individual statistics would never be mentioned. What counted was whether the team won.

The 1961–62 season began in a contentious manner when some Celtics black players were denied admission to an Indiana bar and a Kentucky coffee shop during an early-season exhibition tour. So Russell, KC Jones, Sam Jones and Satch Sanders – all African-Americans – boycotted a game in Lexington. Russell never seemed overly eager to be a role model for African-Americans, but often spoke about racial issues, and complained that in the United States of the 1960s all the emphasis was on being white.

In 1966, Auerbach stunned America by announcing he was handing the team to Russell, who would become player-coach. Russell thus became the first African-American head coach in any major American sport in the post-Depression era. People were keen to laud him as a pioneer for blacks, but he wanted to be praised only as a great basketballer.

Russell never appealed as a fun guy. He seemed complex, prickly, introspective, enigmatic and aloof. He refused to sign autographs, saying: 'You owe the public the same thing it owes you – nothing.' Inducted to the Hall of Fame in 1975, he did not attend the ceremony. There were suggestions he was troubled that no African-American player had been elected previously. He had also shunned the ceremony to retire his No 6 shirt at Boston Garden in 1972.

Russell took two coaching jobs after retiring as player-coach in 1969. He led the Seattle SuperSonics to their first play-off berth, leaving in 1977 with a four-year win-loss record of 162-166. For the next decade his main link with basketball was as a TV commentator. Then he resurfaced as coach of the Sacramento Kings. A disastrous 17-41 record led to his move from the bench to the front office, and he was fired in late 1990. He has continued to make good money, however, endorsing products in commercials.

The taciturn Russell has mellowed since the early days, as do so many sportsmen once they've retired – just think of John McEnroe and George Foreman. These days he seems pleased at how many people recall him as a basketball legend. He is more willing to take part in various basketball ceremonies and has shown a pleasant side of his personality. In May 1999, when Russell's No 6 shirt was re-retired during a public ceremony in Boston (to raise money for the National Mentoring Partnership, dedicated to having adults help youngsters), Chamberlain turned up to salute his close friend. Those fierce NBA battles were just a memory and they seemed to revel in each other's company.

Chamberlain, born in Philadelphia, started his career in high school, leading Overbrook High School of Philadelphia to three city championships. After being one of the most recruited high school players ever (more than 100 colleges sought his signature), Chamberlain, already 7ft tall, chose the University of Kansas.

In 1955, Chamberlain scored 42 points and grabbed 29 rebounds to lead the Kansas freshmen past the KU Varsity 81-71. It was the first time in a series begun in 1923 that the freshmen had won. (Lew Alcindor, better known as Kareem Abdul-Jabbar, did the same thing at UCLA in 1965.) Chamberlain had two successful seasons at Kansas, but was frustrated in the 1958 NCAA final when Kansas lost in triple overtime to the University of North Carolina. He was the best player on the court, but his team didn't win. The pattern was to haunt him throughout his career.

Chamberlain decided to wait out for a year until he was eligible to turn pro. By the time he was 21, he had been featured in four national magazines – *Life*, *Time*, *Look* and *Newsweek*. He spent 1958 with the Harlem Globetrotters, then signed for the Philadelphia Warriors.

It was amazing how quickly Russell and Chamberlain, pro fledglings, dominated the NBA. Fans quickly warmed to their unprecedented rivalry. Here's how they matched up during their years in the NBA:

1959–60

Chamberlain joined the Philadelphia Warriors on a salary of $65,000, twice as much as Bob Cousy was getting as the highest-paid Celtic. The Warriors didn't boast the stars the Celtics were fielding, but still had Paul Arizin, Tom Gola and Joe Graboski of their 1956 championship team. Chamberlain played 48 minutes of nearly every game and averaged 37.6 points a game, astounding for a rookie. On the season's points-scoring list, he was well clear of second-placed Jack Twyman of Cincinnati. He scored 50 or more points seven times and took Rookie of the Year and MVP honours in the same season. He also out-rebounded everybody, averaging 27 a game. Russell was second in rebounds, with 24 per game.

Despite Chamberlain's brilliance, Boston was the best team. It won 59 games, 10 more than the Warriors in the Eastern Division. In the semis, Boston eliminated Philadelphia in six games. Strike one to Russell. In the Finals, the Celtics beat the Hawks 122-103 in the seventh game, in which Russell grabbed 35 rebounds and scored 22 points.

1960–61

The same story. Chamberlain raised the scoring average record to 38.4. He was the only leading shooter with a field goal percentage in excess of .500. Again he led the rebound figures from Russell, 27.2 to 23.9.

Despite Chamberlain's heroics, Russell again guided Boston to the NBA championship. His defensive play revolutionised the game. Previously, big men had been more like shot-swatters, batting the ball out of bounds or into the open court. But Russell turned shot-blocking into an art. His ability to block shots and set off a fast-break offence helped make the Celtics a terrific team. This was emphasised by their spread of leading points-scorers – Tom Heinsohn, Cousy, Russell, Sharman, Frank Ramsey and Sam Jones all averaged 15 or more points a game. The Celtics won 11 more games than the second-placed Warriors in the regular season, beat Syracuse in six games in the Eastern Division Finals and St Louis 4-1 in the Finals.

1961–62

Chamberlain's individual statistics during this season will never be beaten. The great night (maybe the greatest) in pro basketball came on 2 March 1962, when he scored 100 points against the New York Knicks at Hershey, Pennsylvania (famous for Hershey candy bars), 31 in the madcap final quarter, despite the Knicks trying everything to deprive him of possession. Many teams don't score 100 points in a game, yet Chamberlain did it by himself.

Of all Chamberlain's amazing statistics that night, perhaps his effort in sinking 28 of his 32 free throws was the most incredible. Chamberlain was generally below average from the free-throw line. He was given all sorts of advice, and even threw underhand for a while, but never came to terms with this facet of the game – but against the Knicks, he was on fire even from the free-throw line.

Besides Chamberlain's 100-pointer, he had totals of 78, 73, 67, 67 and 65 and averaged a staggering 50.4 points a game for the season. Yet despite also leading the rebound stats, in the end there was frustration.

Boston again won the championship. It dominated the regular season, and in the Eastern Division finals edged out Philadelphia 4-3, winning the seventh game 109-107, courtesy of a Sam Jones basket with two seconds remaining. In the Finals, it was pushed even closer, beating the Lakers 110-107 in overtime in the seventh game. Again the Celtics showed the quality of champions – winning the close ones.

There were some great points-scorers in the NBA that season, including Walt Bellamy, Oscar Robertson, Bob Pettit and Jerry West, but everyone paled in comparison to the astounding Chamberlain. He scored 4029 points; Bellamy was next best with 2495. While Chamberlain was named as centre in the All-NBA First Team, the players themselves voted for Russell as MVP.

1962–63

The Warriors moved from Philadelphia to San Francisco, finishing fourth in the Western Division. Boston dominated the Eastern Division regular season, winning 10 more games than second-placed Syracuse, but was pushed hard in the Eastern Division finals, finally beating Oscar Robertson's Cincinnati 4-3. (The Cincinnati Royals had been placed in the Eastern Division after the Warriors' departure.)

In the Finals, Boston beat Los Angeles 4-2 and Russell was more effective than ever. He was chosen MVP by his peers for the third straight year and displaced Chamberlain on the media-chosen All-NBA First Team. Chamberlain averaged 44.8 points a game to easily lead the scoring from Elgin Baylor (34.0). He also led the rebounds, with 24.3 a game, shading Russell (23.0).

1963–64

One of the most interesting seasons in their rivalry. Warriors coach Alex Hannum asked Chamberlain to concentrate more on defence, which he did to great effect, lifting an underrated Warriors side all the way to the NBA Finals. Chamberlain still led the scoring, but at a reduced average of 36.9, and dipped to second on the rebounds table, behind Russell.

The Celtics faced a difficult year, having lost Cousy and with Cincinnati looking especially strong. In the regular season Boston edged Cincinnati 59 wins to 55, then outplayed it in the Division Finals, winning in five games. Chamberlain's Warriors did well to reach the NBA Finals, but could not contain the slick Boston side and lost in five games.

1964–65

Chamberlain was traded to the Philadelphia 76ers (the transplanted Syracuse Nats) for $150,000 plus three players, Connie Dierking, Lee Shaffer and Paul Neumann. The 76ers played out a sensational Eastern Division final against Boston. The home teams won the first six matches. The seventh, in Boston, looked to be going Boston's way when it led 110-103 with two minutes remaining. But Chamberlain struck with six points, giving him 30 for the game, and it was 110-109 with five seconds to play. Russell's inbound pass hit a guywire supporting the basket and suddenly Philadelphia had the ball. A basket now would end the Celtics' long reign. Then Havlicek stole the ball – he stepped in front of Chet Walker to pick off Hal Greer's inbound pass. Boston had saved the game. It went on to win the anti-climactic NBA Finals 4-1 over Los Angeles.

As usual, Chamberlain led the scoring with an average of 34.7. But Russell shaded him on the rebounds (24.1 to 22.9).

1965–66
Chamberlain's Philadelphia really took it to the Celtics this season. For the first time in 10 years, Boston did not finish the regular season top of the Eastern Division. Philadelphia won 55 games to Boston's 54. But Boston ruled in the play-offs, beating Cincinnati 3-2 and Philadelphia 4-1. It then edged out Los Angeles 95-93 in the seventh game of the NBA Finals.

Chamberlain led the scoring and rebounds. Russell was second in rebounding. Chamberlain had now won the scoring title for seven straight years and was the NBA's all-time scoring leader. He had been chosen MVP by his fellow players for the second time, but still his team couldn't beat Russell's Celtics.

1966–67
As the saying goes, 'All good things come to them that waits.' Chamberlain finally won a Championship ring, as part of a talent-packed Philadelphia 76ers unit that also included Wally Jones, Bill Melchionni, Hal Greer, Lou Costello, Luke Jackson, Chet Walker and Billy Cunningham. Making the victory even sweeter was the fact that Russell was now not only the Celtics' major on-court presence, but also the coach. Philadelphia was far too good. It won eight more games than Boston in the Eastern Division and breezed past Cincinnati 3-1 and Boston 4-1 in the play-offs. In the NBA Finals, Philadelphia beat San Francisco 4-2. The Celtics' glorious run was finally over.

A new Chamberlain revealed himself this season. He scored 1956 points, at just (!) 24.1 points per game, third among points-scorers. But he was third in the assists table and led the rebounds. He was also a clear leader in the field goal percentage (.683 against the next best .521). He seemed intent on making every second on court count for more. His work on defence was outstanding.

At last Chamberlain was the king. This was the first year in his rivalry with Russell that he could claim to have clearly come out on top.

1967–68
Chamberlain's superiority didn't last long. True, the 76ers ruled the regular

season, winning eight more times than second-placed Boston. In the play-offs, the 76ers dispatched the Knicks and led Boston 3-1 in the best of seven series. At this point Russell really proved himself. He lifted his own game and energised his team. The Celtics won three straight games to charge into the NBA Finals, then beat the Lakers 4-2.

Chamberlain was again impressive – third in points-scoring, top in assists and rebounds. Russell's on-court productivity slipped (career-low 18.6 rebounding average and 12.5 points), but he won the big one again.

1968–69

The final season of direct Russell-Chamberlain head-to-head rivalry. It seemed primed for a Chamberlain triumph but, as usual, Russell found a way to thwart him.

Chamberlain transferred to the Los Angeles Lakers, whose ranks included West and Baylor. It was tipped to be an unbeatable combination. On the other coast Russell, now 35, was trying to hang on for one more season. This was an ageing Celtics team, for Sam Jones was 36, Bailey Howell 32 and Satch Sanders 30. The omens didn't look good. In the regular season, Boston could manage just fourth in the Eastern Division, far behind Baltimore, Philadelphia and New York. Los Angeles, by contrast, was seven victories better than any other team in the Western Division.

In the play-offs, Boston upset the form book, beating Philadelphia 4-1 and winning a tight contest over the New York Knicks 4-2. But Los Angeles was untroubled in advancing past San Francisco and Atlanta and was favoured to win the NBA Finals.

The Lakers won the first two games at home, but the Celtics took the next two, the fourth right on the buzzer, 89-88. The Lakers won the fifth but lost the sixth when Russell outplayed an injured Chamberlain. The seventh game was in Los Angeles, where the Celtics stormed to the front and hung on to win 108-106. It was Russell's 11th NBA title and his last hurrah. He retired two months later.

That seventh game caused a rift in what had been a strong friendship. Chamberlain and Russell had been good enough friends for Chamberlain to host Russell to dinner at his house in Philadelphia on occasion. With five minutes left and the Celtics leading by 13 points, Chamberlain took himself out of the game with a bruised shin. A few minutes later, the game closed right up and Chamberlain wanted to return, but Lakers coach Bill van Breda Kolff wouldn't send him back out. Many observers felt the Lakers might have won if Chamberlain had stayed on court.

Russell was annoyed at Chamberlain leaving the game. After his retirement, he said that if Chamberlain had to leave the court, it should only have been because he had to be taken straight to hospital – you couldn't quit and win championships. The news services relayed Russell's comments to Chamberlain, who sniped back. Their friendship was severely dented and it took years to be repaired.

Chamberlain carried on for another four seasons. There was more frustration in 1970 when the Lakers lost 4-3 to the New York Knicks in the NBA Finals. In 1971 the Lakers bowed out 4-1 to Milwaukee in the Western Conference Finals. In 1972, Chamberlain finally got his hands on a second Championship ring when the Lakers beat the New York Knicks 4-1 in the Finals. Chamberlain was no longer chief points-scorer, but he led the league in rebounding for the tenth time and proved an intimidating and ever-present force on defence. The following season the Lakers lost the NBA Finals to New York 4-1. Chamberlain, now 37, left to coach the San Diego Conquistadors in the ABA. Chamberlain departed with mind-boggling statistics – more than 31,000 points and 23,000 rebounds. He owned 49 of the top 57 single-game scoring performances and set records that Abdul-Jabbar and Michael Jordan were to target in the years ahead.

Chamberlain was such a force that the NBA changed some of its rules, including widening the lane to try to keep him and his famous finger-roll further away from the goal. He also prompted the sport to institute offensive goaltending and revise rules governing inbounding the ball and shooting free throws. Chamberlain was also a revolutionary player in that he popularised the dunk shot. But he never won enough. Red Auerbach said in his autobiography, *On and Off the Court*: 'He was much more interested in his own contributions than in the welfare of his team. That's why Russell was better. Russell played with his head. He was better motivated. And, most of all, he had the bigger heart.'

Basketball might have been the sport that brought him fame, but Chamberlain was also a fine all-round athlete, starring at college in events as diverse as cross-country, shot put and high jump. He turned down offers to box (a fight against Muhammad Ali was mooted) and to play football professionally. After his retirement from the NBA, he starred in the short-lived International Volleyball Association. Not long before his death from heart failure in 1999, he ran a marathon in Hawaii, and competed in a 50-mile race in Canada.

Outside sport, Chamberlain remained busy. He honed his investment abilities, wrote books – his first was called *Wilt: Just Like Any Other 7-Foot Black*

Millionaire Who Lives Next Door – and did some acting. In the 1984 movie *Conan the Destroyer*, he received third billing behind Arnold Schwarzenegger and Grace Jones.

In 1991, Chamberlain stirred controversy by claiming in his biography that he'd had sex with 20,000 women, which, statisticians told us, was an average of 1.2 women a day from the age of 15. He later regretted making the claim. (When Magic Johnson revealed shortly after the book was published that he had contracted the AIDS virus, he commented, 'I'm no Wilt Chamberlain, but I was never at a loss for female companionship.')

Russell and Chamberlain had felt their individual rivalry keenly – how could they not when it was a major focus of the American sports media for a decade? In 1965, Chamberlain signed a contract with the San Francisco Warriors for $100,000. Russell promptly had his Celtics contract renegotiated for $100,001.

Despite the rivalry, there was genuine respect. When Chamberlain died, Russell said: 'I feel unspeakably injured. I've lost a dear and exceptional friend in Wilton Norman Chamberlain and an important part of my life. Our relationship was intensely personal.

'Many have called our competition the greatest rivalry in the history of sports. I agree with that. If either of our coaches had told one of us he couldn't guard the other guy, he would have lost that player forever. But we didn't just have a rivalry; we had a genuinely fierce competition that was based on friendship and respect. We loved playing against each other. The fierceness of the competition bonded us for eternity.

'Wilt was the greatest offensive player I have ever seen. Because his talent and skills were so superhuman, he forced me to play at my highest level. If I didn't, I'd risk embarrassment and our team would likely lose.'

Russell tried to describe what it had been like to play against such an awesome offensive force: 'After I played him for the first time, I said, "Let's see. He's four or five inches taller. He's 40 or 50 pounds heavier. His vertical leap is at least as good as mine. He can get up and down the floor as well as I can. And he's smart. The real problem with all this is I have to show up!"

'He sent me through hell so many nights. As we got older, we liked each other more because we knew, basically, we were joined at the hips. We were important to each other. I knew how good he was and he knew that I knew how good he was. As far as I'm concerned, he and I will be friends through eternity.'

Chamberlain had been equally praising of Russell in their post-retirement years. He said one time: 'We were forced to play against the Celtics 11 to 13 times during the regular season. And if you think that wasn't enough, then we had another seven games against them in the play-offs, if it went seven games. So I had a chance to see William Felton Russell much more than I wanted to.' Another time, he said: 'The man is greedy. He has 11 [Championship] rings and 10 fingers.' Where winning was concerned, enough was never enough for Russell.

	Wilton Norman Chamberlain	William Fenton Russell
Born	21 August 1936, Philadelphia, Pennsylvania Died: 12 October 1999, Los Angeles, California	12 February 1934, Monroe, Louisiana
NBA career	1959–73	1956–69
NBA titles	1967 (Philadelphia 76ers), 1972 (Los Angeles Lakers)	1957, 1959, 1960, 1961, 1962, 1963, 1964, 1965, 1966, 1968, 1969 (Boston Celtics)

HEAD TO HEAD

Russell's teams beat Chamberlain's 91 times and lost 60 times.

They clashed in 48 play-off and Finals games, with Russell holding a 29-19 edge.

Russell's teams beat Chamberlain's twice in NBA Finals – in 1964 when Boston downed San Francisco 4-1, and in 1969 when the Celtics beat the Lakers 4-3.

They opposed each other in four All-Star games. Russell's team won all four.

When they were playing simultaneously, Russell won nine NBA championships to Chamberlain's one.

While Russell and Chamberlain were both playing, the Celtics had a 32-19 edge over the Philadelphia Warriors and 21-6 superiority over the San Francisco Warriors, tied with the Philadelphia 76ers 28-28, and trailed the Los Angeles Lakers 7-6.

Records and honours

Wilton Chamberlain:

During the 1961–62 season, played 3882 minutes, averaging 48.5 minutes a game (including overtime).

31,419 points (fourth behind Kareem Abdul-Jabbar, Karl Malone and Michael Jordan).

Career scoring average 30.07 (second behind Jordan's 30.12).

Holds highest scoring average for a single season, 50.4.

Led the NBA in scoring seven straight seasons, 1960–66.

Scored 4029 points in 1961–62, the record for a season.

Scored 50 or more points in a game 45 times in 1961–62 (the record).

Scored 50 or more points in 118 games through his career (the record).

Scored 100 points in the Philadelphia Warriors' 169-147 defeat of the New York Knicks in March 1962, 26 points more than the next highest total in an NBA game.

The only player to attempt at least 15 shots in a game and make them all. He did it three times within a two-month period in 1967 – going 18-for-18, 16-for-16 and 15-for-15.

23,924 rebounds (the record). Career rebound average 22.9 (the record).

Most rebounds in a season, 2149. Most rebounds in a game, 55.

Led the league in rebounding in 11 seasons (the record).

Has the highest rebounding average for a single season, 27.

Led the league in assists in 1967–68, with 602, the only centre to do so.

MVP honours in 1960, 1966, 1967 and 1968.

Elected into NBA Hall of Fame in 1978.

Played in 13 All-Star games.

William Russell:

Two NCAA titles (University of San Francisco): 1955, 1956.

1125 NBA games. 14,522 points. Points average 15.1.

21,721 rebounds (second to Chamberlain). Rebound average 22.5 (second to Chamberlain). Four times the league's leading rebounder.

MVP honours in 1957, 1961, 1962, 1963, 1965.

Elected into NBA Hall of Fame in 1974.

Played in every All-Star Game after his rookie year (12).

Named Athlete of the Decade by *The Sporting News* in 1970.

Named in the NBA's 25th and 35th anniversary all-time teams.

In 1980 named the NBA's Greatest Player in a poll of basketball writers.

11 Rise and Fall

Jack Nicklaus v Arnold Palmer

Have a look at any of the golf celebration books that are so regularly churned out and chances are that there'll be photos of Jack Nicklaus and Arnold Palmer on the cover. Tiger Woods might be there as well, to give the book a more modern look.

While there have been a dozen truly legendary golfers, it's hard to go past Nicklaus and Palmer as the Big Two in the pre-Woods era. Nicklaus earns such celebrated status because he was the greatest player ever. Not only did he win a record 18 Majors (the next most successful man is Walter Hagen with 11), but he was runner-up in a further 19.

For nearly 30 years, Nicklaus was a major factor on the pro golf tour. His longevity was remarkable. He was second in the 1960 US Open when he was 20, and in 1998, at 58, finished equal sixth in the US Masters. His status as a golf icon is unchallenged.

Palmer may have been an even more significant figure. He, too, belongs near the top of any golf honours board, with seven victories in Majors and a period in the late 1950s and early 1960s when he bestrode the game. Palmer was the first player to win $1 million in prizemoney on the PGA Tour, and these days the Arnold Palmer Award honours the year's leading money-winner on the tour. However, his record in Majors – he was a runner-up on 10 occasions, and never did win the US PGA title – does not reflect his ability or influence.

Palmer was important for other reasons. He was such a popular figure that he revolutionised world golf. He made the game appealing to people who were not golf fanatics. When we look at the vast amounts of money on offer worldwide for golfers these days, we should think of Palmer. It was his appeal to sponsors and advertisers that led directly to the golf boom.

Both Nicklaus and Palmer have remained close to golf, continuing to play the Majors into theirs 60s and 70s. They have become golf course designers of world renown. They have featured prominently on the Seniors tour. They have lent their names and energy to running PGA Tour events. They are so famous and respected that they have become Jack and Arnie. Last names are not necessary.

It was a fortunate quirk of timing that they arrived as champion golfers just as television was taking off. The same thing happened in boxing, where Muhammad Ali and television were made for each other. Palmer was the fans' favourite, the chain-smoking golfer built like a footballer. He had daring and charisma and, for a champion golfer, a rather agricultural swing. Nicklaus was chubby but more talented, the young kid intent on knocking the champ off his pedestal. The rivalry was always respectful, but Nicklaus would have liked Palmer's popularity, just as Palmer would surely have liked Nicklaus's matchless skill. Their match-up brought golf to the masses.

In most rivalries there has to be a villain, and in the early days that was Nicklaus. His 'crime' was to challenge the superiority of the People's Champion. Palmer made no effort to mask his emotions on the course, so the ordinary punters could identify with him. They loved seeing him hack the ball out of the long grass, and grimace or leap for joy after an important putt. He made golf look like fun. And he was amazingly personable. He would walk along the rope barrier line after teeing off and talk to the spectators, even shaking their hands. Nicklaus was seen as more clinical and obviously ambitious, a usurper.

In the one-dimensional manner in which these things are sometimes viewed, Palmer was the working class hero, Nicklaus the privileged youngster. After Arnold and his girlfriend Winnie Walzer eloped, they lived in a trailer. When Nicklaus and his fiancée Barbara Bash married, his parents gave them the deposit on a house. (Both proved to be long-term marriages. The Palmers had two children: Peggy and Amy. The Nicklauses had five: Jack – who became a good golfer – Steven, Nancy Jean, Gary and Michael.)

It must have been terribly difficult for the emerging Nicklaus to be so unpopular with Arnold's fans. How must he have felt to see someone standing in the rough holding a banner that read, 'Hit it here, Ohio fats'? People spat and cursed as he walked down the fairway. 'I'd be less than candid if I didn't say that there have been moments when I wished I'd come up when golf had a less glamorous idol,' he once said. Through the 1960s, Nicklaus changed his image, growing his hair longer, losing weight and wearing more stylish clothes. How much of this was a response to the public jibes he continually had to endure?

While the rivalry was hotly contested on the world's great golf courses and spilt over into other areas, it should be stated immediately that this was a gentlemen's rivalry. Just as golf is a game for gentlemen, not tantrum-throwers, so Nicklaus and Palmer fought each other tooth and nail, but always in the best possible spirit. Trawl the newspaper files and the Internet and you won't find examples of them trash-talking each other. It has never been their way. Both are immensely proud of their achievements and their place in the pantheon of golf, but they accept that even at their elevated level there is room for both of them.

Palmer is the older by 10 years, so the sharp peak of their rivalry existed for just a few years. Palmer was the world's best player while Nicklaus was still an amateur. A decade later, when Nicklaus was still the world No 1, Palmer had stopped winning big tournaments. For a while there though, the on-course rivalry burned fiercely. Sure, there were other great golfers about – Peter Thomson, Gary Player, Billy Casper and, a little later, Lee Trevino and Tom Watson. But the media and public focus was inevitably on Nicklaus and Palmer. They were the best of the best. They had stature and colour. Theirs was the greatest personal competition in golf.

Palmer was born in 1929. His father, Deacon, was a golf pro and Arnold, who'd done a stint in the US Coast Guard as a teenager, turned pro in 1954, shortly after winning the US Amateur championship. It was in 1954 that Palmer and Nicklaus's paths first crossed. 'I saw Arnold for the first time when I was 14 years old,' Nicklaus recalled. 'I was entered in the Ohio State Amateur championship at the Sylvania Country Club in Toledo. It was late one afternoon and the only other person on the course was a fellow hitting nine irons in the rain. And he was drilling them. I was impressed. I remember asking myself, "Who is this guy? Boy, is he strong." I learned it was Arnold Palmer, the defending champion. He won the tournament again that year and the rest is history.'

After a year on the pro tour, Palmer won the 1955 Canadian Open, the first of 61 PGA tour events he was to win over the next two decades. In 1958, he began to put some distance between himself and other leading players, and confirmed his superiority by winning the US Masters for the first time, by one stroke. The Palmer reputation was established. He would never shirk a challenge and opponents began to fear his final-round charge, just as the increasingly large galleries, which came to be known as Arnie's Army, thrilled at his shot-making and daring.

Palmer's great year was 1960, when he won eight times, including the US Masters and US Open. At the Masters, Ken Venturi was sitting in Butler Cabin with a one-stroke lead. But Palmer, with those muscular drives and pigeon-toed putts, tied him by rolling in a 27-footer on 17. Another birdie on 18 gave him a stunning victory. It was the sort of finish that led the legendary Bobby Jones to say: 'If I ever had to have one putt to win a title for me, I'd rather have Arnold Palmer hit it than anybody I ever saw.'

At Cherry Hills, where the 1960 US Open was played, Palmer scored a memorable victory after an amazing final day when he began the last round six strokes off the pace. He burnt up the course, going out in 30 to catch the leaders, and then parred his way home to win by a couple of strokes while his challengers, including a young amateur named Jack Nicklaus and an ageing genius named Ben Hogan, faltered.

Such was Palmer's confidence and ability to rise to the occasion that there was speculation he could win the mythical Grand Slam of the Majors that year. He went to St Andrews for the British Open and chased the leader, Australian Kel Nagle, for the entire final day, eventually failing by one stroke after beginning the day four behind.

There were to be other fantastic moments in Palmer's career. He recovered from a four-stroke deficit to win the US Masters in 1962, and he won the British Open in 1962 and the US Masters in 1964 in spectacular fashion, leaving fine players trailing far behind. But unlike Nicklaus and, a generation later, Woods, Palmer never seemed invincible. In Majors he had moments of utter disaster that served only to increase public affection for him. In 1961, needing a par four at the last to win the Masters, he carded a six. In 1966, he led the US Open by seven shots with nine holes to play, but blew it and lost in a play-off to Billy Casper.

Palmer always seemed to play with vitality. Crowds loved his high-risk, attacking style. When he was around, things happened. Either he was hunched over a long putt in that unique style of his, or he was preparing to smash a ball out of impossibly thick rough. 'In Arnold's early years,' said Nicklaus, 'he was not a good driver. He had to hit it out of the trees and the woods, and he kept making the shots. People loved it because he won doing that.'

Palmer was a pivotal figure in other ways. It was when he decided to tackle the British Open that US players really began to cross the Atlantic regularly. Previously, few Americans had bothered with the British Open, and those who did played the tournament only sporadically. Palmer changed that. He finished 2, 1, 1 at the Open in 1960–62 and brought renewed prestige and glamour to the tournament. Once the world's best player took the Open seriously, others could not ignore it.

Palmer was a leader in the business world as well. In 1959 he linked with young lawyer Mark McCormack's fledgling International Management Group. IMG became Palmer's agent, marketing and negotiating on his behalf after a handshake agreement between the principals. They made each other many millions of dollars and soon other leading golfers, then stars from other sports, and finally celebrities from all walks of life, followed Palmer to IMG and to other marketing companies. The Palmer-IMG relationship was so successful that even into his 70s, Palmer remained one of world sport's biggest earners. He enjoys an annual income of about US$20 million, generated mainly through sponsorship, endorsements and course design.

His golf career enjoyed a renaissance in 1980, when he won the PGA Seniors Championship on the increasingly popular over-50s circuit. A year later, he became the first former US Open champion to win the US Senior Open. And Arnie's Army remained as big and loyal as ever.

Arnie's Army was heard from again in January 1997, when it was disclosed Palmer was suffering from prostate cancer. On the mend from surgery early in the year, Palmer said: 'I've got so much mail from people that it's unbelievable.' He played in the US Masters just three months later.

Palmer's ability and personality transformed golf in the 1950s and 1960s from a sport once enjoyed by a generally privileged minority in only a few countries to a game played by all classes all over the globe. While in terms of golf, 1960 was Palmer's peak, it was also important for another reason: it signalled the beginning of his rivalry with Nicklaus.

Golf followers had known for some years about Nicklaus. He was born in Columbus, Ohio in 1940, the son of a wealthy pharmacist, and grew up in a prosperous area. By his early 20s, he was already fashioning a formidable amateur reputation. He was the US Amateur champion in 1959 and 1961, and the NCAA champion in the second of those years. He'd also appeared on two winning US Walker Cup teams (for amateur competition between the United States and Britain) and had helped his country to a record 42-stroke winning margin in the 1960 Eisenhower Trophy.

Without the aid of today's pepped-up clubs and balls, which reduce most courses in length almost farcically, Nicklaus was a huge hitter. Over the years, he added subtlety and finesse to his game, and developed an extraordinary ability to 'will' putts into the hole. But in his early years it was his immense power that took the breath away.

It was at the epochal US Open in 1960 that Nicklaus served notice that he meant business. It was a famous day for golf because three leading contenders on the final afternoon were Ben Hogan, Palmer and Nicklaus. One was an iconic figure of a few years earlier, one was the current king and the third was surely destined to be at least as great as either. Palmer won the tournament by shooting a final-round 65.

Hogan was never the most effusive of people. He seldom spoke unless spoken to, and even then would often elect not to bother. He gave praise sparingly. But after that final round at Cherry Hills, he would tell anyone who would listen: 'I tell you, I've just played with a kid who, if he had been a couple of years older, would have won this thing by 10 shots.' Hogan wasn't the only famous golfer to be awed by Nicklaus's ability. Three years later, Bobby Jones said, 'He plays a game with which I am not familiar.'

Palmer might have been top dog in 1960, but he wasn't blind. He'd known that very soon the kid from Ohio was going to figure large in his life. He'd first become aware of Nicklaus in 1956, at an exhibition in Athens, Ohio, to celebrate Dow Finsterwald Day. Nicklaus was 16, Palmer 26. 'We had a driving contest,' Palmer recalled, 'and I beat him by a bit. After that I kept an eye on him and was aware of what he was doing. You never know how someone's game will develop, but with Jack, I figured it was just a matter of time.'

It took Nicklaus little time to make a significant impression in the pro ranks. He didn't turn pro until 1962, but by then he was already one of the world's leading players. In the 1960 US Masters, while all eyes were on Palmer, Nicklaus finished 13th equal. The following year, still an amateur, he improved to seventh equal, six shots behind Palmer. In the 1961 US Open, at Oakland Hills, Birmingham, he was fourth equal on 284, heading Palmer by five strokes.

By 1962, Nicklaus, just 22, was playing Palmer on level terms, which made him a villain in the eyes of Arnie's Army. At a tournament in New York, Nicklaus spotted a banner being held by a spectator standing in the deep rough. It read: 'Put it here fat boy.' Palmer fans would boo and spit when Nicklaus was about to putt, or shout, 'Miss it, Jack!' and cheer when he hit the ball poorly.

The Palmer–Nicklaus rivalry, however, helped the professional game become ever more popular. At the 1962 US Open at Oakmont, their first real one-on-one match-up, more than 72,000 spectators came out to watch. This bettered the attendance record by more than 25,000. Before the tournament, Palmer said, 'Everybody says there's only one favourite, and that's me. But you'd better watch the fat boy.'

Nicklaus and local hero Palmer were paired for the first two rounds. The match had the atmosphere of a heavyweight title fight. Arnie's Army took to stomping on the ground in unison as Nicklaus was trying to putt, holding aloft signs with messages like 'Nicklaus is a pig' and 'Miss it fat-gut'.

Palmer opened with 71-68 to lead at the halfway stage, but managed just 73-71 over the closing two rounds. Nicklaus closed with 72-69 to tie him and won the 18-hole play-off by three strokes, after holding off a typical mid-round Palmer surge. 'I'll tell you something. Now that the big guy is out of the cage, everybody better run for cover,' was Palmer's post-tournament summation.

Palmer was notably gracious towards Nicklaus, even when the younger player began knocking him off his perch. He certainly never gave Nicklaus the cold shoulder when he burst on the scene as the 'next great player', something Ben Hogan had done to Palmer in the 1950s.

At the 1962 PGA, Nicklaus finished third equal, seven strokes ahead of Palmer. But still Palmer shaded him for the year, winning the Masters, with Nicklaus second equal, and the British Open, where Nicklaus was not a factor.

In 1963, Nicklaus outplayed Palmer at the British Open (third against 26th equal), the US Masters (first against ninth equal), and the PGA (first against 40th), while Palmer had the better only of the US Open (third after Nicklaus failed to make the cut). In *A Golfer's Life*, co-written with James Dodson, Palmer recalled that year's Masters tournament:

> As if taking a US Open trophy out from under me and my Army at Oakmont wasn't enough, Jack Nicklaus now had the temerity to stroll on to the hallowed grounds of Augusta National as a Tour sophomore and simply lay waste to the course in a devastating display of shotmaking not seen in that part of Dixie since a fellow named Sherman made his way from Atlanta to Savannah.

Time magazine summed it up like this after the tournament: 'Whatever Arnie wants, Jack gets.' Leading golf pro Doug Sanders spoke for most when he said: 'Baby Beef is doing to Arnie what Palmer did to all of us.'

In 1964, the last year Palmer won a Major, there wasn't much in it. Nicklaus was second in the British Open, with Palmer way off the pace. But Palmer won the US Masters, with Nicklaus second equal. In the US Open, Palmer was fifth equal to Nicklaus' 23rd equal, and they were second equal behind Bobby Nichols in the PGA.

In the 1960s, long before there were computers working out these things, the end-of-year golf rankings were determined by prizemoney. In 1964, as Palmer and Nicklaus traded blows like two boxers, the prizemoney race see-sawed and there was intense interest in who would finish top. Was the king dead? It all came down to a rather minor tournament called the Cajun Classic, held in Louisiana right at the end of the PGA year, when winter had arrived and many leading golfers were beginning their end-of-year sabbaticals. Going into the Cajun Classic, Palmer had earned $111,703 and Nicklaus was a mere $319 behind. The first-place prizemoney for the tournament was a miserly $3300, but it was enough to entice both Palmer and Nicklaus to the Oakbourne Country Club in Lafayette.

The weather was shockingly cold and the first day was washed out by torrential rain, so 36 holes had to be played on the Sunday. Players wore three sweaters, thick gloves, hats … anything to stay warm. In these miserable conditions, no one really wanted to play golf, but Palmer and Nicklaus were on a mission. Palmer finished fourth in the tournament, won by Miller Barber, and earned $1500. Would this be enough to leave him top of the 1964 money list?

It came down to a 16ft putt by Gay Brewer on the final hole. If Brewer made the putt, he finished second and Nicklaus third. That would leave Palmer as the leading money-earner. But if Brewer missed the putt, Nicklaus would move to second equal and the $1900 he would get would lift him top of the money list. Brewer lined up his putt, then jokingly asked Nicklaus what it was worth for him to miss it. Nicklaus, entering into the spirit of things, pulled out a wad of notes. Brewer's putt eventually came up short and Nicklaus finished the year as the top money-winner – by $81. It was just a small amount, but it was symbolic: Nicklaus was now top dog.

Thereafter, Nicklaus moved steadily away from Palmer, though it took the public a long time to accept that the rivalry was over. Palmer finished second equal (with Gary Player) behind Nicklaus at the 1965 Masters, but he was a long way adrift – nine strokes. At the same tournament the following year, Palmer got within two strokes of Nicklaus at one stage, but as Nicklaus added another Major to his list, Palmer could manage just fourth equal. In the 1967 US Open, Palmer played a great last round of 69 to finish with 279. His problem? Nicklaus shot a final-day 65 to win the tournament by four strokes and leave Palmer runner-up again. Arnie's Army always hoped for one last hurrah, but it never came, though Palmer continued winning on the PGA tour until 1973.

Palmer's trouble was that his game was never as sound as Nicklaus's. He didn't have an effortless swing like Sam Snead, and once he lost a little of his athleticism and confidence, the standard of his golf fell away. He could not compensate for technical deficiencies with brute strength. Nicklaus, on the other hand, had a game that was built to last. His swing and putting stroke remained models of consistency until finally a bad hip slowed him down in his 50s.

Nicklaus moved on to fight other battles. He built such a fine record that he left even immortals like Walter Hagen, Gene Sarazen, Snead and Hogan in his wake. He took on the emerging stars, Trevino and Watson, and even into the 1980s, when he should have been past his prime, was still snatching Majors from the likes of Severiano Ballesteros and Greg Norman. He won the US Open and the US PGA in 1980 and the US Masters in 1986, at 46. At the 1998 Masters, his total of 283 put him ahead of Tiger Woods, Colin Montgomerie, Jose-Maria Olazabal, Phil Mickelson, Ernie Els and a clutch of other modern stars who were not even born when he began winning Majors.

Quite apart from his sublimely good golf, Nicklaus was always a magnificent sportsman. There are many examples. He never showed a flicker of anger after losing a riveting last-day duel with Tom Watson at the British Open at Turnberry in 1977, or when Watson stole the US Open from him at Pebble Beach in 1982 in the unlikeliest of circumstances.

And, of course, there was the famous incident at the end of the 1969 Ryder Cup contest at Royal Birkdale when Nicklaus and Tony Jacklin went head-to-head in a stirring contest that would decide the Cup's outcome. When Nicklaus and Jacklin, the last pairing on the course, played the final hole the scores were locked at 15$\frac{1}{2}$-15$\frac{1}{2}$. It all boiled down to Jacklin's final three-foot putt. Jacklin was at his peak, having won the British Open a couple of months previously, and was a golf idol in Britain. A huge crowd of 10,000 swarmed around the 18th green to watch their hero sink the putt that would mean the Ryder Cup was shared. But a three-footer is no gimme in those circumstances, and Nicklaus knew it. He looked around at the sea of expectant faces and made the sudden and bold decision to concede the putt, thereby relieving Jacklin of the pressure. 'I don't think you would have missed it, but I didn't want to give you the chance,' said Nicklaus as he picked up Jacklin's marker.

In the clubhouse, Snead, the US captain, fumed, and refused to speak to Nicklaus all evening. But Nicklaus had exhibited sportsmanship at its finest. Nicklaus and Jacklin embraced and Jacklin later called it the most sporting gesture in the history of golf. In hindsight, Nicklaus's decision, instinctively made in that most torrid of circumstances, has come to be seen as one of the great moments in golf history and speaks volumes for his innate sense of sportsmanship.

Golf followers gradually came to accept Nicklaus and forgive him for knocking their beloved Palmer off his pedestal. He became universally known as the Golden Bear. By the 1980s, Jack was revered, though Arnie remained something special.

In *My Story*, written with the help of Ken Bowden, Nicklaus reflected on why it took him so many years to be forgiven by Arnie's Army:

Although the goals I set for myself probably were acceptable to everyone – maybe, even, to many of Arnie's Army – the fact is I marched toward them along too straight and narrow a path for the majority of observers to want to applaud my passage.

Sure, I was overweight and crew-cut, and sure, I dressed like a guy painting a porch, and sure, I had a squeaky voice and didn't laugh and joke a lot in public … All those failings might have been forgiven in a young and unsophisticated individual if he had simply papered over the raw intensity of his will to win – including, particularly, trying to knock the game's best-loved idol off his throne.

The media loves a golf rivalry, but they come about surprisingly seldom. Norman, Nick Faldo, Nick Price and Woods have each clearly been the world's best player for sizeable periods over the past two decades. Not often do two players jostle at the top. As Nicklaus explained:

The reason Arnie and I became such a rivalry was because Arnie was winning most of the Major championships and then I came along in 1962 and won my first Major by beating Arnie in a play-off at the US Open and then came back and won the Masters. So, all of a sudden, there were two fellows winning Major championships against each other.

The rivalry went way beyond the golf course:

Arnold and I have had a rivalry in everything we've done. We're competitive in golf, in business, in endorsing products. And in most respects it's been a very healthy rivalry. We've both benefited from the competition. But I've said it before and I'll say it again, I don't like to be beat by Arnold and I'm sure he feels the same way about me. There's no one in the world I'd rather beat than Arnold.

Their rivalry was often raised during press conferences. Palmer summed it up once by saying: 'The competition has been there from the very beginning, and in my mind, it will go on for as long as we live. We don't socialise, we don't spend a lot of time together. But Jack and I have a deep-seated respect for one another. And if you stop and reflect upon how long we've been at it, I think we've gotten along pretty well over the years. I consider us friends.'

Since their playing days, Palmer and Nicklaus have reigned over business empires, designed courses and created their own line of products. And, of course, both host PGA Tour tournaments. Nicklaus is the proud chief of the Memorial Tournament, held at the Muirfield Village Golf Club. Palmer's pride and joy is the Bay Hill Invitational. There is strong rivalry to see which tournament can attract the most top ten and top 100 players. And in designing courses throughout the world, stretching their imaginations and using their experience and flair, both, no doubt, keep an eye on what the other is up to.

The important factor, though, is that while the rivalry has been competitive, it has never been bitter. Nicklaus: 'It was and still is a friendly rivalry. I consider

Bill Russell, 21, celebrates the first of his two NCAA titles with the San Francisco Dons.

Below: Wilt Chamberlain spearheaded Overbrook High School to three Philadelphia city championships in the mid-1950s and foretold greatness.

Bill Russell shoots over his arch-rival Wilt Chamberlain during a Celtics-Lakers play-off match in 1969. The Celtics won the series 4-3. FOTOPRESS

Arnold Palmer (rear) helps Jack Nicklaus line up a putt during Ryder Cup duty for the US. FOTOPRESS

Jack Nicklaus (left) and Arnold Palmer, rivals and friends for more than half a century. FOTOPRESS

Noted American sports artist Ron Lewis captures the Muhammad Ali-Joe Frazier rivalry perfectly in this signed, limited edition print. JOSEPH ROMANOS COLLECTION

George Foreman splits Joe Frazier (left) and Muhammad Ali in this happy reunion photograph of the three great heavyweight boxers of the 1970s. PHOTOSPORT

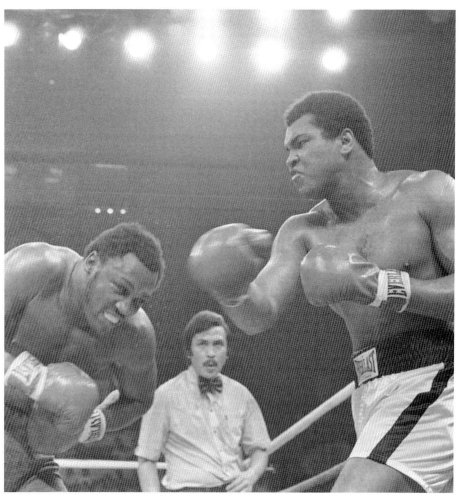

A boxing epic. Muhammad Ali on his way to a memorable 14th round technical knockout win over Joe Frazier in Manila in 1975. TRANZ/CORBIS

Arnold one of my closest friends in the game. We did many things together and our wives were the closest of friends. That doesn't mean that every time we went out there, we didn't want to beat each other's brains in. We're both competitors – always have been and still are – and we enjoy competing against each other on and off the golf course.'

Palmer smiles now when he reflects on the rivalry. Asked about it when he was in his 70s, he said: 'At times we became so hyper about beating each other that we let someone else go right by us and win. But our competition was fun and good for the game.'

	Arnold Daniel Palmer	Jack William Nicklaus
Born	10 September 1929, Latrobe, Pennsylvania	21 January 1940, Columbus, Ohio
Major championships		
US Masters	1958, 1960, 1962, 1964	1963, 1965, 1966, 1972, 1975, 1986
British Open	1961, 1962	1966, 1970, 1978
US Open	1960	1962, 1967, 1972, 1980
US PGA		1963, 1971, 1973, 1975, 1980
Other titles and honours	US Amateur champion: 1954. US Ryder Cup team: 1961, 1963, 1965, 1967, 1971, 1973, 1975. Non-playing captain: 1963, 1975. US Player of the Year: 1960, 1962. Vardon Trophy: 1961, 1962, 1964, 1967. US Tour leading money-winner: 1958, 1960, 1962, 1963. Won 61 US Tour events and 19 outside the US.	US Amateur champion 1959, 1961. US Ryder Cup team: 1969, 1971, 1973, 1975, 1977, 1981. Non-playing captain: 1983, 1987. US Player of the Year: 1967, 1972, 1973, 1975, 1976. US Tour leading money-winner: 1964, 1965, 1967, 1971, 1972, 1973, 1975, 1976. Won 71 US PGA Tour events, and 18 outside the US.

12 Still Smokin' After
All These Years

Muhammad Ali v Joe Frazier

Joe Frazier was the one boxer Muhammad Ali could never tame. Sure, Ali won two of their three famous duels, but Frazier – short, stocky, powerful, proud and courageous – would never concede best to Ali.

The pair had three wonderful heavyweight battles full of urgency and breathtaking audacity. At the end of the third, in Manila in 1975, Ali, the winner after a 14th round stoppage, said he felt 'near death'. Asked about the possibility of Ali–Frazier IV, he shook his head. 'That's it. We don't owe each other nuthin'.'

Ali had arguably the most famous boxing career ever. He fought heavyweight champions Sonny Liston, Floyd Patterson, Frazier, George Foreman, Leon Spinks and Larry Holmes, plus fighters who held portions of the heavyweight title, such as Jimmy Ellis, Ken Norton and Trevor Berbick. There were memorable contests, too, against the likes of Henry Cooper, Oscar Bonavena, Joe Bugner, Earnie Shavers and Jimmy Young. He ducked no one. He loved the spotlight and he loved boxing.

There will always be arguments about the merits of respective fighters. The problem is how to compare boxers of different generations. But the consensus is that Ali, before his enforced three and a half year lay-off, was at least as good as any heavyweight who ever lived. The boxer who twice beat Liston and who humbled Patterson, Cleveland Williams, Ernie Terrell, Zora Folley, Henry Cooper and the rest of them was so quick he may have been too good even for much-touted former champions such as Jack Johnson, Jack Dempsey, Joe Louis and Rocky Marciano. The young Ali had speed of hand, head and foot that defied belief.

After the lay-off, imposed because he refused to be inducted into the US

Army, Ali fought for another decade, which was when he achieved most of his enduring fame. Boxing by then had entered the live video-link era and – partly because of the influence of Ali – the multimillion-dollar pay-packet stage, and world heavyweight title fights stopped the world.

Throughout most of the 1970s, Ali was a terrific boxer. He could take a punch as well as any heavyweight ever, was accurate with his punches, was big, and could dominate an opponent by sheer force of personality. In truth, though, he wasn't the boxer of the 1960s. That said, it was Ali's three fights with Frazier, in 1971, 1974 and 1975, that did the most to cement his reputation. They were brutal contests. Ali had shocked the pundits with his upset victories over Liston in 1964 and Foreman in 1974, he'd performed Houdini-type miracles of endurance and escapism to beat Ken Norton (two out of three times), Young and Shavers, and come back from a comprehensive defeat to win a return bout against Leon Spinks despite carrying 36 years.

Even without Frazier, the Ali dossier was pretty full. But it was the Frazier component that really made him. An international sports star is fortunate if his career clashes with another who brings out the best in him. Thus John McEnroe had Bjorn Borg as a measuring stick, and Bill Russell and Wilt Chamberlain lined up against each other each year chasing NBA honours.

As much as Ali benefited from Frazier, though, the truth of it, unpalatable as it may be, is that Frazier needed Ali more than Ali needed him. If we take away the three Ali fights, Frazier's CV looks a little thin. There were two humbling knockout losses to George Foreman and not many wins over really good fighters in their prime. He knocked out Jimmy Ellis, won two hard-fought decisions over Oscar Bonavena and beat Joe Bugner on points, but really, Ali excepted, he never scored a win over a super-boxer. Even so, theirs was a wonderful rivalry and, certainly in Frazier's eyes, it has continued to this day.

Ali said some hurtful things about Frazier during their fighting days, calling him an 'Uncle Tom' and 'the white man's champion', saying he looked like a gorilla and so on. He devised poems belittling Frazier and repeated them often. Two examples:

The referee wears a worried frown
Cause he can't start countin' till Frazier comes down.
Who would have thought
When they came to the fight
They'd witness the flight
Of the first coloured satellite?

And:

Joe's gonna come out smokin',
And I ain't gonna be jokin',
I'll be peckin' and pokin'.
This might shock and amaze ya,
But I'm gonna retire Joe Fray-shuh!

Ali got lots of laughs, but Frazier took it all personally. He'd been generous and respectful during Ali's time in exile, and now he found himself the target of intense personal abuse. Frazier channelled his resentful feelings into his fighting, boxing with the conviction of someone who had been grievously insulted. For many years he refused to call Ali by his chosen name, referring to him instead as Cassius Clay, a name Ali had renounced in 1964 because, he said, it was a slave name.

It's doubtful Ali meant half of the things he said. He might now claim he was trying to jack up ticket sales and raise interest in the fight, but things were at a fever pitch anyway. More likely, he was trying to motivate himself.

After the fights, Ali was happy just to move on. Not Frazier. He has harboured resentment ever since. This became evident in 1996 when Ali was chosen to light the flame during the Atlanta Olympics opening ceremony. Ali, as the world knows, has been ravaged by Parkinson's syndrome since the early 1980s and can hardly speak. He moves in a ponderous manner and it was quite an effort to get him onto the platform and have him light the flame.

The people in the Atlanta stadium, and the hundreds of millions watching around the world, felt for Ali. He remains the ultimate sports hero and there is tremendous goodwill towards him, the more so because his present plight contrasts so utterly with the fast-talking, fun-loving man he was in his boxing prime.

Frazier shared none of the joy of seeing Ali honoured on the Olympic stage. He wished, he said, that Ali would fall into the flame, and wondered what he'd done to be chosen for such an honour. Usually old warriors put their past battles behind them. When Ali meets George Foreman or Ken Norton, they genuinely rejoice in each other's company. They had torrid fights and tested each other in the most punishing circumstances. Now they're happy to reminisce and give each other the credit they deserve. But Frazier is different. He is as bitter today as ever. Maybe that's a pointer to just what an incredible rivalry he had with Ali through the early 1970s.

Their first clash, which took place on 8 March 1971 at Madison Square

Garden, New York, was about the most eagerly awaited fight in history. Ali–Frazier I was billed, appropriately, as The Fight. Nothing more needed to be said. There were so many angles. Frazier and Ali were former Olympic gold medallists, so had served their apprenticeships in the amateur ranks. By 1971, both could claim to be legitimate world heavyweight champions, and both were unbeaten. That hadn't happened before.

Ali was the king from 1964 to 1967 and was streets ahead of the field. But then came the induction fiasco. He was sentenced to five years' jail and his boxing licence was revoked. With the benefit of hindsight, this was incredibly harsh, but in 1967 Ali was branded a coward and a traitor for refusing to fight in Vietnam. 'I ain't got to quarrel with them Viet Cong,' he said.

These days Ali is loved all over the world, but in the late 1960s, having embraced the teachings of Elijah Muhammad and become a Black Muslim, and refused to enlist, he was the subject of incredible scorn, hatred even. While he didn't actually serve time in jail, for three years he lost his primary ability to earn money and made a living speaking on college campuses. This brought him closer to many young Americans, but he remained extremely unpopular with most older white Americans.

When he won his last fight before his enforced exile, a seventh round knockout of Zora Folley on 22 March 1967, Ali was unbeaten. As no one took the title off him in the ring, and he wanted to continue boxing, it was easy to claim that he deserved to be regarded still as the champion. He toured the United States touting himself as the People's Champion, a tag that stuck.

Frazier, too, had legitimate claims to the heavyweight title. After winning the Olympic gold medal in 1964, he had turned professional and risen quickly through the ranks. Less than 15 months after his pro debut, he had scored a tough 10-round points decision win over Oscar Bonavena and a tenth round technical knockout of rugged Eddie Machen. In early 1967, he dealt summarily with Doug Jones and George Chuvalo. With Ali shunted off the scene, Frazier became the leading heavyweight. What to do? Some preferred to keep Ali installed as champion, but several of the emerging boxing organisations began looking about for a new champion.

In 1970 Frazier scored a fifth round technical knockout over Jimmy Ellis and won the vacant world title, at least according to most organisations. A two-round knockout later that year over light-heavyweight king Bob Foster cemented his standing. So by the end of 1970, when Ali returned to the ring, Frazier's title claims were certainly legitimate.

Beside the intriguing situation of having two unbeaten champions, the other appealing aspect of the fight was the contrast between them, as people and as boxers. Ali was a showman, charismatic, brash, noisy, colourful. Frazier was equally proud, but he was not as ebullient or as quick with words. He was a real worker. During Ali's exile, the pair had been relatively friendly, but once Ali got his licence back, the relationship changed. The jesting was gone. Now it was deadly earnest.

In early 1971, no one was sure how Ali would fight, probably not even the man himself. Would he be the quicksilver, flashy boxer of the mid-1960s, or would he be slower, and therefore present an easier target for Frazier? He would certainly have height and reach on his side, and it was clear he would have hand speed and variety of punches in his favour. Would he be able to absorb the sledgehammer hooks of Frazier?

Frazier was obviously going to ensure he was busy in the ring, a sort of heavyweight version of Henry Armstrong, a three-minutes-a-round man. He would bull his way in, willingly absorbing some blows to get close enough to land his own. Would his height disadvantage be telling? Would Ali be able to hurt him?

These were the sorts of questions boxing fans asked before the two gladiators met at Madison Square Garden. Never before had two fighters commanded such colossal pay packets – $2.5 million each. The black market for tickets was frantic. Anyone who was anyone was there. Frank Sinatra was accredited as a photographer for *Life* magazine! Norman Mailer was there writing for *Life*, Budd Schulberg for *Playboy*. There were 760 requests for media credentials approved and another 500 turned down. Celebrities were out in force – Aretha Franklin, Bing Crosby, Ed Sullivan, David Frost, Joe Namath, Diana Ross, Ted Kennedy, Diahann Carroll, Burt Lancaster, Count Basie, Alan King. There were 20,455 spectators crammed into the Garden that night. The fight was shown in more than 50 countries on either satellite TV or closed circuit sites.

Before the fight, Ali got intensely personal. He projected himself as a persecuted black man, standing up for his race. But hold on … Joe Frazier had even blacker skin. That didn't concern Ali, who said: 'Joe Frazier is no representative of the black people … Anybody who thinks Frazier can whup me is an Uncle Tom … All those people from Georgia, they will say to Joe Frazier, "Stop that nigger! You gonna be white tonight! Stop the draft-dodging nigger."' Ali rounded on Frazier's looks: 'Joe Frazier is too ugly to be champ. Joe Frazier is too dumb to be champ. The heavyweight champion should be smart and pretty like me. Ask Joe Frazier how do you feel, champ, and he'll say, duh, duh, duh.' Understandably, Frazier felt the taunts were cruel and unworthy.

Ali, 6ft 3in and 215 lb, and Frazier, 5ft 11in and 205 lb, turned on a great fight. In retrospect, Ali was still on the way back. He was not the boxer of a few years before, nor was he quite the boxer he would be a couple of years later. He had had just two fights – a quick dismissal of Jerry Quarry and a 15-round knockout of Oscar Bonavena – in the lead-up and needed more ring action. That said, he was still some fighter. He threw hundreds of strong left jabs and put together some great combinations.

Frazier was never greater than on this night. As the fight wore on, his face became swollen and bleeding, but he thrived on the pain. He seemed energised by the action. He was able to transfer his personal grudge into frenetic activity in the ring. Though Ali had some good rounds, and was superior early on, Frazier wore him down. Ali, with nowhere near as much gas in the tank as Frazier, was forced to rest on the ropes and to showboat to eat up time. He threw away rounds by doing so. Frazier threw away nothing.

By the 15th round, the fight had swung Frazier's way, though Ali supporters were still claiming their man could win. Then Frazier snaked out a whiplash left hook that hit Ali flush on the jaw and sent him sprawling on his back. How Ali rose at the count of four is beyond comprehension. He survived the final two minutes, but was a beaten man at the finish.

All three officials gave Frazier the bout, though by widely varying margins. Judge Artie Aidala scored it 9-6, Judge Bill Recht scored it 11-4 and referee Arthur Mercante scored it 8-6 with one even.

Ali had said he would crawl across the ring and kiss Frazier's feet if he lost. Well, there was none of that. There was no need for a show of public humility because both boxers had turned on the performance of a lifetime. Ali's jaw swelled alarmingly afterwards. Frazier needed several days in hospital. The sports world drew breath. Would there ever be a fight like that again?

Amazingly, there was, and between the same two boxers. It happened in Manila on 1 October 1975.

But before that, the two men met again in New York in a 12-rounder on 28 January 1974. Now neither was the champion. Ali had been beaten by Ken Norton, who had broken his jaw, and desperately needed a good showing against Frazier to regain credibility as a top boxer. And a year before, Frazier had lost his title when he was smashed to pieces in Kingston, Jamaica by big George Foreman, who knocked him down six times in less than two rounds. After such a demoralising defeat, many wondered if Frazier would ever come back – but he outpointed Joe Bugner a few months later, then set his sights on Ali. Again there were insults, threats, taunts and trash talk. Ali started most of it, but Frazier invariably responded. A week before the fight, the pair came to blows during a televised interview with noted broadcaster Howard Cosell.

The second fight drew strong interest among boxing fans, but did not stop the world as their first meeting had done. Each fighter was paid $850,000, though once TV rights kicked in their income rose to $2.6 million each. This time Ali was the winner, by quite a margin. He might have knocked out Frazier in the second round, but for a timekeeping mistake that resulted in the bell being rung too soon, but just soon enough for Frazier.

Ali was busier throughout this fight, and piled up points with his educated left jab. Frazier fought a tough, honest bout, but was frustrated by the end of the 12th. When he wasn't throwing left jabs, Ali clinched. Though Frazier later claimed he was robbed, the decision went to Ali, as it should have. The judges scored it 8-4, 7-4-1, 6-5-1, all for Ali.

Over the next year, remarkable things happened in heavyweight boxing. Ali defied the sands of time to topple the mighty Foreman in the eighth round in Zaire (the fight Ali tagged the Rumble in the Jungle) and so reclaim the crown that had been his a full decade earlier. Frazier got himself back into contention with technical knockouts of Jerry Quarry and Jimmy Ellis.

So Ali–Frazier III became a natural. Usually sequels do not live up to expectations. With the exception of *Godfather II*, has a movie sequel ever been as good as the original? In boxing, Leonard-Duran I was a wonderful bout. By their third meeting, they were just going through the motions. That's generally the way it is in boxing. By 1975, Ali was 33, old for a heavyweight. Frazier was 31, and had been pummelled mercilessly by Foreman, the sort of thrashing that haunts boxers forever.

Ali did his best to hype up the Manila fight. 'It'll be a chilla and a thrilla when I get the Gorilla in Manila,' he would shout. There were side-issues. Ali was between wives at the time, and this caused embarrassing scenes in the Philippines. But as he had done throughout his career, Ali seemed able to shrug off the chaos of his private life, and the bedlam in his corner if his trainer Bundini Brown started shooting off at the mouth, to box calmly and skilfully once out in the middle.

Frazier trained as never before, and he was always a great trainer. At the weigh-in Ali tipped the scales at 224$\frac{1}{2}$ lb, Frazier at 215$\frac{1}{2}$ lb. Still, people looked at their ages and their recent defeats and wondered if the fight would turn out to be a stinker.

In fact, it was one of the all-time classics. There wasn't quite the build-up to it that had preceded the New York clash in 1971. How could anything match that? But in terms of quality of boxing, the Manila fight, in front of 27,000 spectators, outshone the other Ali-Frazier meetings.

By the time the fight came round Frazier was burning with hatred for Ali.

Boxers sometimes say a fight is nothing personal, but for Frazier it undoubtedly was. He'd been insulted too many times. He was out to kill. 'No question about it. It's real hatred. I want to hurt him. If I knock him down, I'll stand back, give him breathing room. I don't want to knock him out in Manila, I want to take his heart out,' said Frazier.

For his part, Ali was back as the heavyweight king, and he liked the feeling. He was never happier than when the spotlight was shining brightly on him, and it never shone as brightly as when he was champion. He knew Frazier would be tough and persistent, and got himself into outstanding shape. He needed to.

The fight see-sawed, each boxer landing sledgehammer blows. It seemed at times as if Ali must surely crumble, so tired did he appear. But he always came back, landing yet more blows to the head, forcing his feet to carry him around the ring, trying to shrug off the pain. 'They told me Joe Frazier was washed up,' Ali rasped as they began the seventh round. 'They lied,' replied Frazier.

As the fight wore on, Ali's eyes sometimes clouded over. He was still fiercely resolute and proud, but he was exhausted. Frazier's face was beaten into a misshapen pulp. After 10 rounds, two judges had the fight even, the third had Ali a shade in front. By the 13th, Frazier was in big trouble. He was still coming in, still swinging, but was getting tagged repeatedly. Ali was dog-tired, but encouraged by the number of clean blows he was landing.

Into the 14th, Frazier could hardly see. His left eye had closed and his right one was shutting fast. It was a cruel round. Frazier became a stationary target, taking blow after blow to the head, nine consecutive right-hands at one point. How he stayed on his feet amazed spectators. Finally he had to withdraw. To see Frazier back-pedalling was such a shock that it must have offered Ali huge encouragement.

At the end of the round, both boxers slumped in their corners. Ali, gasping for breath, had all but punched himself out, and he hadn't been able even to floor Frazier. He wondered if he had enough strength for the final round. Frazier was in serious trouble. His eyes were nearly shut. The hammering he'd just taken had so unnerved his veteran trainer Eddie Futch that Futch called over referee Carlos Padilla and told him the fight was over. This was the act of a real trainer. Futch felt his man was leading on points, but still conceded the fight. Another round like the 14th might leave Frazier permanently damaged. As much as Futch wanted Frazier to beat Ali and reclaim the title, he wouldn't risk that. Frazier rose to begin the final round, but Futch put his hand on his shoulder and said: 'Sit down, son. It's all over. No one will ever forget what you did here today.'

Ali looked across the ring and saw that Frazier's corner had conceded. He dragged himself to his feet and thrust an arm in the air in triumph. But that was just about it. This wasn't the brash youngster who'd outdazzled Sonny Liston and then shouted repeatedly at the TV cameras: 'I shook up the world, I shook up the world …'

This Ali was so utterly spent he slumped to the canvas and lay on his back. A reporter asked him about Frazier and Ali gasped, almost inaudibly: 'He's the greatest fighter of all time … next to me.' Then he was helped to his dressing room, where he lay quietly and hoped he wouldn't die. He asked that Frazier's young son, Marvis, be brought in, and said to him: 'Tell your father the stuff I said about him, I didn't mean. Your father's a helluva man. I couldn't have taken the punches he took today.' The words meant a lot to young Marvis but, when relayed to Frazier, were quickly dismissed.

Ali had been guaranteed a purse of $6 million and Frazier $2 million for the fight, and they'd had a $1 million side-bet, the loser to pay the winner. After the fight, Philippines President Ferdinand Marcos reminded Ali of the money he was owed. Ali shook his head: 'Joe don't owe me nuthin'. We've paid all the dues we're ever going to pay each other.'

There have been some wonderful heavyweight fights down the years. Ring pundits will talk about Fitzsimmons–Corbett, Dempsey–Tunney, Louis–Conn, Marciano–Walcott, Holmes–Norton and Holyfield–Bowe, but there was never a fight that was more brutal, more intense, more gruelling, that contained more enmity or better encapsulated a rivalry than Ali–Frazier III in Manila.

Neither boxer was ever the same again. How could they be? Frazier fought just twice more. He took another hiding from George Foreman in 1976, this time being knocked out in the fifth round, and reappeared in the ring five years later, a shell of the once mighty warrior, to win in 10 rounds over one Jumbo Cumming.

Ali kept fighting, but the magic had gone. There were easy wins over patsy opponents like Jean-Pierre Coopman, Richard Dunn and Alfredo Evangelista. But he was fortunate to get decisions over Jimmy Young, Ken Norton and Earnie Shavers. Then he lost his title to a novice named Leon Spinks, who only 18 months earlier had been boxing at the Olympics. He regained the title from Spinks and retired.

The lure of the ring, and the limelight, however, drew him back and in 1980 an Ali whose energy had been sapped by diet pills was given a comprehensive beating by Larry Holmes, being forced to retire in the 11th round. It was the first time Ali had been unable to finish a fight.

Even that was not the end. Though by now he was dyeing his hair to try to look younger, and was displaying the early signs of his debilitating illness, Ali was allowed to fight again. Dr Ferdie Pacheco, a friend as well as a fight doctor, had long since walked out on his camp, appalled at the permanent damage Ali was sustaining while his so-called friends watched.

Ali travelled to Nassau in the Bahamas and took on Trevor Berbick, an energetic and sizeable youngster who would a short time later gain a part-share of the world title. Ali was hardly even a shadow of the great fighter of earlier years and Berbick beat him on points over 10 rounds. It was a sad way for the self-styled Greatest to close his stellar career.

Before long, Ali had bigger battles to fight. His speech became slurred, his movement restricted, and a series of tests revealed he was suffering from Parkinson's syndrome. Boxing apologists claimed it was a naturally occurring physical phenomenon and that Ali had simply been unlucky. But most people thought back to his terrible battles with Frazier, Foreman, Norton and the rest of them, the pummelling he'd taken in training year after year, and conceded that Ali was now paying the price. And what a price.

Frazier remained involved in boxing, for a while training his son Marvis, who reached world title challenger status before Larry Holmes disabused him of any ideas of claiming the crown that had once belonged to his father. Frazier then got into management and looked after several leading boxers.

Ali and Frazier ran into each other surprisingly often, at big fights where they would be introduced to the crowd, and at reunions of champions. It was noticeable that Ali was, to the best of his limited physical ability, always ready to play-act and ham it up. Frazier seldom seemed as at ease. It became clear to him that whereas he was saluted as a former champion, Ali was revered as one of the greatest sports figures of all time. Frazier was acknowledged as a terrific boxer, but Ali was up there among legends like Pele, Jack Nicklaus, Jesse Owens, Babe Ruth, Michael Jordan and Rod Laver.

That rankled with Frazier. He had fought three super fights with Ali and felt he had won two of them. He knew he had given as good as he had received. On top of that, he had acted with dignity and class. Ali had said some terrible things. Why was Ali so adored? In 1996, Frazier's autobiography, *Smokin' Joe*, was released. In it we learned just how embittered the rivalry had made him:

> It'd be easy for me to fall in line and act as if Clay [he still referred to him as Clay, even after all these years] was some fuzzy old saint to me, like he is to so many others. I know that's what people would like to hear. Forgive and forget. But I'd be shuckin' you if I told you that. Truth is, I'd like to rumble with that sucker again – beat him up piece by piece and mail him back to Jesus. No, I ain't forgiven him for what he said and did.

Frazier said people asked him if he felt bad for Ali, with his medical problems:

> Nope, I don't. Fact is I don't give a damn. Clay always mocked me like I was the dummy. Now look at him: he can hardly talk and he's still out there trying to make noise … he's a ghost and I'm still here.

Asked recently about Ali, Frazier said: 'I don't think nothin' about him, but I know one thing. He thinks about me every day when he gets out of bed.' It was as if Frazier was proud that his huge left hooks might have played their part in Ali's infirmity.

For Ali, the fights with Frazier had been defining moments. 'I have nothing bad to say about Joe Frazier,' Ali explained. 'Without him I couldn't be who I am and without me he couldn't be who he is. We were a pretty good team for four, five years.' Ali had moved on. Frazier never did.

On 8 June 2001, there was a bizarre footnote to this great boxing rivalry when the daughters of Ali and Frazier met in the ring in New York. Boxing promoters, ever on the lookout for an angle, billed ther fight as Ali–Frazier IV. Others tagged it Dames with Names.

Laila Ali, 23, was the strong favourite. She'd had a short but impressive pro career and shown her father's poise and timing in the ring. Jacqui Frazier-Lyde was regarded as a novice, and not a very skilled one at that. At 39, she might have been a good lawyer in Philadelphia, but wasn't seen as any sort of boxer.

In personality, the women were the opposites of their fathers. Ali was quiet and dignified, Frazier-Lyde extroverted and glib. But they fought just as their dads had. Over eight action-packed rounds, Ali moved and flicked punches, and Frazier hustled and charged and thrived on the pain and savagery.

Ali won a majority decision but Frazier-Lyde took Ali's best shots and pressured her into fighting in her own brawling style much of the way. It was like the 1970s all over again.

	Muhammad Ali (changed name from **Cassius Marcellus Clay**)	**Joe Frazier**
Born	17 January 1942, Louisville, Kentucky	12 January 1944, Beaufort, South Carolina
Pro career	Won Olympic light-heavyweight gold medal, 1960. 1960–81 Bouts 61, wins 56 (37 by knockout), losses five (one by knockout).	Won Olympic heavyweight gold medal, 1964. 1965–81 Bouts 37, wins 33 (27 by knockout), losses four (three by knockout).
Ali-Frazier I, II and III		
8 March 1971, New York:	Frazier won on points over 15 rounds.	
28 January 1974, New York:	Ali won on points over 12 rounds.	
1 October 1975, Manila:	Ali won by technical knockout after 14 rounds.	

13 Great Gareth, Super Sid

Gareth Edwards v Sid Going

They're proud of their rugby in New Zealand. It's the national sport. In 1987 the New Zealand team, the famed All Blacks, won the first rugby World Cup.

New Zealanders will concede that other countries have produced excellent rugby players, but that's generally about as far as it goes. Asked to nominate the best rugby players of all time, they don't tend to look offshore, and start reciting names like George Nepia, Colin Meads and Sean Fitzpatrick – all of them All Black legends.

There is one overseas player, though, who even the most avid All Black supporters will admit belongs on the highest pedestal: Gareth Edwards, the Welsh scrum-half from 1966–78. It is a point of considerable debate in New Zealand whether Edwards was as good a player as his major All Black rival of that era, Sid Going. Their individual battles in the late 1960s and early 1970s encapsulated the magnificent rivalry of the time between the All Blacks of New Zealand and the Red Dragons of Wales.

There are all sorts of private clashes in a game of rugby union. Fullbacks will match themselves against their opposites, as will wingers, centres, No 8s, flankers and so on. But the battle between scrum-halves is often the most fascinating. These two players are continually harassing each other. At every scrum they set out to make the other's task that much more difficult. They tackle each other, try to jink past each other, kick over each other. Their confrontation is an obvious physical battle that employs most of the skills demanded of a rugby player – kicking, running, passing, tackling – but it's also like chess. The ability to think quickly and to produce the unexpected is vital.

When Edwards was in his prime, Wales was in the middle of a golden era, dominating the Five Nations Championship and playing sublimely good rugby. Some of the all-time Welsh greats of that time formed the nucleus of the brilliant British and Irish Lions teams that made triumphant tours of New Zealand in 1971 and South Africa in 1974.

Edwards' credentials seem difficult to dispute. In 1996, British magazine *Rugby World* compiled a list of the top 100 players of all time and placed the Welsh scrum-half at No 1. Edwards comes out top in virtually every poll. He was the British rugby personality of the 1970s and became so famous in his own country that he was known simply as Gareth.

All Black Chris Laidlaw, who played against the young Edwards and was himself one of the finest scrum-halves about, is unequivocal when asked about the Welshman. 'He's a bit like Bradman,' says Laidlaw. 'He could do everything and was well ahead of the field. That doesn't mean that some of us didn't have our good days against him, but overall, he was the master.'

Arguably the two most famous television commentators in rugby history have been Bill McLaren of Scotland and Keith Quinn of New Zealand. Both have in recent years named their best-ever selections. Both had Edwards as their scrum-half.

McLaren wrote in *Rugby's Great Heroes and Entertainers*:

Gareth Edwards was the complete scrum half with the build of a bison, a rifled pass, control of the punted ball, impressive power on the run that rendered him lethal from close range, a highly competitive temperament, a strong helping of self-belief and a punishing tackle. He had the physical strength of the gymnast he had been, which gave him resilience and power. He revelled in taking on bigger opposing forwards … he was special, the best ever.

Quinn echoed these sentiments in *A Century of Rugby Greats*:

I have certainly never seen a better scrum-half. He was a star even in great teams; the teams he played for won major titles and series; he had every facet of his position mastered; he made the players around him better; he could dominate a match; he had longevity and durability.

Such praise. How could even passionate New Zealand rugby followers mount a case for Going after all that? Well, without too much difficulty, if you ask them. They don't mind conceding that Edwards was a marvellous player, but better than their Sid? … just hold on a minute!

Their records are remarkably similar. Edwards played test rugby over 12 seasons, Going over 11. Edwards, though never a great on-field leader, captained Wales. Going, though not outgoing enough to be a captain, was Ian Kirkpatrick's All Black vice-captain in 1972–73. Edwards scored 85 points in 63 tests, including 20 tries. Going, from less than half as many tests, scored 10 tries. Both were part-time goal-kickers.

One crucial difference was that within Wales, Edwards was praised unstintingly. He was never dropped from the test team, became Wales' youngest test captain (at 20 years, 7 months) and was revered. Going had battles with New Zealand selectors throughout his career. He was dropped several times from the All Blacks and while sections of the rugby public idolised him, others criticised supposed deficiencies in his play. Apparently, if you listened to some media analysts, he could be selfish and run too much, without looking to service his outside backs. Such critics, of course, ignored the matches Going won with his flair and try-scoring.

Sometimes it needs the dust to settle on a rivalry before we can decide who came out on top. Edwards and Going departed test rugby in the late 1970s. We can see now what brilliant players they were. They played in an era of great scrum-halves – others of the highest calibre included Ken Catchpole and John Hipwell of Australia, Laidlaw, South African Dawie de Villiers and Frenchman Max Barrau. Yet Edwards and Going are the two whose reputations have been enhanced by the passing years.

Gareth Owen Edwards, born at Gwaun-cae-Gurwen in 1947, was educated at Pontardawe Technical School, Millfield and Cardiff Training College, where he studied physical education. He joined the Cardiff club, where he remained until his retirement. As a youngster, he dreamed of playing rugby for Wales, though he was a good soccer player (he was offered a soccer contract by Swansea City) and won the All-England Schools 200-yard hurdles title, beating by 15 yards Alan Pascoe, later an Olympic Games hurdles finalist.

Edwards was 19 when he won his first cap, against France in 1967. Soon after, he linked with fly-half Barry John at Cardiff, for Wales, and in South Africa for the 1968 British and Irish Lions. The young Edwards was no great passer, but was put at ease by the nonchalant John and a famous partnership was born. They played 23 tests for Wales, and five for the Lions. When John retired, Edwards formed another enduring combination, with Phil Bennett.

New Zealanders first glimpsed Edwards in 1967. He was in the Welsh side that was beaten 13-6 by Brian Lochore's All Blacks, he captained East Wales to a 3-3 draw with the tourists and played for the Barbarians in the last game of the tour.

That All Black tour was also the first for Sid Going, but he was Chris

Laidlaw's understudy and never met Edwards on the field. He was 24 by then, four years older than Edwards, and had been around in representative rugby for several years.

Sidney Milton Going was born at Kawakawa, North Auckland, in 1943. His father, Cyril, was of Irish descent and his mother, Mary, was full Maori. Cyril married twice and in all Sid had seven half-brothers and half-sisters and six brothers and sisters. He was always a little bloke, but very strong. When he first donned a rugby jersey he weighed a forbidding 3st 3lb! Going had one year at Northland College, then attended Church College in Hamilton from 1958–60. At 17, and back in Northland working on the family farm, Going made the Whangarei team and in 1962 made his representative debut for North Auckland. He was clearly a star in the making, but missed the next three years of rugby while based in Alberta, Canada, doing Mormon missionary work.

He made his test debut in 1967 when he was picked to replace the injured Laidlaw for the Jubilee test against Australia at Athletic Park. On the 1967 All Black tour, Going was given only one test, against France at Paris. There were arguments over whether Laidlaw, with his magnificent passing, or Going, with his body strength and brilliant individualism, was the better player. Laidlaw generally got the nod, yet coach Fred Allen has since said that Going was the better footballer.

Edwards, already a big name in world football, toured New Zealand with the Welsh national side in 1969. It marked the first occasions that Going and Edwards clashed on the field. This is how their rivalry progressed over the next five years:

31 May 1969: New Zealand v Wales, first test, Christchurch
The All Blacks utterly dominated proceedings, scoring four unanswered tries, and romping to a 13-0 halftime lead. Going, playing behind one of the greatest forward packs of all time, was given a joyride, whereas Edwards, who played the match with a suspect right hamstring, was under incessant pressure. Wales' touring team included greats like J.P.R. Williams, Gerald Davies, John Dawes, Phil Bennett, Barry John, Edwards, Mervyn Davies, Brian Price and John Taylor, but few of them showed even glimpses of their home form while on tour. New Zealand won 19-0.

14 June 1969: New Zealand v Wales, second test, Auckland
This test was even more lopsided than the first. Wales trailed only 14-6 at halftime, but was blown away in the second spell. The Welsh team, Five Nations champions, was exceedingly disappointing in New Zealand that year.

Going, anxious to cement his All Black spot ahead of Laidlaw (who was now at Oxford University, having been awarded a Rhodes Scholarship), played outstandingly, setting up a try for George Skudder, but faced little opposition from Edwards. At this point, New Zealand rugby followers couldn't see what all the fuss was about with Edwards, who had a poor tour. Fergie McCormick scored a world record 24 points in the match. New Zealand won 33-12.

2 June 1971: New Zealand Maori v British and Irish Lions, Auckland

It was only the fourth match of the Lions tour. Rugby followers still did not quite appreciate what a brilliant team the Lions would turn out to be, though 48,000 of them at Eden Park that day were given a glimpse of what was to come. The New Zealand Maori side was a strong one. It was captained by Going and included other All Blacks or future All Blacks in Ken Going, Ken Carrington, Terry Mitchell, Mac Herewini, Buff Milner and Tane Norton. The Lions forwards dominated proceedings, though it was a rugged, physical battle. Barry John scored the only try of the game and kicked six penalties. Of the Maori players, the star was Sid Going, who made several trademark runs and fired out some brisk passes. The Lions won 23-12.

26 June 1971: New Zealand v British and Irish Lions, first test, Dunedin

The Lions won a tight match mainly because of the tactical genius of fly half John, who made All Black fullback Fergie McCormick's job a nightmare with his pinpoint kicking. Edwards hurt his hamstring soon after play began and was replaced after seven minutes by Ray Hopkins. Going had a good match, but the All Black forwards surprisingly struggled. The Lions won 9-3.

10 July 1971: New Zealand v British and Irish Lions, second test, Christchurch

Needing victory to square the series, the All Blacks came out firing and dominated the match, scoring five tries to two. Going scored his first try against his scrum-half rival and set up two others. It was one of his finest matches for the All Blacks and he outplayed Edwards. New Zealand won 22-12.

31 July 1971: New Zealand v British and Irish Lions, third test, Wellington

The Lions took advantage of a poor All Black performance and produced their finest match of the series. Edwards turned on his best test performance in New Zealand and gave his fly-half, John, a dream ride. John responded with a try (set up by Edwards' strong run from a lineout), a drop goal and two conversions. Going ran well, but the Lions forwards and Edwards pressured him into making some wayward passes. The Lions won 13-3.

7 August 1971: North Auckland v British and Irish Lions, Whangarei

This was an entertaining match in which the three Going brothers, Sid, Ken and Brian, pulled off some outrageous inter-passing manoeuvres, including their famous triple scissors. The Lions had too much discipline, but Going, who captained his province, was outstanding. Edwards played solidly, without producing Going's fireworks. The Lions won 11-5.

14 August 1971: New Zealand v British and Irish Lions, fourth test, Auckland

The two great scrum-halves met for the sixth time in 11 weeks. With the result of the test series at stake, it was a tense affair with the forwards battling for supremacy and Going and Edwards both playing well. Lions fullback J.P.R. Williams dropped a long-range goal midway through the second spell, which broke All Black supporters' hearts. It proved to be a decisive moment of the match, and the tour. Match drawn 14-14.

4 November 1972: Cardiff v New Zealand, Cardiff

Going was vice-captain of the All Black touring side, a strange appointment considering his quiet and rather introverted personality. Certainly his ebullience on the field was not matched by any gregariousness off it. It was a young team, under Ian Kirkpatrick's leadership, and the 32-match tour turned out to be only moderately successful by All Black standards. The team lost five matches, and drew two more, and powerhouse prop Keith Murdoch was sent home for misbehaviour. In the Cardiff game, a spiteful affair, New Zealand, smarting after a loss four days earlier to Llanelli, applied remorseless pressure. Its forwards were too strong and Going controlled matters at scrum-half, setting up two tries. Near fulltime, Edwards ran the blind from a scrum, linked with his loose forwards, regathered the ball and scored wide out, his first try against Going. New Zealand won 20-4.

2 December 1972: Wales v New Zealand, Cardiff

These were the days when Wales–New Zealand test matches were close, unpredictable affairs. This one was a torrid battle that was finally tipped New Zealand's way by the place-kicking of Joe Karam, who slotted five penalties. The only New Zealand try was scored by prop Murdoch, following a Going virtuoso display that involved a kick, chase, tackle and pass. Edwards evened matters early in the second half when he tackled Going hard and the ball bounced loose. The Welsh backs streamed through and winger John Bevan scored in the corner. New Zealand won 19-16.

27 January 1973: Barbarians v New Zealand, Cardiff

This match has been cited as the greatest game of rugby ever played. Perhaps the only ingredient missing was the sharp edge of test match atmosphere. Certainly for movement, flair and daring, it was decades ahead of its time. The fixture gave British rugby fans the opportunity to see what was virtually the 1971 British and Irish Lions team in action. The individual star of the match was Edwards, who scored one of the most famous tries of all time. It has become the most replayed moment in rugby television history. Early in a sweeping end-to-end movement, which began with a catch and run deep in his own territory by Phil Bennett, Edwards sprinted through, then sent out a perfect pass as he sprawled on the ground. Yet there he was, 30 seconds later, up with the action, having watched J.P.R. Williams, John Pullen, John Dawes, Tom David and Derek Quinnell handle the ball to take the final pass, sprint 30 metres and score. Those who have watched the thrilling try on television will have noticed that just as Edwards takes the final pass and dives over for the try, there is a blip in the picture. The capacity crowd of 60,000 at Cardiff that day roared so loudly that they distorted forever the television recording. As a straight match-up between scrum-halves it was no contest, because Going began the match with a suspect ankle injury and became progressively more handicapped as the match advanced, eventually being replaced by Lin Colling midway through the second spell. The Barbarians won 23-11.

27 November 1974: Wales XV v New Zealand, Cardiff

This match should have been accorded test status. The Welsh, captained by Edwards, fielded a full-strength selection and would go on to win the Five Nations championship that season. Going had been dropped from the New Zealand team, then recalled, during the previous season, and played as if he had a point to prove. The All Black forwards dominated throughout and their controlled, disciplined play was augmented by Going's good performance behind the scrum. New Zealand won 12-3.

30 November 1974: Barbarians v New Zealand, London

Having beaten Ireland and what was effectively Wales within four days, the All Blacks faced a tough assignment in taking on what was virtually a British and Irish Lions team under a different banner just three days later. The Barbarians team included the complete pack from the unbeaten 1974 Lions team in South Africa and a backline that boasted six internationals. The match was not as free-flowing as the Barbarians-New Zealand points-fest two years earlier, but was hard-fought and entertaining. New Zealand led 7-3 at halftime, and during the second spell both teams held the lead and looked sure winners. Finally, four minutes from time, No 8 Mervyn Davies dived over for a try that levelled the scores. Match drawn 13-13.

That was the extent of the Edwards-Going rivalry. They met 13 times. Going won six, Edwards five and two matches were drawn. On paper, the rivalry was, as horse-racing commentators love to say, 'too close to call'.

Both players wrote best-selling biographies. In Edwards' case, he wrote two, *Gareth* in 1978 and *Gareth Edwards: The Autobiography* in 1999. He wrote other books as well, including the eminently readable *Gareth Edwards' 100 Great Rugby Players*.

His comments on Going in *100 Great Rugby Players* were interesting:

I played against him more than against any other test scrum-half. It could well be that I was his most frequent opposite at representative level, too. Sid must be one of the most perfect products of the New Zealand scrum-half factory. A chunky, strong man with a low centre of gravity, he was a difficult target for big, tall back-row forwards. His main thought was always for his forwards. Therefore, he would make breaks close to the scrum, which his own flankers and No 8 could support. Another attribute, which made him invaluable to the All Black sides in the seventies, was accuracy of kicking, especially into the box – that is, the vulnerable area guarded between an opposing pack and its own corner flag.

Edwards was interviewed by Keith Quinn in 1999 for the television series *Legends of the All Blacks*. He told Quinn:

Without doubt, Sid Going was the best player I played against. The fact that I was able to play against him on so many occasions meant that we really did have a battle over a period of time. Some he won, some I think I won. But it wasn't about winning and losing because we were so dependent on our forwards.

I admired Sid because he was such an outstanding player, a great competitor, so dangerous, a match-winner. You had to keep such a close eye on the man. I admired his skills whenever I played against him.

Edwards was even more generous when being interviewed by Ron Palenski in 2002 for *Century in Black* and conceded that overall, Going came out on top in their personal rivalry:

Yes, I would say that. Mind you, I remember playing against the All Blacks once thinking that I wouldn't have minded playing with the back row the All Blacks had … then Sid might not have come out on top.

I played against Chris Laidlaw, Dawie de Villiers and of course any number of European scrum-halves, but over that period Sid would have been the most difficult I played against. They were great confrontations. Of course, I didn't go out on the field with the aim of beating Sid Going. I went out with the aim of beating the All Blacks and I'm sure Sid would have felt the same way. And I'm sure he would also agree that for a scrum-half to shine, he had to be behind the better pack. In 1971, for example, Sid had the benefit of a better pack performance in the second test and I had the benefit in the third and that was the way the results went.

Going, in his biography, *Super Sid*, was equally complimentary of Edwards, choosing him for a world team from players he'd faced. In the *Legends of the All Blacks* series, Going said:

Oh, he was a tremendous player, a great player. The first time I came up against him was in 1969 when Wales toured New Zealand. We had a fantastic forward pack and never let them into the game. But I saw the best of Gareth over the next few years.

He was a chirpy, cocky sort of guy and he was a bit bigger than me, probably faster and as strong. The media always made a huge amount out of the Going-Edwards rivalry, and it worked on me. I guess I've got a bit of stubbornness and anyone who pushes something against me makes me perform a bit better. I loved the thrill of test rugby and when I was facing Gareth, that was the biggest challenge of all.

I've heard Gareth speak very kindly of my play and of our battles, and I feel the same. I prided myself because I feel I probably got the better of him in most of the tests we met. But on some days he was wonderful. I remember the third test against the Lions at Wellington in 1971. They blew us away and Gareth had a great game. I didn't see which way he went.

The other really great day Gareth had against us was the Barbarians game in 1973, when he scored his famous try. I've seen it from time to time on television. It's a terrible thing for me to watch, but what a brilliant try. They ran at us with such pace and their timing was excellent – they kept passing before they got tackled. Then Gareth snuck in there at full steam and there was no stopping him.

There are some surprising opinions on the Going–Edwards rivalry. Generally, each player is strongly supported by his countrymen. Bryan Williams, Ian Kirkpatrick and Grant Batty, All Black stars of the 1970s, rated Going well ahead. 'They met many times,' said Batty, 'and Sid usually came out on top. They possessed similar qualities of strength and attacking skill. Edwards had the better pass, but Sid was stronger and therefore handled the loose forwards better. Edwards didn't possess Going's guile.'

Welshmen championed Edwards equally strongly. Brilliant fullback J.P.R. Williams, in his autobiography, simply entitled *JPR*, wrote: 'Gareth is such a natural athlete and ball player that he could have been a top class soccer or tennis player as well as the most complete rugby player I have ever seen.'

Welsh test player and later leading journalist Clem Thomas wrote in a retirement tribute to Edwards:

> Gareth Edwards is a legend, one of the great patron saints of Welsh rugby, elevated not only by contributing massively to three Grand Slams and five Triple Crowns over a period of eleven years, but by his ingenuous charm and gentle modesty … Sid Going was more aggressive and durable, but I believe that in the end Gareth had it over all other scrumhalves, as since 1974 there was not a weakness in his game, and he had such an armoury of skills that he could produce more firepower than any other scrum-half.

Going attracted more criticism than did Edwards. Terry McLean, the doyen of New Zealand rugby writers for half a century, sometimes paid credit to Going's match-winning ability, but it was at best only muted praise and was often stained by criticism of Going's personality. McLean wrote that having Going as vice-captain of the 1972–73 All Black touring team was 'a misfortune, if not a disaster', that Going was neither warm nor friendly, and was 'often taciturn, churlish and sullenly indifferent'. McLean accused Going of destroying his backs by not giving them enough ball and said Going had a preoccupation with himself on the field. 'Going has been the greatest attacking half I have ever seen; there is no limit to his courage. His brilliance is incomparable. But where is the team?'

Leading British rugby observers such as Welsh writer J.B.G. Thomas and Lions coach Carwyn James echoed such sentiments. But counterbalancing such opinions are the observations of John Reason, who for many years infuriated New Zealand rugby fans with his stringent criticisms in the *Daily Telegraph* of most aspects of All Black rugby. When talking to Quinn for the

Legends of the All Blacks series, Reason stated emphatically that Going was the better player:

> They met 13 times and Going outplayed him 12 times. On the 13th occasion, Going was carrying an injury so bad nobody else would have gone on the pitch without a crutch. Sid Going was a better player than Gareth Edwards. Everyone raved about Edwards, but he had his faults. For instance, he couldn't pass off his left hand, never could.

Even the greats cop a bit of criticism now and then, and perhaps it's churlish to even mention it. At this distance, it is safe to say that Edwards and Going were two of the greatest scrum-halves in history, and that it was fortunate for rugby watchers that they opposed each other so often.

As personalities, Edwards was more outgoing. There is a lovely story, which may or may not be apocryphal, told by Carwyn James about an occasion when his team had been having all sorts of lineout problems. James devised a simple solution. A word sign beginning with the letter 'p' was the call for the forwards to go right. James: 'When Gareth Edwards, typically, called PSYCHOLOGY, half the forwards went left!'

It would be impossible to overstate the popularity Edwards has enjoyed in Wales, as this well-worn joke illustrates: Wales and England were playing a test at Twickenham. A young Welsh fan couldn't get a ticket, so stood outside the ground in the pouring rain. He would repeatedly call up to the England supporters inside the ground: 'What's happening?' Finally the English supporters, tiring of the youngster, told him all the Welsh team except Edwards had been carried off injured. A few moments later there was a roar from the crowd. The Welsh fan called out: 'What's happening? What's happening? Did Gareth score?'

Edwards has stayed close to rugby since his retirement, and not only with his writing (his first autobiography is said to be the highest-selling rugby book ever). He worked with Bill McLaren for a time in the BBC TV commentary box and is a regular sight at big games. He was one of the First XV chosen for the International Rugby Hall of Fame. In his spare time he is an avid fisherman.

Going, too, has remained near rugby, but he is by nature quieter and has not become involved with the media. He is busy working on his farm in the far north of New Zealand, but coached the North Auckland representative team in the early 1990s. For 15 years Going took the Rugby News Youth team overseas, and on 13 of those occasions the team travelled to the United

Kingdom. He ran into Edwards only once in that time, though. 'We were both busy and our paths hardly ever crossed,' said Going.

Sid and his wife Colleen had five children. Their eldest daughter was killed in a car accident. Two of their sons, Jared and Milton, have played rugby to a high level. Milton played for Northland and at Super 12 level and then took up a professional contract in France. Jared is a New Zealand sevens and Northland representative. In addition, several nephews have played top rugby, including All Black Todd Miller.

Going and Edwards, while so closely linked on the field, never spent much time together socially. Going, because of his religious beliefs, didn't drink alcohol and tended to shy away from some of the normal boisterous after-match behaviour of the time, while Edwards, though not a rabble-rouser, was always an exceedingly popular team man.

Perhaps their strong rivalry on the field prevented them from being closer off it. 'You read stuff about a person and form an impression of what he's like,' said Going. 'I spoke to Gareth cordially at after-match functions, but apart from that I can't say I ever really got to know him.'

It was warming, then, that in early 2003 these two great players came together as part of a 30-year anniversary celebration of the unforgettable Barbarians–New Zealand match of 1973. Ian Kirkpatrick and Sid Going represented the New Zealand team, while most of the surviving Barbarians players were present at a massive gathering at London's Hilton Hotel. It was a splendid occasion, a reminder of rugby in its pre-professional days. One of the nicest sights in an evening of nostalgia was seeing Edwards and Going chatting away. They had a lot of catching up to do.

'It was a really fantastic occasion,' said Going. 'Kirky and I went over there with our wives. We arrived one day, had the evening at the Hilton, then left the next day. We joked that it was a long way to go for dinner, but wouldn't have missed it. I was really pleased I got to spend some time with Gareth and his wife. I think we saw a different side of each other. You spend so long on the field trying to win and make their life a misery. It's wonderful years later to be able to sit down and really talk to someone.'

	Gareth Owen Edwards	**Sidney Milton Going**
Born	12 July 1947, Gwaun-cae-Gurwen, Wales	19 August 1943, Kawakawa, New Zealand
Test debut	Wales v France, Paris, 1967	New Zealand v Australia, Wellington, 1967
Test career	1967–78 (63 matches – 53 for Wales, 10 for the British Isles).	1967–77 (29 matches).
Test points	85 (20 tries, 2 conversions, 3 dropped goals).	44 (10 tries, 1 conversion, 2 penalties).

14 When Opposites Attract
Chris Evert v Martina Navratilova

W omen's tennis has provided a number of wonderful rivalries, full of tension and drama. Americans Helen Wills and Helen Jacobs hardly spoke a civil word to each other while locking horns at Wimbledon and the US Nationals through the 1930s. Quiet, athletic Australian Margaret Court and extroverted Californian Billie Jean King had some titanic struggles in the 1960s and 1970s. In modern times, Steffi Graf and Monica Seles vied for the world No 1 status in an absorbing battle of wills through the early 1990s. Now Justine Henin-Hardenne and Kim Clijsters, from towns just 15 miles apart in Belgium, scrap not just for supremacy in their own country, but for Grand Slam titles and the No 1 world ranking.

All these confrontations offered quirks of personality and style that make them special. But there has never been a women's tennis rivalry as enduring as that between Martina Navratilova and Chris Evert, who faced each other 80 times from 1973 to 1988. Usually they met in tournament finals, often in Grand Slam events, so there was always extra spice in their battles. Though Navratilova came out on top narrowly (43-37) both enjoyed plenty of golden moments. Each won 18 Grand Slam singles tournaments.

Their rivalry was marked by deep mutual respect. Evert hated losing to Navratilova as much as Navratilova hated losing to Evert, but, as Evert said: 'I think we both realised that we pushed each other and, in the end, made the other one a much better player. Martina and I are linked, whether we like it or not.' Navratilova summed it up like this: 'Everywhere I went, Chris was there to meet me. Everywhere she went, I was there to meet her. It was easy emotionally to get up for matches against Chris. She was a champion.'

Besides the sheer number of matches they played against each other, other elements made the Evert–Navratilova rivalry unique. For a start, their styles were complementary. Evert was the first really famous female tennis player to wield a two-fisted backhand – look at the women's tour today to see her influence. She was a safety-first baseliner who masked her emotions and won because of her steadiness and relentless concentration. Navratilova was an explosive net-rusher. She hit a one-handed backhand, loved to slice the ball and follow it to the net to set up her lethal volley. She wore her emotions on her sleeve and her play was marked by bursts of brilliance followed by lapses in concentration.

Off the court, too, they were opposites.

Navratilova was born in Czechoslovakia, but became an American. She loved being the centre of attention, and loudly supported all manner of causes, including many of a political nature. And she was a lesbian who had a series of high-profile relationships with well-known women. The tennis public had a love–hate relationship with her – they admired her tennis, but for many years seldom rooted for her.

Evert, two years older, was as American as apple pie. She grew up in Florida and was the essence of femininity. She played her cards much closer to her chest, seldom alienating people, and throughout her career was a crowd favourite. She had a series of liaisons with well-known men. She and brash men's champion Jimmy Connors were engaged when they won the Wimbledon singles titles in 1974, but the planned marriage never took place. Later in the 1970s, Evert had relationships with actor Burt Reynolds, US President Gerald Ford's son Jack, and British rock star Adam Faith, before marrying English Davis Cup player John Lloyd. That marriage broke up, and Evert is now married to Olympic skier Andy Mill. They have three sons.

Navratilova and Evert were remarkably evenly matched on court. Evert won 154 career singles titles, Navratilova 167. Evert was the better clay-court player, but reached at least the semis on Wimbledon's grass a staggering 15 times. Navratilova excelled on grass, but twice won on the red clay of Roland Garros at the French Open.

In spite of their intense sporting rivalry, Evert and Navratilova became friends. For some years tennis followers wondered how much of their 'friendship' was for public effect, but it became clear eventually that they enjoyed each other's company and that there was genuine mutual respect. And they remain friends. They competed on the Legends Tour, with Team Evert playing Team Navratilova. After retiring from the women's tour, they even chose to settle in the same community – Aspen, Colorado. As Evert joked, 'We just can't seem to shake each other.'

In recalling Evert's early tennis years, it is important to note how the professional tennis scene has changed. When Evert, who'd been coached by her father Jimmy, burst on to the scene at the 1971 US Open, she was a phenomenon. She was just 16, and what was that two-handed backhand all about?

This was a turbulent time for women's tennis, with big names like Billie Jean King, Françoise Durr, Julie Heldman and Rosie Casals locking horns with male-dominated tennis officialdom about such matters as the inequality of men's and women's prizemoney. There were boycott threats from the top women, who formed their own pro tour, sponsored by Virginia Slims.

The arrival of the shy, blonde, pony-tailed, high-school girl from Florida was both a blessing and a curse. King and her cohorts knew that Evert would give women's tennis a fresh marketing tool. But Evert was no activist and it was important she not be so dominant a player that tennis officials could shrug their shoulders and scoff at the women's tennis 'trouble-makers'. Already the women's tour leaders were having problems because Australians Margaret Court and new star Evonne Goolagong were anything but militant trade unionists.

So Evert's appearance at the 1971 US Open was surrounded by intrigue, though much of it bypassed the teenager. These days, a 16-year-old playing at the top level is normal. Martina Hingis was the world No 1 when she was 16. Nearly three decades earlier, Evert was regarded as a freak of nature.

Evert was born in Fort Lauderdale, Florida and raised on the clay of that city's tennis courts, where her father was a teaching pro. While a 4ft 11in eighth-grader in 1969, she was mentioned in *Sports Illustrated*'s Faces in the Crowd section for being ranked No 1 nationally in girls' under-14 tennis.

Evert arrived at Forest Hills, where the US Open was held in those days, riding a 42-match seven-month winning streak. She had during 1971 become the youngest player to represent the US on the Wightman Cup team, beating Winnie Shaw and Virginia Wade on a slow synthetic surface in Cleveland to spearhead America's defence of the Cup.

At Forest Hills, Evert looked at home even on grass courts, though her baseline game was much more suited to clay. She made her tournament debut against former German No 1 Edda Budding, and mowed her down for the loss of one game. That was the beginning of a fairytale fortnight. In the second round she survived six match points to beat No 4 American Mary Ann Eisel in three sets.

In the next two rounds, Evert, with huge crowds screaming support, dispatched fiery Frenchwoman Françoise Durr 2-6, 6-2, 6-3 and Australian Lesley Hunt 4-6, 6-2, 6-3. Both players belonged in the exclusive world top 10 category. In the semi-finals, Evert's golden run ended when a fired-up Billie Jean King beat her 6-3, 6-2. But the Evert legend had been created.

For the next two decades the tennis public adored Evert. There was a slight cooling in the mid to late 1970s, mainly because she was so supreme. Tennis fans wished, too, that she would show a little more emotion on court, and she was dubbed the Ice Maiden. But generally she was enormously popular. Sponsors and advertisers swarmed to be linked with her and tournament organisers knew if they could secure Evert, they would be guaranteed full houses. Evert was an inviting mixture of femininity and grit. She would never concede a point, but never lost her poise and charm.

Her list of accomplishments makes astounding reading:

- She was the first player to win 1000 singles matches.
- Her .900 winning percentage (1309-146) is the best in pro tennis history.
- She won 125 straight matches on clay, the longest winning streak on any surface.
- Her record of 55 consecutive victories, set in 1974, stood until Navratilova broke it 10 years later.
- She had 154 tournament singles victories, second (among men and women) only to Navratilova's 167.
- Evert was the first female player to win US$1 million. She earned US$8,896,195 in career prizemoney, and several times that in endorsements.
- She won 18 Grand Slam singles titles – six US Opens, three Wimbledons, seven French Opens and two Australian Opens.
- She won at least one Grand Slam tournament for 13 consecutive years (1974–86).
- In 52 of her 56 Grand Slam events, including her first 34, she reached at least the semis.

While this list of achievements takes the breath away, it would have been even more impressive but for the presence of Navratilova, who beat her on 43 occasions, including 14 times in Grand Slam tournaments. If Evert had won most of the tournaments in which she lost to Navratilova, it would have taken her tournament victory tally close to 200.

Navratilova's story could hardly be more different. She was born Martina Subertova in the Republic of Czechoslovakia, and lived initially in Prague. Her parents divorced when she was three and her mother moved the family to rural Revnice, just outside Prague. In 1962 she remarried, to Marislav Navratil. Martina took the name of her stepfather, adding the feminine -ova.

Martina's stepfather became her first coach. She played her first tournament in 1964, at the age of seven, and began working with George Parma. At 15 she won the Czech national championship. A year later she turned pro, reaching the quarter-finals of her first Grand Slam event, the 1973 French Open, in which she beat fifth-seeded American Nancy Gunter and then lost a close match to Goolagong. After losing to Evert in the semi-finals of the 1975 US Open in New York, the 18-year-old Navratilova crossed the East River to the offices of the Immigration and Naturalizations Service in Manhattan. Within a month, she received her green card.

In her autobiography, *Being Myself*, Navratilova wrote:

> For the first time in my life I was able to see America without the filter of a Communist education, Communist propaganda. And it felt right … I honestly believe I was born to be an American. With all due respect to my homeland, things never really felt right until the day I got off the plane in Florida.

Navratilova initially struggled to adjust to Western life. She enjoyed fast foods, bought sleek cars, sported garish-looking jewellery. She fell in love with hamburgers, fries and milkshakes. She beefed up to 167 pounds, when tennis media personality Bud Collins famously described her as 'the Great Wide Hope'.

It wasn't until 1978 that Navratilova buckled down to being a serious tennis player. She ate better and centred her life around tennis. The results followed quickly, for the left-handed Navratilova had exceptional talent and an attacking game that could take apart the best opponents. On 10 July 1978, Navratilova reached the world No 1 ranking, immediately after winning her first Grand Slam singles title. She'd beaten Evert in the Wimbledon final and replaced her at the top of the rankings. For the next 15 years Navratilova was a focal point of any tournament.

Off the court, she made even more headlines. Navratilova's prominence in the tennis world prompted the tabloid press to take an interest in her private life. She had been seen in the company of the proudly lesbian novelist Rita Mae Brown, and newspapers speculated about the nature of their relationship. Martina ended the speculation by confirming that the papers had guessed right – she was a lesbian and she and Brown were a couple.

This openness about her sexual orientation earned her respect, but cost her millions of dollars, with some potential sponsors fearing a backlash from intolerant consumers if they associated their company's name with someone who was openly homosexual. Nonetheless, Martina was able to gain the unequivocal acceptance of the US immigration service. On 21 July 1981, she became an American citizen.

After splitting with Brown, Navratilova moved to Dallas to live with basketball star Nancy Lieberman, who became her personal trainer and hardened her physically and mentally. Navratilova also hired transsexual player Renee Richards as coach.

A couple of years later, Navratilova began a long-term relationship with another writer, Judy Nelson, and would often run into the crowd to hug her after winning tournaments. These public displays of affection seemed to make television commentators uncomfortable. They struggled for an acceptable way to describe the relationship, often hesitantly referring to Nelson as Navratilova's 'friend'.

These days players have had whole careers by their early 20s. Martina Hingis retired in 2002 at the age of 22 after a brilliant career that included five Grand Slam singles titles and 40 singles titles in total. Navratilova was a late bloomer by comparison. She'd won only three Grand Slam singles titles by 25, yet finished with 18.

After she dedicated herself to being a great tennis player, Navratilova built a fantastic record. Among her achievements:

- She won 167 singles titles, the most of any professional player.
- She won at least one tour event for 21 consecutive years.
- Navratilova broke Evert's record of 1309 singles match wins, raising the mark to 1440.
- She won singles and doubles titles at the same event 84 times.
- Her 18 Grand Slam singles titles place her fourth equal among women players, behind Margaret Court (24), Steffi Graf (22) and Helen Wills Moody (19), and tied with Evert.
- She completed a singles non-calendar year Grand Slam sweep at Roland Garros in 1984 during a run of six consecutive Grand Slam singles victories.
- She achieved three non-calendar year doubles Grand Slams with Pam Shriver.
- With Shriver, Navratilova holds the record of 109 consecutive doubles matches victories.
- She won a record nine Wimbledon singles titles.
- She won the singles, doubles and mixed titles at every Grand Slam event.
- In 2003, in her 47th year, she reached three Grand Slam finals, winning the Australian and Wimbledon mixed titles. During the year she became the oldest Grand Slam title winner.
- She was ranked No 1 for 331 weeks, second only to Steffi Graf's 373 weeks since rankings began in 1975.

Gareth Edwards passes, Sid Going chases. How often was this scene repeated during their 13-match rivalry? PHOTOSPORT

Gareth Edwards at an International Rugby Hall of Fame function, with his Lions team-mates Barry John (left) and Willie John McBride. KEITH QUINN COLLECTION

After retiring as a player, Sid Going became a provincial rugby coach and took youth teams overseas for 15 years. PHOTOSPORT

Pick the winner. Martina Navratilova (left) and Chris Evert battled each other 80 times. They both seem happy with the outcome this time. FOTOPRESS

It doesn't matter what they do, Chris Evert (left) and Martina Navratilova will always be competitive. But wasn't Navratilova supposed to have the muscles? FOTOPRESS

Seoul Olympics, 100m final: Ben Johnson raises his finger in triumph and beaten finalists Carl Lewis (right) and Linford Christie look stunned. All three place-getters would fail drugs tests during their careers. PHOTOSPORT

Carl Lewis wins the long jump at the 1996 Olympics, his ninth gold medal. PHOTOSPORT

Ben Johnson looks proud and confident, but what secrets is he hiding? PHOTOSPORT

- Her earnings of $20 million stood as a record until surpassed by Graf in 1998. Graf finished her career with $21.89 million. Midway through 2004, Navratilova's earnings were $21.02 million.
- Navratilova had consecutive match-winning streaks of 74 (the women's record), 58 and 54.
- She had years with singles records of 86-1, 78-2, 90-3 and 89-3.

Evert and Navratilova's marvellous tennis records stand proudly alongside the best in tennis history. But the point here is not their individual brilliance, but their rivalry, which can be broken into three stages.

It began on 19 March 1973, when the 18-year-old American princess beat the wide-eyed 16-year-old from Prague 7-6, 6-3 on an indoor court in the first round of a tournament at Akron, Ohio. The rivalry endured until 13 November 1988, in the final of the Virginia Slims of Chicago, when Navratilova won 6-2, 6-2.

Of their 80 meetings, 60 were finals. Evert won the first stage 21-4. In the middle section Navratilova held a 14-9 edge. Navratilova dominated the last stage, winning 13 straight at one point and taking 25 of their final 32 matches. But Evert had her moments, even late in her career. She scored exciting three-set victories over Navratilova on the Paris clay in the 1985 and 1986 French Open finals.

Evert won their first five encounters and also their first clash on grass, in the semi-finals of Wimbledon in 1976. By 1978, however, Navratilova was beginning to turn things around. She won a fascinating battle at Eastbourne that year, 6-4, 4-6, 9-7, and a couple of weeks later repeated the dose in the Wimbledon final, winning 2-6, 6-4, 7-5. Their longest match was the 1979 final at Eastbourne when Evert won 7-5, 5-7, 13-11. Evert won more of their meetings every year until 1979 and it wasn't until late 1984 that Navratilova caught her in terms of overall matches between them.

Perhaps the lowest moment for Navratilova came at Amelia Island, Florida in 1981, when Evert won their final 6-0, 6-0. As Navratilova was by then playing Evert on equal terms, this result on Evert's favoured clay surface must have taken some digesting. But Navratilova won some quick matches, too. In 1984 she beat Evert 6-2, 6-0 at Amelia Island and a few weeks later beat her 6-3, 6-1 at Roland Garros. Both these lopsided results came on clay, especially galling for Evert.

Their greatest match? It would have to come from one of their 22 Grand Slam clashes, where the stakes are highest.

Three that stand out are the 1981 US Open semi-final that Navratilova won

7-5, 4-6, 6-4, the 1985 French Open final thriller that Evert won 6-3, 6-7(4-7), 7-5, and the 1988 Wimbledon semi-final that Navratilova won 6-1, 4-6, 7-5. The 1981 US Open was particularly important to Navratilova. She was by then a US citizen, and that meant a lot to her, yet still had not won the US national title. Their semi-final meeting see-sawed until Evert led 3-2 in the final set. Then there was an interruption while security guards ejected two men who had been disrupting play by making too much noise. When the match resumed, Navratilova regained her composure better and rushed to victory. She leapt in the air when she won the match to make it to her first US Open final. (Tracy Austin beat her in the final in a third set tiebreaker.)

The 1985 French Open final was a cracker. Navratilova had won 15 of their previous 16 encounters, but Evert had gathered herself for the challenge. She had increased her training workload in the gym and looked fitter and stronger. The match went to the wire. Navratilova hung in by winning the second set tiebreaker, but Evert was fractionally too steady in the closing minutes of the third set. 'I don't know what I'd have done if I'd lost today,' she said afterwards. 'It's my best surface and I'm playing as well as I ever have in my life. It feels great to have a win over Martina in a Grand Slam.'

By the time they met in the 1988 Wimbledon semi-final, Steffi Graf was the new queen of the tour (she would go on to complete a Grand Slam that year) and Navratilova was struggling to hold her. Evert was in the twilight of her career. And yet, in this semi-final, Evert used her experience and court craft to push Navratilova all the way. All things considered, this might have been the highest quality tennis Evert played on grass, and at a time when she was considered past her best.

There were other aspects to their rivalry. For two such apparently good friends, they often sniped at each other. For instance, in 1981, when stories of Navratilova's various liaisons were being devoured by the media, Evert said: 'Her tennis isn't going to straighten out until she straightens out her life. Martina is in a slump. Two years ago, she was playing real well. I don't think she's really working that hard right now and practising the way she used to … If she wants to be Number One, she has to change something.'

Navratilova quoted this passage in her autobiography, *Being Myself*, and added: 'She was legitimately concerned about me. How was she to know I had already changed my training so drastically that within two years she would be unable to beat me on any surface, even clay?' A little barb?

The pair jostled for the prized No 1 ranking, with only a short interlude by Tracy Austin to break 12 years of domination. It went like this:

3 November 1973–9 July 1978 (140 weeks)	Evert
10 July 1978–13 January 1979 (26 weeks)	Navratilova
14–27 January 1979 (2 weeks)	Evert
28 January–24 February 1979 (4 weeks)	Navratilova
25 February–15 April 1979 (7 weeks)	Evert
16 April–24 June 1979 (10 weeks)	Navratilova
25 June–9 September 1979 (11 weeks)	Evert
10 September 1979–6 April 1980 (31 weeks)	Navratilova
7–20 April 1980 (2 weeks)	Tracy Austin
21 April–30 June 1980 (10 weeks)	Navratilova
1 July–17 November 1980 (20 weeks)	Austin
18 November 1980–2 May 1982 (76 weeks)	Evert
3–16 May 1982 (2 weeks)	Navratilova
17 May–13 June 1982 (4 weeks)	Evert
14 June 1982–9 June 1985 (156 weeks)	Navratilova
10 June–13 October 1985 (18 weeks)	Evert
14–27 October 1985 (2 weeks)	Navratilova
28 October–24 November 1985 (4 weeks)	Evert
2 November 1985–16 August 1987 (90 weeks)	Navratilova
17 August 1987–10 March 1991 (186 weeks)	Steffi Graf

This battle for the No 1 ranking produced interesting side-issues. In 1985, the Wimbledon committee, which maintains the right to deviate from computer rankings in finalising its seedings, allocated Navratilova and Evert joint top seeding. This irritated both of them. Evert was ranked No 1 when the seedings were done and felt she should be accorded top seed status. Navratilova had won Wimbledon the previous three years and felt the honour should have been hers.

It was a curious time. Not only were they fighting for Grand Slam titles, the world No 1 ranking and top seeding at Wimbledon, but both released books to coincide with Wimbledon. Navratilova's *Being There* was a gritty, warts and all effort that spoke frankly about lesbianism, the homophobia of the commercial world and other issues about which she felt strongly. Evert's *Lloyd on Lloyd* (written with her husband and the help of Margaret Thatcher's daughter Carol) was altogether sweeter. The cover had a touched-up photo of Chris and John Lloyd smiling happily and the book generally presented a glowing picture of bliss that did not always tie in with the facts. The books epitomised their rivalry. Released in opposition to each other, they captured perfectly the principals' personalties.

Evert retired from the tour after losing a quarter-final match to Zina

Garrison at the 1989 US Open, leaving with dignity. She had changed over the years. The shy schoolgirl of the early 1970s had been transformed into a confident public speaker, eager to use her name and stature to assist the game. She was president of the Women's Tennis Association Players Association in 1975–76 and 1983–91.

In 1995, Evert was only the fourth player to be elected unanimously into the International Tennis Hall of Fame. She serves as the business advisor to the board of directors for the WTA Tour Players Association. She has commentated extensively for American television and brings to the task professionalism, knowledge and a nice touch of humour – she was always one of the funnier, if more ribald, joke-tellers in the women's locker room. She founded Chris Evert Charities in 1989 and her efforts have raised more than $12 million to fight drug abuse and assist neglected, drug-exposed and abused children. In 1996 she opened and now actively oversees the Evert Tennis Academy in Boca Raton, Florida, which specialises in junior tennis development. She is the publisher of the American magazine *Tennis*.

Navratilova stayed very close to tennis. In fact, she remained so fit that she seemed to regret her decision to retire from the pro tour at the end of 1996. She'd quit singles in 1994, when she held a world ranking of eighth. She dipped her toe in the water again in 2000, playing six doubles tournaments. In 2001 she upped the number to 12. In 2002, on the improve again, she and Natasha Zvereva captured the Madrid doubles title. Navratilova was aged 45 years, seven months, seven days.

She then astounded everyone by returning to singles at Eastbourne. In her first singles tournament in seven and a half years, she scored a notable three-set first-round win over world No 22 Tatiana Panova to become the oldest woman on the tour to win a singles match. She lost in three sets in the second round to world No 13 Daniela Hantuchova.

Into 2003, Navratilova played even more and scored even better results, teaming with Indian Davis Cup player Leander Paes to win the mixed doubles at the Australian Open and Wimbledon, and with Svetlana Kuznetsova, the promising 18-year-old Russian, to finish runner-up in the US Open doubles. These successes meant that by the end of 2003, Navratilova had a total of 58 Grand Slam titles, only four behind the leader, Margaret Court.

Perhaps more incredibly, Navratilova returned to Fed Cup play in 2003, after an interval of eight years. She and Lisa Raymond won their doubles match against Elke Clijsters and Caroline Maes 6-1, 6-4 in the semi-final against Belgium to help put the US into the Cup final against France in November. France proved too good, beating the US 4-1, but 47-year-old Navratilova kept her unblemished Fed Cup record, combining with Raymond to beat Stephanie Cohen Aloro and Emilie Loit 6-4, 6-0 for the US's only win. Navratilova finished the year saying she would be chasing a spot on the US team for the 2004 Athens Olympics. She began 2004 well, reaching the Australian Open mixed doubles final with Paes, who was returning to the game after a major illness. She even played some singles events, including the French Open. In the US's first Fed Cup outing of 2004, Navratilova and Raymond won their doubles match in a 4-1 US victory over Slovenia. It lifted Navratilova's overall Fed Cup record to 40 wins and no defeats.

Navratilova was non-playing captain of the US Fed Cup team in 1997. Never one to shy away from the politics of a situation, she was an active Women's Tennis Association president in 1979–80, 1983–84 and 1994–95. She was inducted into the Tennis Hall of Fame in 2000.

In addition to rekindling her interest in competitive tennis, Navratilova is also an accomplished golfer and skier, co-wrote three mystery novels in the late 1990s and remains vigorous in her support of lesbian and gay rights groups, as well as several other charitable causes.

	Chris Evert	Martina Navratilova
Born	21 December 1954, Fort Lauderdale, Florida	18 October 1956, Prague, Czech Republic
WTA Tour titles	154 singles, 8 doubles.	167 singles, 173 doubles.
Grand Slam titles	18 singles, 3 doubles.	18 singles, 31 doubles, 9 mixed.
Federation Cup	(US) 1977–89: 57-4 (40-2 singles, 17-2 doubles).	(Czechoslovakia and US) 1975–2004: 40-0 (20-0 singles, 20-0 doubles).

HEAD TO HEAD

Year	Place	Winner	Score
1973	Akron, Ohio	Evert	7-6, 6-3
	St Petersburg, Florida	Evert	7-5, 6-3
1974	San Francisco	Evert	6-7, 6-4, 6-1
	Italian Open	Evert	6-3, 6-3
1975	San Francisco	Evert	6-4, 6-3
	Washington, DC	Navratilova	3-6, 6-4, 7-6
	Akron, Ohio	Evert	6-3, 6-1
	Chicago	Navratilova	6-4, 6-0
	Philadelphia	Evert	7-6, 6-4
	Los Angeles	Evert	6-4, 6-2
	Amelia Island, Florida	Evert	7-5, 6-4
	Italian Open	Evert	6-1, 6-0
	French Open	Evert	2-6, 6-2, 6-1
	US Open	Evert	6-4, 6-4
	Atlanta	Evert	2-6, 6-2, 6-0
	Orlando, Florida	Evert	walkover
1976	Austin, Texas	Evert	6-0, 6-3
	Houston	Navratilova	6-3, 6-4
	Wimbledon	Evert	6-3, 4-6, 6-4
1977	Washington, DC	Navratilova	6-2, 6-3
	Seattle, Washington	Evert	6-2, 6-4
	Los Angeles	Evert	6-2, 2-6, 6-1
	Philadelphia	Evert	6-4, 4-6, 6-3
	Tucson, Arizona	Evert	6-3, 7-6
	Colgate Series Championships	Evert	6-4, 6-1
1978	Eastbourne	Navratilova	6-4, 4-6, 9-7
	Wimbledon	Navratilova	2-6, 6-4, 7-5
	Atlanta	Evert	7-6, 0-6, 6-3
	Palm Springs, California	Evert	6-3, 6-3
	Tokyo, Japan	Evert	7-5, 6-2
1979	Oakland, California	Navratilova	7-5, 7-5
	Los Angeles	Evert	6-3, 6-4
	Dallas	Navratilova	6-4, 6-4
	Eastbourne	Evert	7-5, 5-7, 13-11
	Wimbledon	Navratilova	6-4, 6-4
	Phoenix, Arizona	Navratilova	6-1, 6-3
	Brighton	Navratilova	6-3, 6-3

HEAD TO HEAD

Year	Place	Winner	Score
1980	Chicago	Navratilova	6-4, 6-4
	Wimbledon	Evert	4-6, 6-4, 6-2
	Brighton	Evert	6-4, 5-7, 6-3
	Tokyo, Japan	Navratilova	7-6, 6-2
1981	Colgate Series Championships	Navratilova	walkover
	Amelia Island, Florida	Evert	6-0, 6-0
	US Open	Navratilova	7-5, 4-6, 6-4
	Tokyo, Japan	Navratilova	6-3, 6-2
	Sydney, Australia	Evert	6-4, 2-6, 6-1
	Australian Open	Navratilova	6-7, 6-4, 7-5
1982	Wimbledon	Navratilova	6-1, 3-6, 6-2
	Brighton, UK	Navratilova	6-1, 6-4
	Australian Open	Evert	6-3, 2-6, 6-3
	Toyota Championships	Navratilova	4-6, 6-1, 6-2
1983	Dallas	Navratilova	6-4, 6-0
	Virginia Slims Championships	Navratilova	6-2, 6-0
	Los Angeles	Navratilova	6-1, 6-3
	Canadian Open	Navratilova	6-4, 4-6, 6-1
	US Open	Navratilova	6-1, 6-3
	Tokyo, Japan	Navratilova	6-2, 6-2
1984	East Hanover, New Jersey	Navratilova	6-2, 7-6
	Virginia Slims Championships	Navratilova	6-3, 7-5, 6-1
	Amelia Island, Florida	Navratilova	6-2, 6-0
	French Open	Navratilova	6-3, 6-1
	Wimbledon	Navratilova	7-6, 6-2
	US Open	Navratilova	4-6, 6-4, 6-4
1985	Key Biscayne, Florida	Evert	6-2, 6-4
	Delray Beach, Florida	Navratilova	6-2, 6-4
	Dallas	Navratilova	6-3, 6-4
	French Open	Evert	6-3, 6-7, 7-5
	Wimbledon	Navratilova	4-6, 6-3, 6-2
	Australian Open	Navratilova	6-2, 4-6, 6-2
1986	Dallas	Navratilova	6-2, 6-1
	French Open	Evert	2-6, 6-3, 6-3
	Los Angeles	Navratilova	7-6, 6-3
1987	Houston	Evert	3-6, 6-1, 7-6
	French Open	Navratilova	6-2, 6-2

HEAD TO HEAD

Year	Place	Winner	Score
	Wimbledon	Navratilova	6-2, 5-7, 6-4
	Los Angeles	Evert	6-2, 6-1
	Filderstadt, Germany	Navratilova	7-5, 6-1
1988	Australian Open	Evert	6-2, 7-5
	Houston	Evert	6-0, 6-4
	Wimbledon	Navratilova	6-1, 4-6, 7-5
	Filderstadt, Germany	Navratilova	6-2, 6-3
	Chicago	Navratilova	6-2, 6-2

Navratilova won head-to-head matches 43-37 (walkovers excluded).

Surface breakdown

Hardcourt: Navratilova 9-7   Clay: Evert 11-3

Grass: Navratilova 10-5   Indoors: Navratilova 21-14

Year-by-year breakdown

1973: Evert 2-0

1974: Evert 2-0

1975: Evert 9-2

1976: Evert 2-1

1977: Evert 5-1

1978: Evert 3-2

1979: Navratilova 5-2

1980: tied 2-2

1981: Navratilova 3-2

1982: Navratilova 3-1

1983: Navratilova 6-0

1984: Navratilova 6-0

1985: Navratilova 4-2

1986: Navratilova 2-1

1987: Navratilova 3-2

1988: Navratilova 3-2

Grand Slam breakdown

Australian Open: tied 2-2

French Open: Evert 3-2

Wimbledon: Navratilova 7-2

US Open: Navratilova 3-1

15 Enhanced Performance
Carl Lewis v Ben Johnson

The 1988 Seoul Olympics 100m final was one of the most famous moments in sports history. It featured three 100m world record-holders – Carl Lewis, Ben Johnson and Calvin Smith – and three sprinters who won successive Olympic 100m finals – Lewis, Johnson and Linford Christie. It was also the culmination of an especially acrimonious rivalry: the battle between Johnson and Lewis to be regarded as the fastest human being on earth.

Their rivalry can be divided into several distinct phases. All were dramatic and headline grabbing:
- Their increasingly frantic struggle over the previous four years to be world sprint king.
- The race itself. Has there been a more talked-about 10 seconds in sport?
- The immediate aftermath, with a sports megastar being branded a cheat after returning a positive drugs test, having his gold medal taken away and being barred from athletics.
- The race's long-term effects, still reverberating 15 years later.

Whole books could be written about that showdown in Seoul. We'll not see its like again. It produced the greatest sprinting that athletics followers had seen. It was followed by a huge scandal that turned athletics upside-down by placing the issue of drugs cheats squarely in the spotlight. Of the eight 100m finalists, five (Johnson, Lewis, Christie, Dennis Mitchell and Desai Williams) would eventually be tainted by drug scandals. The race is sprinting's entry into the Hall of Shame.

Lewis and Johnson possessed all the ingredients necessary to be rivals. Lewis was American; Johnson, born in Jamaica, ran for Canada. Lewis was boastful, showy, well spoken and craved the limelight. Johnson was introverted, sullen, a reticent speaker with a bad stammer. Lewis never used 10 words if 100 would do. Johnson wouldn't use 10 if he didn't have to. Lewis was tall and rangy, Johnson shorter and heavily muscled. Lewis ran with grace, Johnson with explosive power.

Though he was the greatest runner the United States had produced since Jesse Owens in the 1930s, King Carl was never an American hero. His countrymen never warmed to his self-promotion and ego. Canada, which had never produced an athletics superstar before, idolised quiet Big Ben, who was feted wherever he went before his spectacular fall from grace. For years the pair slugged it out, eyeing each other off before big races, sprinting for glory, then chipping at each other in the media. The rivalry peaked on that famous day in Seoul – 24 September 1988.

Lewis, born in Birmingham, Alabama in 1961, was always going to be a champion athlete. His parents, Bill and Evelyn, were coaches and his sister Carol was selected for the long jump at three Olympics. The well-to-do Lewis family moved to Willingboro, New Jersey, when Carl was two. At 10 he was introduced to Jesse Owens while competing at a junior meet in Philadelphia. It was a meeting of the ages – Owens was Bill Lewis's athletics hero and throughout his career Carl would be compared to Owens, who won four golds at the 1936 Berlin Olympics.

Even at high school, Lewis was an exceptional athlete. He shone first in the long jump and then, as he grew, in sprints as well. Colleges from all over the United States tried to recruit this teenager who was destined for athletics superstardom, and sports product companies aggressively chased him. Eventually Lewis chose Houston University, because he clicked with track coach Tom Tellez, and signed for Nike. Lewis resided in Texas after leaving college, but became the biggest name in the Santa Monica Track Club in California, which was started by Joe Douglas in the early 1970s.

But for the Americans' 1980 Olympic boycott, Lewis's record might have been even more spectacular. He won a long jump bronze medal at the 1979 Pan American Games. At the 1980 US Olympic trials, Lewis, just 18, qualified for the American team in the long jump and finished fourth in the 100m sprint, which would have qualified him for the sprint relay team.

Through 1980-81, Lewis improved so dramatically that by 1982 he was named Athlete of the Year. He was the world's best sprinter and in 1981 began a streak of long jump wins that would eventually reach 65 and not be broken until a magnificent contest with Mike Powell at the 1991 world championships in Tokyo.

At the inaugural world championships at Helsinki in 1983, Lewis was sensational. He won the 100m in 10.07s, anchored the 4 x 100m relay team to gold and won the long jump. This set him up for the 1984 Los Angeles Olympics, where Lewis emulated Owens' feat, scooping the 100m, 200m, sprint relay and long jump gold medals.

While Lewis was vastly admired as an athlete, he was not popular. Many were turned off by his showboating, vanity and love of the spotlight. However, there was no denying his class as an athlete. After the 1984 Olympics, when Lewis had just turned 23, he was already being ranked alongside Owens, Zatopek, Nurmi and other legends.

So dominant was Lewis that few paid attention to the minor place-getters in that 100m sprint in Los Angeles. If only they'd known. The bronze medallist was a rising Canadian named Ben Johnson who, with a placing that surprised even his staunchest supporters, had announced his arrival as a top sprinter. Johnson, born into semi-poverty in the port town of Falmouth, Jamaica, moved to Toronto with his mother and five siblings in 1976, when he was 14. He tagged along with older brother Eddie to the Optimist club, where he ran into mercurial coach Charlie Francis, a leading Canadian sprinter a few years earlier. Francis became a father figure to Johnson.

Until he had a growth spurt in his mid-teens, Johnson didn't seem to have the makings of a top athlete, but he stuck with it and by 1978 the first inklings of ability surfaced. Johnson, just 16, ran last in the Commonwealth Games trials that year.

Once he began to mature physically, his times improved quickly. He made the Canadian Olympic team in 1980, though the team never competed in Moscow because of the American-led boycott. The first time he faced Lewis was in August 1980 at the Pan Am juniors in Sudbury, Ontario. Lewis won the 100m in 10.43s. Johnson was sixth in 10.88s.

At the 1982 Brisbane Commonwealth Games, Johnson ran a surprising second in the 100m, with a wind-assisted 10.05s. It seemed he might even steal the gold from Scotland's Olympic champion Allan Wells, but Wells ran him down to win by 0.03s. Johnson was also part of the Canadian 4 x 100m relay team that took the silver.

Johnson made further advances over the next year, placing in (and once winning) some big races in Europe. His explosive start gave him an edge at the beginning of any 100m race and as he built his strength, it took even the best longer to catch him. Those who follow these things closely felt that a time would come when he would start fast and would simply stay in front. In the meantime, though, all eyes remained on Lewis.

At the 1983 world champs at Helsinki, Johnson ran poorly and failed to get past the semi-finals, but at the 1984 Olympics, he moved up another notch. In the 100m final, he ran exceptionally well for 70 metres and though Lewis jetted by and another American, Sam Graddy, pipped him on the line, he still ran 10.22s for the bronze.

Johnson ended 1984 ranked fourth in the world in the 100m by the authoritative *Track and Field News*. Lewis was way clear in first, but the pair had a terrific race at the Zurich Grand Prix meet, when Johnson led for much of the journey before being passed by Lewis and Harvey Glance. This Zurich race was the sixth straight time Lewis had beaten Johnson – but the greatest rivalry in sprinting history had only now begun in earnest.

The next four years provided marvellous drama. Whenever Johnson and Lewis faced each other, their clash was the focal point of the meeting. Here's how they fared in those four seasons:

1985

Many people, used to Lewis being undisputed No 1, ranked him top of the 100m for the year, but a case can be made for placing Johnson first.

Lewis won an early-season clash in Modesto in 9.98s, with Johnson third in 10.16s. Johnson evened the score by winning their 100m clash at the prestigious Zurich meet. Running into a headwind, Johnson outpaced a class field, winning in 10.18s from Calvin Smith (10.19s), Desai Williams (10.26s) and Lewis (10.31s). The pair had another meeting that year, at Cologne, where the Pole Marian Woronin upset them both, with Lewis second and Johnson third. Johnson then took the gold medal in the season's most important 100m race, the World Cup at Canberra, which Lewis bypassed.

Track and Field News ranked Lewis first (for the fifth consecutive year) and Johnson second, but Johnson had won the year's two most important races, in Zurich and Canberra. Despite Johnson's rise, there was still no argument about their commercial value. Lewis was pulling up to $25,000 a race while Johnson was often running for less than $1000.

This was the year that the words 'Johnson' and 'drugs' began to be mentioned in the same sentence, though the nickname Benoid was yet to be invented. When asked about drugs, Johnson replied: 'Drugs are demeaning and despicable and when people are caught they should be thrown out of the sport for good … I want to be the best on my own natural ability and no drugs will pass into my body.'

1986

One appealing aspect of the Johnson–Lewis battle was that they met several times a year, unlike other famous runners of this period. Their 1986 season began in earnest at the Bruce Jenner meet in San Jose in May. Johnson sizzled to a 10.01s victory. Lewis was a long way back in second in 10.18s.

Attention turned to the Goodwill Games in Moscow in July. The Goodwill Games, a Ted Turner brainchild, evolved because of the 1980 and 1984 Olympic boycotts. Turner wanted to bring together Soviet Union and American athletes. Somehow leading athletes from other countries got roped in.

Johnson spreadeagled the field in Moscow with a breathtaking run of 9.95s, the fastest sea-level 100m. Lewis struggled home third, the pair split by Nigeria's Chidi Imoh. Lewis complained that his preparation had been affected by the recent US Nationals and refused to attend the medal ceremony. He was beginning to show signs of a man under pressure. Lewis was still an athletics megastar – don't forget, he was the world's best long jumper through the 1980s – but Johnson now owned the title of World's Fastest Human. Johnson then travelled to Edinburgh to win the 100m and finish third in the 200m at the boycott-blighted Commonwealth Games.

The season climaxed at the Zurich Grand Prix, where the strongest 100m field of the year assembled – Johnson, Lewis, Christie, Smith, Woronin, Kirk Baptiste, Harvey Glance and Imoh. Johnson finished easing up with his arm hoisted in triumph, but still won in 10.03s, a spectacular time into a headwind. Imoh was second in 10.23s and Lewis a distressed third. As the man who had ended the reign of the great Lewis, Johnson was elevated to celebrity status.

1987

It transpired that 1986 was but a tasty appetiser for the fireworks of 1987. Johnson had a long season, winning 21 finals, from January in Perth to September in Tokyo. He also set several world indoor records. Johnson was the Athlete of the Year in 1987. It's doubtful if there had ever been a more impressive season of sprinting.

At the 1987 world championships in Rome, Johnson ran supremely well. His winning time of 9.83s knocked a full tenth of a second off Calvin Smith's altitude-assisted world record. Lewis also ran outstandingly at Rome, his time for second place being 9.93s, yet he finished a metre down on the flying Johnson, having also lost to him earlier at Seville.

The world championships final was one of those special athletics moments. Lewis centred his season around those 10 seconds, even bypassing the 200m to focus on the 100m. Lewis had suggested during the season that Johnson would be 'dead meat' in Rome and the face-off was eagerly awaited.

Lewis flew through the preliminary rounds, running 10.03s in the semi-final, while Johnson was content with 10.15s for second place in his semi. In the final, on 31 August, Johnson made a brilliant start, while Lewis was away sluggishly. The race was effectively decided within the first 20 metres. Johnson's sprinting was so powerful and compelling that it took time to realise he'd not only scored a stunning victory, but had obliterated the world record.

The after-race comments were fascinating. Lewis spoke about the negative effects of drugs in sport and accused (unnamed) athletes of cheating. He implored officials to act more decisively to weed out the cheats. He never mentioned Johnson's name, but didn't need to. No journalist who heard the interview was in any doubt about Lewis's target. For instance: 'There are medallists in this meet who are definitely on drugs. That race [the 100m] will be looked at for many years, for more reasons than one … There's a problem and I just want to take a stand … If I were to jump to drugs, I could do 9.8 right away.' Lewis also claimed later that Johnson should have been called for a false start, saying Johnson had found a way to beat the electronic false-start test. Many dismissed his comments as sour grapes.

Johnson was interviewed for NBC by former high jump star Dwight Stones. 'You said you'd run 9.85 and you ran 9.83,' Stones said. 'Yeah. I don't talk shit,' Johnson replied matter-of-factly. But he was riled by Lewis's accusations, saying: 'When Carl Lewis was winning everything, I never said a word against him. He won and that was it. And when the next guy comes along and beats me, I won't complain about that either.'

1988

Johnson had taken Lewis's world title from him in 1987. Could he relieve Lewis of his Olympic crown at Seoul in 1988?

This was to be a year of incredible twists and turns. Johnson tore a hamstring early in the season and suffered his first defeat by Lewis in three years when they met in Zurich five weeks before the Olympics. But at Seoul, Johnson, in lane six, turned himself into a human bullet and blitzed the field in the final, winning in a scarcely believable 9.79s. Lewis, in lane three, was a long way back second in 9.92s, just ahead of Christie and Smith. For the first time since 1968, the world 100m record was broken in the Olympic final. This was also the first time four runners had broken 10s in the same 100m race.

It's difficult to portray the media frenzy created around Johnson and Lewis in Seoul, and that was *before* they raced. Johnson addressed a packed press conference and raised a laugh when, asked if he disliked Lewis, he replied: 'I like everyone.' Lewis marched in the opening ceremony and caused a stir by reporting by cell-phone (a newfangled gadget in those days) what it was like to be part of the big show.

The 100m final was Johnson's greatest moment. The *Toronto Star* labelled him 'a national treasure'. Wearing his national team's white and red tracksuit, he looked serene on the victory dais. He had the gold medal and Lewis, for all his talk, was No 2. At the press conference, Johnson spoke from the heart when he said: 'My name is Benjamin Sinclair Johnson Junior and this world record will last 50 years, maybe 100. The important thing was to beat Carl.' (It took only until 2002, when Tim Montgomery ran the 100m in 9.78s, for Johnson's mark to be beaten legally.)

Yet within two days, Johnson's world was in a spin. The Canadian tested positive for the anabolic steroid stanozolol, the 43rd Olympian to return a positive since Olympic drug testing started in 1968. He had his gold medal removed, returned to Canada in disgrace and was banned from the sport for two years. Lewis was elevated to first, was proved right about Johnson and drugs and finished 1988 as Male Athlete of the Year (he also won the Olympic long jump and was second to clubmate Joe DeLoach in the 200m).

The Johnson affair marked the end of the age of innocence for athletics. We look back now at the times and distances achieved by the 1980s champions and can conclude that many were drugs assisted. Two decades later, world champions are often unable to match marks set in the drugs-soaked 1980s. The 100m final lasted less than 10 seconds, but the fallout continued for years. Random out-of-competition testing was introduced worldwide and sports officials were forced – often reluctantly – to take a harder line on drugs cheats.

Chaotic images from Seoul remain seared in the mind: Johnson's muscular body as he settled on his marks before the final, gold chain swinging around his neck; his breathtaking sprinting; his finish with one finger in the air to signal victory; a beaten and frustrated Lewis grabbing Johnson's hand immediately afterwards to offer perfunctory congratulations; Frenchwoman Michelle Verdier, the IOC's Information Director, announcing to a stunned media conference that Johnson had tested positive for steroids; the black-tracksuited Johnson being hustled through airport security and out of Seoul hours later …

The Johnson–Lewis show dominated the Olympics despite the presence in Seoul of such superstars as tennis player Steffi Graf, weightlifter Naim Sulemanoglu, swimmers Michael Gross and Kristin Otto, and athletes Florence

Griffith Joyner, Said Aouita and Edwin Moses. As Linford Christie said later: 'The 100m wasn't just a sporting event. It was news.'

In Canada, Johnson plunged from hero to villain. The *Ottawa Citizen* headlined one story, 'Thanks a Lot, You Bastard'. Another paper said, 'From Hero to Zero in 9.79s'. Several ran the one-word banner headline 'Cheat!'

At the time, Lewis, apparently drugs free, looked snow white. When his autobiography, *Inside Track*, was published a couple of years later, he described his feelings before the 100m final: 'It was hard to focus when I saw Ben Johnson on the track. I noticed that his eyes were very yellow. A sign of steroid use. "That bastard did it to me again," I said to myself.' According to his book, he said to a friend that evening: 'It is so unfair. You try to do the right thing, you try to be honest and hardworking ... but there seems to be no justice.' Such comments were to look extremely hypocritical once the truth surfaced years later.

Even after 1988 and all that momentous year entailed, there was much distance to be travelled in the intertwined Johnson and Lewis stories. The Canadians launched an inquiry into drugs in sport. Run by Ontario's associate chief justice, Charles Dubin, it became known as the Dubin inquiry. It unearthed a wealth of information, most of which had previously only been hinted at behind cupped hands.

Johnson's coach, Charlie Francis, was the frankest of witnesses. He outlined the drugs programmes his athletes, including Johnson, had followed through the 1980s. Francis asked what would have been the point of his athletes training hard but disadvantaging themselves by not following drugs programmes when their major rivals did. 'You take drugs and try to win or resign yourself to losing forever by staying away from them.' He portrayed athletics as a sport in which drug-taking was routine.

After the inquiry, Johnson was retrospectively deprived of his 1987 world title and the world record he'd set in that race in Rome. It was a decision that is difficult to justify. He passed drugs tests at the time. Many other famous athletes have returned positive dope tests without suffering that sort of over-the-top retrospective reaction.

Johnson duly served his two-year suspension. Initially he had denied the drug allegations. His standard quote was: 'I have never knowingly taken illegal drugs.' But after Francis's testimony, he was left with no choice but to admit his guilt. Watching from the United States, Lewis and his camp lapped it up. The revelations merely reinforced Lewis's standing as the world's greatest sprinter.

Though he returned to the sport in 1991 and ran at both the 1991 world championships in Tokyo and the 1992 Barcelona Olympics, Johnson was never a factor again. He went from being the world's greatest sprinter to someone who might make the semis of a major meet on a good day, 'a mediocre athlete who just became great with drugs', as Lewis described him.

Lewis himself defied the march of time. He won the world 100m title in 1991 in world record time. In 1992 he did not qualify for the US Olympic team in the 100m sprint, but ran a superb anchor leg to power the Americans to the 4 x 100m relay gold medal at that year's Barcelona Olympics. And there was always his long jumping. Mike Powell broke his decade-long unbeaten streak at the 1991 world championships, but only after the greatest long jump competition of all time, during which Lewis put together the best sequence of jumps ever seen at one meet. Lewis went on to win the 1992 and 1996 Olympic long jump gold medals, meaning he joined discus thrower Al Oerter as an athlete who had won the same event at four successive Olympics. By the time Lewis drifted out of athletics in 1998, after a series of farewell meets around the world, the American's record was unmatched for longevity and versatility.

Lewis always claimed he had other strings to his bow. He had recorded music even while a top athlete, and after departing track and field pursued an acting career. The spotlight always drew him.

For Johnson, the 1990s brought more disgrace. After disappointing in his comeback, he failed a drugs test for a second time in 1993 and was banned from track and field for life. His other headline-grabbing activities did not reflect particularly well on him, but then again, a man's got to make a living. On one occasion, he ran against horses for charity. In 1997 he was employed to be fallen Argentine soccer star Diego Maradona's trainer during a short-lived Maradona comeback. Later Libyan leader Muhammar Gaddafi hired him to be the personal trainer of his son, Al-Saad, a member of the national soccer team.

Then, in early 2003, came the latest and most intriguing twist in the entire Johnson-Lewis saga, with revelations of a massive American cover-up of positive drugs tests stretching back 15 years.

There'd been dark stories floating about for years about Americans testing positive before major meets and having the results quashed. The Santa Monica Track Club (Lewis's club) was said to be a drugs club. US track stars like Lewis, Mary Decker, Florence Griffith Joyner, Andre Phillips, Joe DeLoach and Butch Reynolds had to fend off drug-cheating allegations. Charlie Francis, among others, had always claimed that if Johnson had been an American, with the full weight of that country's powerful Olympic Committee behind him, he'd never have been exposed.

Then, in April 2003, came revelations from Wade Exum, the US Olympic Committee's director for drug control from 1991–2000. He provided more than

30,000 pages of documents and his evidence was explosive. Exum contended that American officials hushed up more than 100 positive tests of athletes who went on to compete at the Olympics, winning 19 gold medals between them. Among those exposed were Lewis (who at the 1988 US Olympic Trials had failed tests for three different banned stimulants – pseudoephedrine, ephedrine and phenylpropanolamine), DeLoach, Phillips, tennis player Mary Joe Fernandez, soccer's Alexi Lalas and wrestling king Dave Schultz. Exum's papers showed that even as Lewis was being informed in writing that he had failed an A test, he was being told he would be let off the infraction.

The duplicity defied belief. The Americans had been vocal critics of the systemised drug cheating of Eastern bloc countries. It's true that Tatyana Kazankina, Renate Stecher, Kristin Otto, Marita Koch and other Eastern bloc stars were almost certainly steroid assisted. Some failed tests, others retired hastily. Some of their records stand today. But the man who epitomised the hypocrisy of it all was Lewis, winner of nine Olympic gold medals. It was Lewis who virtually pointed at Johnson while imploring officials to catch the drugs cheats. He was saluted for his bravery and for being an upright person. Lewis portrayed himself as a moral guardian. At the 2000 US Olympic trials in Sacramento, he refused to attend a champions dinner as an anti-drugs protest. If US officials had done their jobs properly, Lewis wouldn't have been at Seoul in 1988; he'd have been under suspension. Not for taking steroids or muscle-building drugs, it's true, but suspended all the same.

On being exposed, Lewis claimed that he had taken the stimulants as a cold cure, but has any cold cure ever included all three active ingredients? First disqualifying Lewis, the USOC later accepted his appeal on the basis of inadvertent use of an over-the-counter health tonic, although he had appeared in a video two years earlier warning of the dangers of supplements.

Lewis said in 2003 that it had all happened a long time ago and wondered why it was still regarded as news. He said the drugs climate was different back in the 1980s. 'There were hundreds of people getting off. We were all treated the same,' he said. Within days of the drugs story breaking, Lewis was involved in a car accident. He was eventually sentenced to three years' probation and fined $500 after pleading guilty to a misdemeanour speeding charge. He was ordered to attend 20 meetings of either Alcoholics Anonymous or Mothers Against Drunk Driving, perform 200 hours of community service and attend 32 hours of a state-approved alcohol education programme.

For Johnson, the Lewis drugs revelations came as sweet revenge. They did not make his own cheating more excusable, but they did indicate he wasn't the only cheat. Johnson threatened to sue Lewis and the US Olympic Committee, which was a nonsense. But it must have been galling to know that he'd lost his gold medal, and an estimated $25 million in endorsement and other commercial opportunities, while drug-users all around him prospered. In 2001, the BBC put together a fine documentary on Johnson called *Lost Seoul*. In it, he said: 'Everybody cheats. Who doesn't cheat in this life? Why Ben Johnson? I'm not the only one in this world.'

The programme closed poignantly when the interviewer asked Johnson what he would do if he could go back to 1982 and have Francis offer him steroids again. 'I get burnt if I say yes and if I say no,' said Johnson. The interviewer pressed him. Finally Johnson said: 'No. I don't need it. I wouldn't take them.'

By 2003 most runners in that historic 1988 Olympic final had been revealed to be drugs cheats. There was Johnson, of course. And Lewis. Desai Williams, Johnson's stable-mate, was exposed at the Dubin inquiry. Dennis Mitchell was caught in 1999 with unnatural levels of testosterone. He claimed he had drunk six cans of beer and had sex four times with his wife, as they celebrated her birthday. ('The lady deserved a treat,' he is said to have told his hearing.) Linford Christie had barely escaped suspension at the 1988 Olympics. He had a suspicious amount of pseudoephedrine in his body when he was tested after the 200m, but claimed it was because he had drunk ginseng tea. Officials, reeling from the Johnson case, let him off after a split vote. In 1999, however, at the tail-end of his career, Christie returned a positive test for the steroid nandrolone. He was suspended and never raced again. Only three of the finalists, Robson da Silva, Ray Stewart and Calvin Smith, still have 'clean' reputations.

So after it all – the running, the records, the talk and the drugs – what are we to make of the Lewis-Johnson rivalry?

It was a rivalry all right. It made headlines on and off the track. It was compelling, exciting and unpredictable. But when all's said and done, it was a tainted rivalry. It always had the whiff of scandal and hypocrisy about it and, after all these years, that's how it's turned out.

	Carl Lewis	Benjamin Sinclair Johnson
Born	1 July 1961, Birmingham, Alabama	30 December 1961, Falmouth, Jamaica
Olympic Games	1980: selected but did not compete owing to boycott 1984: 1st 100m 1st 200m 1st long jump 1st 4 x 100m relay 1988: 1st 100m (promoted from 2nd after Johnson failed drugs test) 2nd 200m 1st long jump 1992: 1st long jump 1st 4 x 100m relay 1996: 1st long jump	1980: selected but did not compete owing to boycott 1984: 3rd 100m 3rd 4 x 100m relay 1988: 1st 100m (disqualified after positive drugs test) 1992: Semi-finals 100m
World championships	1983: 1st 100m 1st long jump 1st 4 x 100m relay 1987: 1st 100m (promoted from 2nd after Johnson admitted long-term steroid use) 1st long jump 1st 4 x 100m relay 1991: 1st 100m 2nd long jump 1st 4 x 100m relay 1993: 4th 100m 3rd 200m	1983: Semi-finals 100m 1987: 1st 100m (title later withdrawn after drugs revelations) 1991: 2nd round 100m 8th in 4 x 100m relay
Commonwealth Games		1982: 2nd 100m 2nd 4 x 100m relay 1986: 1st 100m 3rd 200m 1st 4 x 100m relay

196

Records and honours
Carl Lewis **World records** 100m: 9.93s, 1987 (came 2nd, but 1st place-getter Johnson had his time withdrawn after admitting drug use. Lewis equalled Calvin Smith's world record.) 9.92s, 1988 (came 2nd, but 1st place-getter Johnson was disqualified and his time discounted). 9.86s, 1991. 4 x 100m relay (5 times from 1983–92). 4 x 200m relay (1989 and 1992). Won 65 successive long jump competitions from 1981–91. Has most 28ft-plus long jumps and had most sub-10s 100m runs. Voted Greatest Athlete of the 20th Century by the IAAF. **Benjamin Sinclair Johnson** **World records** 100m: 9.83s, 1987 (record later withdrawn after drug revelations). 9.79s, 1988 (time never ratified after failing drugs test).

Bibliography

Chapter 1

ATP, *Association of Tennis Professionals Media Guide* (various editions)

Barrett, John, *100 Wimbledon Championships: A Celebration*, Willow Books, 1986

Borg, Bjorn and Scott, Gene, *My Life and Game*, Sidgwick & Jackson, 1980

McEnroe, John and Kaplan, James, *You Cannot Be Serious*, Putnam, 2002

Chapter 2

Bannister, Roger, *First Four Minutes*, Putnam, 1955

Giller, Norman, *The Golden Milers*, Pelham Books, 1982

Matthews, Peter (ed.), *Athletics: The International Track and Field Annual*, Simon & Schuster/Sports Books, various editions

Nelson, Cordner and Quercetani, Robert, *Runners and Races: 1500m/Mile*, Tnfnews Press, 1973

Chapter 3

Auerbach, Red and Fitzgerald, Joe, *On and Off the Court*, MacMillan, 1985

Bird, Larry and Ryan, Bob, *Drive: The Story of My Life*, Doubleday, 1989

Garber, Greg, *Basketball's Legends*, Friedman/Fairfax Publishing, 1993

Hollander, Zander and Sachare, Alex, *The Official NBA Basketball Encyclopedia*, Villard Books, 1989

Wolff, Alexander, *Sports Illustrated 100 Years of Hoops*, Crescent Books, 1991

Chapter 4

Court, Margaret and McCann, George, *Court on Court*, W.H. Allen, 1976

King, Billie Jean and Deford, Frank, *Billie Jean King: The Autobiography*, Granada, 1982

Lichenstein, Grace, *Behind the Scenes in Women's Pro Tennis*, Robson Books, 1975

Smith, Margaret and Lawrence, Don, *The Margaret Smith Story*, Stanley Paul, 1965

WTA, *Women's Tennis Association Media Guide*, various editions

Chapter 5

Barrow Junior, Joe Louis and Munder, Barbara, *Joe Louis: The Brown Bomber*, McGraw-Hill Book Company, 1988

McRae, Donald, *In Black and White*, Scribner, 2003

Mead, Chris, *Champion*, Robson Books, 1986

Schmeling, Max and Von Der Lippe, George, *Max Schmeling: An Autobiography*, Bonus Books, 1998

Chapter 6
Hilton, Christopher, *Alain Prost*, Partridge Press, 1992
Nye, Doug, *Formula One Legends*, Magna Books, 1994
Small, Steve, *Grand Prix Who's Who*, Travel Publishing, 2000
Walker, Murray, *Unless I'm Very Much Mistaken*, CollinsWillow, 2002

Chapter 7
Barrett, Norman (ed.), *Purnell's Encyclopedia of Association Football*, Purnell Books, 1972
Hart, Graham (ed.), *The Guinness Football Encyclopedia*, Guinness Publishing, 1995
Murray, Bill, *The Old Firm: Sectarianism, Sport and Society in Scotland*, Birlinn Ltd, 2001

Chapter 8
Coe, Sebastian and Miller, David, *Born To Run*, Pavilion, 1992
Matthews, Peter (ed.), *Athletics: The International Track and Field Annual,* Simon & Schuster/Sports Books, various editions
Ovett, Steve and Rodda, John, *Ovett: An Autobiography*, Grafton Books, 1985
Walker, John and Palenski, Ron, *John Walker: Champion*, Moa, 1984

Chapter 10
Auerbach, Red and Fitzgerald, Joe, *On and Off the Court*, MacMillan, 1985
Garber, Greg, *Basketball's Legends*, Friedman/Fairfax Publishing, 1993
Hollander, Zander and Sachare, Alex, *The Official NBA Basketball Encyclopedia*, Villard Books, 1989
Nadel, Eric, *The Night Wilt Scored 100*, Taylor Publishing, 1990
Wolff, Alexander, S*ports Illustrated 100 Years of Hoops*, Crescent Books, 1991

Chapter 11
Alliss, Peter and Hobbs, Michael, *The Who's Who of Golf*, Oris Publishing, 1983
Alliss, Peter and Hobbs, Michael, *Peter Alliss's 100 Greatest Golfers*, Macdonald Queen Anne Press, 1989
Hauser, Thomas, *Arnold Palmer: A Personal Journey*, Collins, 1994
Lawrenson, Derek, *The Complete Encyclopedia of Golf*, Carlton Books, 1999
Nicklaus, Jack and Bowden, Ken, *Jack Nicklaus: My Story*, Simon & Schuster, 1997
Palmer, Arnold and Dodson, James, *A Golfer's Life*, Ballantine Books, 2000
Stanley, Louis T., *Legends of Golf*, Salamander Books, 1997

Chapter 12
Brunt, Stephen, *Facing Ali,* Pan, 2002
Frazier, Joe and Berger, Phil, *Smokin' Joe*, MacMillan, 1996

Chapter 13
Chester, Rod and McMillan, Neville, *Centenary*, Moa, 1984
Chester, Rod and McMillan, Neville, *The Visitors*, Moa, 1990

Edwards, Gareth, *Gareth Edwards' 100 Great Rugby Players*, Macdonald Queen Anne Press, 1987

Howitt, Bob, *Grant Batty*, Rugby Press, 1977

Howitt, Bob, *Super Sid*, Rugby Press, 1978

John, Barry (ed.), *Barry John's World of Rugby*, W.H. Allen & Co./Christopher Davies Publishers, 1978

McLaren, Bill, *Rugby's Great Heroes and Entertainers*, Hodder & Stoughton, 2003

McLean, Terry, *They Missed the Bus*, Reed, 1973

Palenski, Ron, *Century in Black*, Hodder Moa Beckett, 2003

Quinn, Keith, *A Century of Rugby Greats*, Celebrity Books, 1999

Quinn, Keith, *Legends of the All Blacks*, Hodder Moa Beckett, 1999

Williams, J.P.R., *JPR*, Collins, 1979

Chapter 14

Barrett, John, *100 Wimbledon Championships: A Celebration*, Willow Books, 1986

Evert Lloyd, Chris and Amdur, Neil, *Chrissie*, Methuen, 1982

Lloyd, Chris and John, and Thatcher, Carol, *Lloyd on Lloyd*, Willow Books, 1985

Navratilova, Martina and Vecsey, George, *Being Myself*, Collins, 1985

WTA, *Women's Tennis Association Media Guide* (various editions)

Chapter 15

Francis, Charlie and Coplon, Jeff, *Speed Trap*, Grafton Books, 1990

Lewis, Carl and Marx, Jeffrey, *Inside Track*, Simon & Schuster, 1990

Matthews, Peter (ed.), *Athletics: The International Track and Field Annual*, Simon & Schuster/Sports Books, various editions

General references

FitzSimons, Peter, *Everyone But Phar Lap*, HarperSports, 1997

Matthews, Peter, Buchanan, Ian and Mallon, Bill, *The Guinness International Who's Who of Sport*, Guinness Publishing, 1993

Wallechinsky, David, *The Complete Book of the Summer Olympics*, The Overlook Press, 2000

Websites

The following websites were also particularly helpful:

www.celticfootballclub.info/

www.footballfancensus.com/

www.formula1.com/

www.nancyfans.com/

www.nba.com/

www.pga.com/home/

www.rangers.co.uk/

www.tonyaharding.com/